THE
DATA
REVOLUTION

LANDON
JUNE
2015

'This is a path-breaking book. Rob Kitchin has long been one of the leading figures in the conceptualisation and analysis of new forms of data, software and code. This book represents an important step-forward in our understanding of big data. It provides a grounded discussion of big data, explains why they matter and provides us with a framework to analyse their social presence. Anyone who wants to obtain a critical, conceptually honed and analytically refined perspective on new forms of data should read this book.'

David Beer, Senior Lecturer in Sociology, University of York

'Data, the newest purported cure to many of the world's most "wicked" problems, are ubiquitous; they're shaping discourses, policies, and practices in our war rooms, our board rooms, our classrooms, our operating rooms, and even around our dinner tables. Yet given the precision and objectivity that the *datum* implies, it's shocking to find such *im*precision in how data are conceived, and such cloudiness in our understandings of how data are derived, analyzed, and put to use. Rob Kitchin's timely, clear, and vital book provides a much needed critical framework. He explains that our ontologies of data, or how we understand what data *are*; our epistemologies of data, or how we conceive of data as units of truth, fact, or knowledge; our analytic methodologies, or the techniques we use to process that data; and our data apparatuses and institutions, or the tools and (often huge, heavy, and expensive) infrastructures we use to sort and store that data, are all entwined. And all have profound political, economic, and cultural implications that we can't risk ignoring as we're led into our "smart," data-driven future.'

Shannon Mattern, Faculty, School of Media Studies, The New School

'A sober, nuanced and inspiring guide to big data with the highest signal to noise ratio of any book in the field.'

Matthew Fuller, Digital Culture Unit, Centre for Cultural Studies, Goldsmiths, University of London

'Data has become a new key word for our times. This is just the book I have been waiting for: a detailed and critical analysis that will make us think carefully about how data participate in social, cultural and spatial relations.'

Deborah Lupton, Centenary Research Professor News & Media Research Centre, University of Canberra

'By carefully analysing data as a complex socio-technical assemblage, in this book Rob Kitchin discusses thought-provoking aspects of data as a technical, economic and social construct, that are often ignored or forgotten despite the increasing focus on data production and usage in contemporary life. This book unpacks the complexity of data as elements of knowledge production, and does not only provide readers from a variety of disciplinary areas with useful conceptual framings, but also with a challenging set of open issues to be further explored and engaged with as the "data revolution" progresses.'

Luigina Ciolfi, Sheffield Hallam University

'Kitchin paints a nuanced and complex picture of the unfolding data landscape. Through a critique of the deepening technocratic, often corporate led, development of our increasingly data driven societies, he presents an alternative perspective which illuminates the contested, and contestable, nature of this acutely political and social terrain.'

Jo Bates, Information School, University of Sheffield

'*The Data Revolution* is a timely intervention of critical reflection into the hyperbolic and fast-paced developments in the gathering, analysis and workings of "big data". This excellent book diagnoses the technical, ethical and scientific challenges raised by the data revolution, sounding a clarion for critical reflections on the promise and problematic of the data revolution.'

Sam Kinsley, University of Exeter

'Much talk of big data is big hype. Different phenomena dumped together, a dearth of definitions and little discussion of the complex relationships that give rise to and shape big data practices sums it up. Rob Kitchin puts us in his debt by cutting through the cant and offering not only a clear analysis of the range, power and limits of big data assemblages but a pointer to the crucial social, political and ethical issues to which we should urgently attend. Read this book.'

David Lyon, Queen's University, Canada

'Data matter and have matter, and Rob Kitchin thickens this understanding by assembling the philosophical, social scientific, and popular media accounts of our data-based living. That the give and take of data is increasingly significant to the everyday has been the mainstay of Kitchin's long and significant contribution to a critical technology studies. In *The Data Revolution*, he yet again implores us to think beyond the polemical, to signal a new generation of responsive and responsible data work. Importantly, he reminds us of the non-inevitability of data, articulating the registers within which interventions can and already are being made. Kitchin offers a manual, a set of operating instructions, to better grasp and grapple with the complexities of the coming world, of such a "data revolution".'

Matthew W. Wilson, Harvard University and University of Kentucky

'With a lucid prose and without hyperbole, Kitchin explains the complexities and disruptive effects of what he calls "the data revolution". The book brilliantly provides an overview of the shifting socio-technical assemblages that are shaping the uses of data today. Carefully distinguishing between big data and open data, and exploring various data infrastructures, Kitchin vividly illustrates how the data landscape is rapidly changing and calls for a revolution in how we think about data.'

Evelyn Ruppert, Goldsmiths, University of London

'Kitchin's powerful, authoritative work deconstructs the hype around the "data revolution" to carefully guide us through the histories and the futures of "big data". The book skilfully engages with debates from across the humanities, social sciences, and sciences in order to produce a critical account of how data are enmeshed into enormous social, economic, and political changes that are taking place. It challenges us to rethink data, information and knowledge by asking - who benefits and who might be left out; what these changes mean for ethics, economy, surveillance, society, politics; and ultimately, whether big data offer answers to big questions. By tackling the promises and potentials as well as the perils and pitfalls of our data revolution, Kitchin shows us that data doesn't just reflect the world, but also changes it.'

Mark Graham, University of Oxford

'This is an incredibly well written and accessible book which provides readers who will be curious about the buzz around the idea of big data with: (a) an organising framework rooted in social theory (important given dominance of technical writings) through which to conceptualise big data; (b) detailed understandings of each actant in the various data assemblages with fresh and novel theoretical constructions and typologies of each actant; (c) the contours of a critical examination of big data (whose interests does it serve, where, how and why). These are all crucial developments it seems to me and I think this book will become a trail blazer because of them. This is going to be a biggie citation wise and a seminal work.'

Mark Boyle, Director of NIRSA, National University of Ireland, Maynooth

THE
DATA
REVOLUTION

BIG DATA, OPEN DATA, DATA INFRASTRUCTURES
& THEIR CONSEQUENCES

Rob Kitchin

Los Angeles | London | New Delhi
Singapore | Washington DC

Los Angeles | London | New Delhi
Singapore | Washington DC

SAGE Publications Ltd
1 Oliver's Yard
55 City Road
London EC1Y 1SP

SAGE Publications Inc.
2455 Teller Road
Thousand Oaks, California 91320

SAGE Publications India Pvt Ltd
B 1/I 1 Mohan Cooperative Industrial Area
Mathura Road
New Delhi 110 044

SAGE Publications Asia-Pacific Pte Ltd
3 Church Street
#10-04 Samsung Hub
Singapore 049483

© Rob Kitchin 2014

First published 2014

Editor: Robert Rojek
Assistant editor: Keri Dickens
Production editor: Katherine Haw
Copyeditor: Rose James
Marketing manager: Michael Ainsley
Cover design: Francis Kenney
Typeset by: C&M Digitals (P) Ltd, Chennai, India
Printed and bound by CPI Group (UK) Ltd,
    Croydon, CR0 4YY

Library of Congress Control Number: 2014932842

British Library Cataloguing in Publication data

A catalogue record for this book is available from
the British Library

MIX
Paper from
responsible sources
FSC
www.fsc.org   FSC® C013604

ISBN 978-1-4462-8747-7
ISBN 978-1-4462-8748-4 (pbk)

CONTENTS

LIST OF TABLES

LIST OF FIGURES

ABOUT THE AUTHOR

Professor Rob Kitchin is an European Research Council Advanced Investigator at the National University of Ireland Maynooth. He has authored or edited 23 other books and was the 2013 recipient of the Royal Irish Academy's Gold Medal for the Social Sciences. He is principal investigator for the Digital Repository of Ireland and the All-Island Research Observatory.

ACKNOWLEDGEMENTS

This book started life in early July 2012 as a discussion in a coffee shop in Edinburgh with Robert Rojek from Sage. I was suggesting he find someone to write a book on big data, open data, and data infrastructures, presenting ideas as to who might be well placed to draft such a text. He felt I was the right person for the job. A couple of months later I decided to juggle round my writing plans and started to draft what was to be a quite short, critical analysis of the changing data landscape. Over time the book developed into a full-length manuscript that sought to do justice to the emerging trends and debates. Along the way, Robert remained a keen sounding board and source of interesting material, and his help has been very much appreciated. At Sage, his colleague Keri Dickens helped shepherd the book into production, where it was admirably guided to production by Katherine Haw.

Martin Dodge and Tracey P. Lauriault kindly undertook a detailed read-through and critique of the entire manuscript. Mark Boyle read the entire second draft. Gavin McArdle and Evelyn Ruppert provided useful critique of individual chapters, and a number of other colleagues and peers engaged in useful discussions and guided me to relevant material, including Mark Graham, Taylor Shelton, Matt Zook, Matt Wilson, Lev Manovich, Cian O'Callaghan, Sung-Yueh Perng, Aileen O'Carroll, Jane Gray, Sandra Collins, John Keating, Sharon Webb, Justin Gleeson, Aoife Dowling, Eoghan McCarthy, Martin Charlton, Tim McCarthy, Jan Rigby, Rob Bradshaw, Alan Moore, Darach Mac Donncha and Jim White. I also received useful feedback at presentations at Durham University, Clark University and Harvard University. Rhona Bradshaw and Orla Dunne minded the office while I tried to keep my head down to conduct research and draft chapters. Justin Gleeson kindly produced some of the diagrams. I owe you all a debt of gratitude. I would also like to thank the many people on Twitter for pointing me to interesting material and engaging in relevant micro-discussions. Lastly, as ever, Cora kept me grounded and provided wonderful support.

The research conducted in writing this book was in part supported by a European Research Council Advanced Investigator Award, 'The Programmable City' (ERC-2012-AdG-323636; www. nuim.ie/progcity) and Programme for Research in Third Level Institutes Cycle 5 funding from the Higher Education Authority to create a Digital Repository for Ireland.

A hyperlinked version of the book's bibliography can be found at http://thedatarevolutionbook.wordpress.com/. Additional sources of information and stories about the data revolution are regularly scooped onto http://www.

scoop.it/t/the-programmable-city. Feedback is also welcome via email (Rob. Kitchin@nuim.ie) or Twitter (@robkitchin).

Some of the material in this book has been previously published as papers and blog posts, though it has been updated, reworked and extended:

Dodge, M. and Kitchin, R. (2005) 'Codes of life: identification codes and the machine-readable world', *Environment and Planning D: Society and Space*, 23(6): 851–81.

Kitchin, R. (2013) 'Big data and human geography: opportunities, challenges and risks', *Dialogues in Human Geography*, 3(3): 262–7.

Kitchin, R. (2014) 'The real-time city? Big data and smart urbanism', *GeoJournal* 79(1): 1–14.

Kitchin, R. (2014) 'Big data, new epistemologies and paradigm shifts', *Big Data and Society*, 1(1) April–June, 1–12.

Kitchin, R. and Lauriault, T. (2014) *Small Data, Data Infrastructures and Big Data*. The Programmable City Working Paper 1. Available at SSRN: http://ssrn.com/abstract=2376148.

Kitchin, R. and Lauriault, T. (in press) 'Small data in an era of big data,' *Geo Journal*.

Figure 1.1 is adapted from InformationisBeautiful.net with the permission of David McCandless.

Figure 1.2 is reproduced with the permission of The Statistical and Social Inquiry Society of Ireland.

Table 2.4 is included with the permission of Neil Beagrie, Brian Lavoie and Matthew Woollard and under a creative commons licence for Fry et al., http://repository.jisc.ac.uk/279/.

Table 3.1 is reproduced from http://opendefinition.org/od/ under a creative commons licence.

Table 3.3 is included with the permission of Michael Hausenblas, http://5stardata.info/.

Table 4.1 is reproduced with the permission of *The Economist*. The Economist Newspaper Limited, London, issued March 11, 2014.

Figure 6.1 is reproduced with the permission of Monica Stephens.

Table 6.1 is reproduced with the permission of Taylor and Francis.

Figure 6.2 is reproduced with the permission of Flightradar24.com.

Figure 6.3 is reproduced with the permission of Andrew Hudson-Smith.

Figures 6.4 and 6.5 are reproduced with the permission of Professor Mikael Jern, National Center for Visual Analytics, Linköping University, http://ncva.itn.liu.se.

Table 7.1 Forms of big data corporate intelligence is included with the permission of McKinsey & Company.

Table 7.2 and Figure 7.1 are reproduced courtesy of International Business Machines Corporation, © International Business Machines Corporation.

Figure 7.2 is reproduced from http://ipprio.rio.rj.gov.br/centro-de-operacoes-rio-usa-mapas-feitos-pelo-ipp/ under a creative commons license.

Tables 10.2 and 10.3 are included with the permission of John Wiley & Sons.

Table 10.4 is included with the permission of Ann Cavoukian, Ph.D., Information and Privacy Commissioner, Ontario, Canada.

NOTE

Throughout this book the term 'data' is expressed in the plural, with datum being used to denote a singular instance. As explained in the *Oxford English Dictionary* (OED):

> In Latin, **data** is the plural of **datum** and, historically and in specialized scientific fields, it is also treated as a plural in English, taking a plural verb, as in *the **data were** collected and classified*.

However, the term is increasingly used in the singular form in popular media and everyday conversation. As the OED details:

> In modern non-scientific use, however, it is generally not treated as a plural. Instead, it is treated as a mass noun, similar to a word like **information**, which takes a singular verb. Sentences such as ***data was** collected over a number of years* are now widely accepted in standard English.

The book therefore follows scientific convention. However, where it is used in the singular in quoted passages, the original text has been retained. As to which version is correct, the grammarians would argue for the plural, but popular opinion is more open and flexible.

PREFACE

There is a long history of governments, businesses, science and citizens producing and utilising data in order to monitor, regulate, profit from, and make sense of the world. Data have traditionally been time-consuming and costly to generate, analyse and interpret, and generally provided static, often coarse, snapshots of phenomena. Given their relative paucity, good-quality data were a valuable commodity, either jealously guarded or expensively traded. Recently, this state of affairs has started to change quite radically. Data have lost none of their value, but in other respects their production and nature is being transformed through a set of what Christensen (1997) terms disruptive innovations that challenge the status quo as to how data are produced, managed, analysed, stored and utilised. Rather than being scarce and limited in access, the production of data is increasingly becoming a deluge; a wide, deep torrent of timely, varied, resolute and relational data that are relatively low in cost and, outside of business, increasingly open and accessible. A data revolution is underway, one that is already reshaping how knowledge is produced, business conducted, and governance enacted.

This revolution is founded on the latest wave of information and communication technologies (ICTs), such as the plethora of digital devices encountered in homes, workplaces and public spaces; mobile, distributed and cloud computing; social media; and the internet of things (internetworked sensors and devices). These new technical media and platforms are leading to ever more aspects of everyday life – work, consumption, travel, communication, leisure – and the worlds we inhabit to be captured as data and mediated through data-driven technologies. Moreover, they are materially and discursively reconfiguring the production, circulation and interpretation of data, producing what has been termed 'big data' – vast quantities of dynamic, varied digital data that are easily conjoined, shared and distributed across ICT networks, and analysed by a new generation of data analytics designed to cope with data abundance as opposed to data scarcity. The scale of the emerging data deluge is illustrated by the claim that '[b]etween the dawn of civilisation and 2003, we only created five exabytes of information; now we're creating that amount every two days' (Hal Varian, chief economist with Google, cited in Smolan and Erwitt 2012).

Big data are not the only components of the data revolution. Rather, there are related initiatives such as the digitisation, linking together, and scaling-up of traditionally produced datasets (small data) into networked data infrastructures; the open data movement that seeks to make as much data as possible openly available for all to use; and new institutional structures that seek to secure common guidelines and policies with respect to data formats, structures, standards, meta-data, intellectual property rights, licensing and sharing protocols. Together, these constitute a set of new data assemblages – amalgams of systems of thought, forms of knowledge, finance, political economies, governmentalities and legalities, mat-erialities and infrastructures, practices, organisations and institutions, subjectivities and communities, places, and marketplaces – that frame how data are produced and to what ends they are employed.

The impact of big data, open data and data infrastructures is already visible in science, business, government and civil society. Used to operating in data deserts, seeking to extract information and draw conclusions from relatively small num-bers of observations, established disciplines are now starting to grapple with a data avalanche (H.J. Miller 2010). They are accompanied by new fields, such as data science, social computing, digital humanities, and computational social sci-ences, that are explicitly concerned with building data infrastructures and finding innovative ways to analyse and make sense of scaled and big data. In business, big data are providing a new means to dynamically and efficiently man-age all facets of a company's activities and to leverage additional profit through enhanced productivity, competitiveness, and market knowledge. And data them-selves have become an important commodity, actively bought and sold within a global, multi-billion dollar market. For governments, widespread, dynamic data are providing new insights about their own operations, as well as reshaping the means to govern and regulate society. Through examining open datasets, citizens and non-governmental organisations (NGOs) are drawing their own conclu-sions, challenging corporate and government agendas, and forwarding alternative visions of how society should be organised and managed.

These new opportunities have sparked a veritable boom in what might be termed 'data boosterism'; rallying calls as to the benefits and prospects of big, open and scaled small data, some of it justified, some pure hype and buzz. In turn, the terms big data and open data have become powerful memes, not just a way of describing data but symbolic of a wider rhetoric and imaginary that is used to garner support and spread their roll-out and adoption. Such boosterism and memes can make it easy to drift into uncritically hyping the changes taking place, many of which raise numerous ethical, political and legal concerns. History, though, does reveal earlier precedents of disruptive information-related innovations – the radical transformation of knowledge production in the wake of the printing press, for example. Indeed, every new era of science has had at its inception new technologies that lead to an information overload and spark a transition to new ways of generating, organising, storing, analysing and interpreting data (Darnton 2000). For example, Strasser (2012) notes, the explorations of the Renaissance, enabled by better navigation, mapping and scientific instruments, yielded vast quantities of new discoveries that led to new methods of categorisa-tion, new technologies of analysis and storage, and new scientific insights.

Given the relatively early point in the present data revolution, it is not at all certain how the present transformations will unfold and settle, and what will be the broader consequences of changes taking place. What is clear is that there is an urgent need to try and make sense of what is happening. Thus, the aim of this book is to provide a synoptic, conceptual and critical analysis of data and the data revolution underway. It seeks, on the one hand, to chart the various ways in which the generation, processing, analysis and sharing of data is being reconfigured, and what this means for how we produce and use information and knowledge; and, on the other, to open up debate and critical reflection about data: their nature, how they are framed technically, philosophically, ethically and economically, and the technological and institutional assemblages that surround them. Rather than setting out a passionate case for the benefits of big data, open data and data infrastructures, or an entrenched critique decrying their more negative consequences, the book provides a contextual, critical appraisal of the changes taking place.

The analysis presented is based on an extensive engagement with the literature from across humanities, social sciences and the sciences, and from popular culture, journalism, and industry publications, and on first-hand experience of working on large-scale data archiving/infrastructure and data analytics projects. The book is divided into eleven chapters. The first provides an overview and critical reflection on the concept of data and how to make sense of databases and data infrastructures. The second examines the continued role of small data and how they are being scaled up into digital archives and infrastructures, and sold through data brokers. Chapter 3 discusses the drive towards creating open and linked data that are more widely shared and reused. Chapters 4 and 5 detail the nature of big data and its enablers and sources. Chapter 6 provides an overview of a new set of data analytics designed to make sense of scaled small data and big data. The next two chapters examine the arguments used to promote big data and their impact on governance and business, and the ways in which the data revolution is reshaping how research is conceptualised and practised. Chapters 9 and 10 discuss the technical, organisational, ethical, political and legal challenges of the data revolution. The final chapter sets out some overarching conclusions and provides a road map for further research and reflection.

1

CONCEPTUALISING DATA

Data are commonly understood to be the raw material produced by abstracting the world into categories, measures and other representational forms – numbers, characters, symbols, images, sounds, electromagnetic waves, bits – that constitute the building blocks from which information and knowledge are created. Data are usually representative in nature (e.g., measurements of a phenomena, such as a person's age, height, weight, colour, blood pressure, opinion, habits, location, etc.), but can also be implied (e.g., through an absence rather than presence) or derived (e.g., data that are produced from other data, such as percentage change over time calculated by comparing data from two time periods), and can be either recorded and stored in analogue form or encoded in digital form as bits (binary digits). Good-quality data are discrete and intelligible (each datum is individual, separate and separable, and clearly defined), aggregative (can be built into sets), have associated metadata (data about data), and can be linked to other datasets to provide insights not available from a single dataset (Rosenberg 2013). Data have strong utility and high value because they provide the key inputs to the various modes of analysis that individuals, institutions, businesses and science employ in order to understand and explain the world we live in, which in turn are used to create innovations, products, policies and knowledge that shape how people live their lives.

Data then are a key resource in the modern world. Yet, given their utility and value, and the amount of effort and resources devoted to producing and analysing them, it is remarkable how little conceptual attention has been paid to data in and of themselves. In contrast, there are thousands of articles and books devoted to the philosophy of information and knowledge. Just as we tend to focus on buildings and neighbourhoods when considering cities, rather than the bricks and mortar used to build them, so it is the case with data. Moreover, just as we think of bricks and mortar as simple building blocks rather than elements that are made within factories by companies bound within logistical, financial, legal and market concerns, and are distributed, stored and traded, so we largely do with data. Consequently, when data are the focus of enquiry it is usually to consider, in a largely technical sense, how they should be generated and analysed, or how they can be leveraged into insights and value, rather than to consider the nature of data from a more conceptual and philosophical perspective.

With this observation in mind, the principal aim of this book is threefold: to provide a detailed reflection on the nature of data and their wider assemblages; to chart how these assemblages are shifting and mutating with the development of new data infrastructures, open data and big data; and to think through the implications of these new data assemblages with respect to how we make sense of and act in the world. To supply an initial conceptual platform, in this chapter the forms, nature and philosophical bases of data are examined in detail. Far from being simple building blocks, the discussion will reveal that data are a lot more complex. While many analysts may accept data at face value, and treat them as if they are neutral, objective, and pre-analytic in nature, data are in fact framed technically, economically, ethically, temporally, spatially and philosophically. Data do not exist independently of the ideas, instruments, practices, contexts and knowledges used to generate, process and analyse them (Bowker 2005; Gitelman and Jackson 2013). Thus, the argument developed is that understanding data and the unfolding data revolution requires a more nuanced analysis than much of the open and big data literature presently demonstrates.

WHAT ARE DATA? /CAPTA

Etymologically the word data is derived from the Latin *dare*, meaning 'to give'. In this sense, data are raw elements that *can be* abstracted from (given by) phenomena – measured and recorded in various ways. However, in general use, data refer to those elements that *are* taken; extracted through observations, computations, experiments, and record keeping (Borgman 2007). Technically, then, what we understand as data are actually capta (derived from the Latin *capere*, meaning 'to take'); those units of data that have been selected and harvested from the sum of all potential data (Kitchin and Dodge 2011). As Jensen (1950: ix, cited in Becker 1952: 278) states:

> it is an unfortunate accident of history that the term *datum* ... rather than *captum* ... should have come to symbolize the unit-phenomenon in science. For science deals, not with 'that which has been given' by nature to the scientist, but with 'that which has been taken' or selected from nature by the scientist in accordance with his purpose.

Strictly speaking, then, this book should be entitled *The Capta Revolution*. However, since the term data has become so thoroughly ingrained in the language of the academy and business to mean capta, rather than confuse the matter further it makes sense to continue to use the term data where capta would be more appropriate.

Beyond highlighting the etymological roots of the term, what this brief discussion starts to highlight is that data harvested through measurement are always a selection from the total sum of all possible data available – what we have chosen to take from all that could potentially be given. As such, data are inherently partial, selective and representative, and the distinguishing criteria used in their capture has consequence.

Other scholars have noted that what has been understood as data has changed over time with the development of science. Rosenberg (2013) details that the term 'data' was first used in the English language in the seventeenth century. As a concept then it is very much tied to that of modernity and the growth and evolution of science and new modes of producing, presenting and debating knowledge in the seventeenth and eighteenth century that shifted information and argument away from theology, exhortation and sentiment to facts, evidence and the testing of theory through experiment (Poovey 1998; Garvey 2013; Rosenberg 2013). Over time, data came to be understood as being pre-analytical and pre-factual, different in nature to facts, evidence, information and knowledge, but a key element in the constitution of these elements (though often the terms and definitions of data, facts, evidence, information and knowledge are conflated). As Rosenberg (2013: 18) notes,

> facts are ontological, evidence is epistemological, data is rhetorical. A datum may also be a fact, just as a fact may be evidence ... [T]he existence of a datum has been independent of any consideration of corresponding ontological truth. When a fact is proven false, it ceases to be a fact. False data is data nonetheless.

In rhetorical terms, data are that which exists prior to argument or interpretation that converts them to facts, evidence and information (Rosenberg 2013). From this perspective, data hold certain precepts: they are abstract, discrete, aggregative (they can be added together) (Rosenberg 2013), and are meaningful independent of format, medium, language, producer and context (i.e., data hold their meaning whether stored as analogue or digital, viewed on paper or screen or expressed in any language, and 'adhere to certain non-varying patterns, such as the number of tree rings always being equal to the age of the tree') (Floridi 2010). Floridi (2008) contends that the support-independence of data is reliant on three types of neutrality: taxonomic (data are relational entities defined with respect to other specific data); typological (data can take a number of different non-mutually exclusive forms, e.g., primary, secondary, metadata, operational, derived); and genetic (data can have a semantics independent of their comprehension; e.g., the Rosetta Stone hieroglyphics constitute data regardless of the fact that when they were discovered nobody could interpret them).

Not everyone who thinks about or works with data holds such a narrow rhetorical view. How data are understood has not just evolved over time, it varies with respect to perspective. For example, Floridi (2008) explains that from an epistemic position data are collections of facts, from an informational position data are information, from a computational position data are collections of binary elements that can be processed and transmitted electronically, and from a diaphoric position data are abstract elements that are distinct and intelligible from other data. In the first case, data provide the basis for further reasoning or constitute empirical evidence. In the second, data constitute representative information that can be stored, processed and analysed, but do not necessarily constitute facts. In the third, data constitute the inputs and outputs of computation but have to be processed to be turned into facts and information (for example, a DVD contains gigabytes of data but no facts or information per se) (Floridi 2005). In the fourth, data are meaningful because they capture and denote variability (e.g., patterns of dots, alphabet letters and numbers, wavelengths) that provides a signal that can be interpreted. As discussed below, other positions include understanding data as being socially constructed, as having materiality, as being ideologically loaded, as a commodity to be traded, as constituting a public good, and so on. The point is, data are never simply just data; how data are conceived and used varies between those who capture, analyse and draw conclusions from them.

KINDS OF DATA

Whether data are pre-factual and rhetorical in nature or not, it is clear that data are diverse in their characteristics, which shape in explicit terms how they are handled and what can be done with them. In broad terms, data vary by form (qualitative or quantitative), structure (structured, semi-structured or unstructured), source (captured, derived, exhaust, transient), producer (primary, secondary, tertiary), and type (indexical, attribute, metadata).

Quantitative and qualitative data

Data can take many material forms including numbers, text, symbols, images, sound, electromagnetic waves, or even a blankness or silence (an empty space is itself data). These are typically divided into two broad categories. *Quantitative data* consist of numeric records. Generally, such data are extensive and relate to the physical properties of phenomena (such as length, height, distance, weight, area, volume), or are representative and relate to non-physical characteristics of phenomena (such as social class, educational attainment, social deprivation, quality of life rankings). Quantitative data have four different levels of measurement which delimit how they can be processed and analysed (Kitchin and Tate 1999, see also Table 1.1). Such data can be analysed using visualisations, a variety of descriptive and inferential statistics, and be used as the inputs to predictive and simulation models.

Table 1.1 Levels of data measurement

Levels of measurement	Definition	Example
Nominal data	Categorical in nature, with observations recorded into discrete units.	Unmarried, married, divorced, widowed
Ordinal data	Observations that are placed in a rank order, where certain observations are greater than others.	Low, medium, high
Interval data	Measurements along a scale which possesses a fixed but arbitrary interval and an arbitrary origin. Addition or multiplication by a constant will not alter the interval nature of the observations. Data can either be continuous (e.g., time or length) or discrete (e.g., counts of a phenomenon) in nature.	Temperature along the Celsius scale
Ratio data	Similar to interval data except the scale possesses a true zero origin, and multiplication by a constant will not alter the ratio nature of the observations.	Exam marks on a scale of 0–100

In contrast, *qualitative data* are non-numeric, such as texts, pictures, art, video, sounds, and music. While qualitative data can be converted into quantitative data, the translation involves significant reduction and abstraction and much of the richness of the original data is lost by such a process. Consequently, qualitative data analysis is generally practised on the original materials, seeking to tease out and build up meaning and understanding rather than subjecting the data to rote, computational techniques. However, significant progress is being made with respect to processing and analysing qualitative data computationally through techniques such as machine learning and data mining (see Chapter 6).

Structured, semi-structured and unstructured data

Structured data are those that can be easily organised, stored and transferred in a defined data model, such as numbers/text set out in a table or relational database that have a consistent format (e.g., name, date of birth, address, gender, etc). Such data can be processed, searched, queried, combined, and analysed relatively straightforwardly using calculus and algorithms, and can be visualised using various forms of graphs and maps, and easily processed by computers. *Semi-structured data* are loosely structured data that have no predefined data model/schema and thus cannot be held in a relational database. Their structure are irregular, implicit, flexible and often nested hierarchically, but they have a reasonably consistent set of fields and the data are tagged thus, separating content semantically and providing loose, self-defining content metadata and a means to sort, order and structure the data. An example of such data are XML-tagged web pages (pages made using Extensible Markup Language [XML] which encode documents in a format that is both human- and machine-readable; Franks 2012; see linked data in Chapter 3).

In contrast, *unstructured data* do not have a defined data model or common identifiable structure. Each individual element, such as narrative text or photo, may have a specific structure or format, but not all data within a dataset share the same structure. As such, while they can often be searched and queried, they are not easily combined or computationally analysed. Such unstructured data are usually qualitative in nature, but can often be converted into structured data through classification and categorisation. Until relatively recently, very large datasets were typically structured in form because they were generally much easier to process, analyse and store. In the age of big data, many massive datasets consist of semi- or unstructured data, such as Facebook posts, tweets, uploaded pictures and videos, and blogs, and some estimates suggest that such data are growing at 15 times the rate of structured data (Zikopoulos et al. 2012), with advances in database design (such as NoSQL databases that do not use the tabular models of relational databases, see Chapter 5) and machine learning techniques (see Chapter 6) aiding storage and analysis.

Captured, exhaust, transient and derived data

There are two primary ways in which data can be generated. The first is that data can be *captured* directly through some form of measurement such as observation, surveys, lab and field experiments, record keeping (e.g., filling out forms or writing a diary), cameras, scanners and sensors. In these cases, data are usually the deliberate product of measurement; that is, the intention was to generate useful data. In contrast, *exhaust data* are inherently produced by a device or system, but are a by-product of the main function rather than the primary output (Manyika et al. 2011). For example, an electronic checkout till is designed to total the goods being purchased and to process payment, but it also produces data that can be used to monitor stock, worker performance and customer purchasing. Many software-enabled systems produce such exhaust data, much of which have become valuable sources of information. In other cases, exhaust data are *transient* in nature; that is, they are never examined or processed and are simply discarded, either because they are too voluminous or unstructured in nature, or costly to process and store, or there is a lack of techniques to derive value from them, or they are of little strategic or tactical use (Zikopoulos et al. 2012; Franks 2012). For example, Manyika et al. (2011: 3) report that 'health care providers ... discard 90 percent of the data that they generate (e.g., almost all real-time video feeds created during surgery)'.

Captured and exhaust data are considered 'raw' in the sense that they have not been converted or combined with other data. In contrast, *derived data* are produced through additional processing or analysis of captured data. For example, captured data might be individual traffic counts through an intersection and derived data the total number of counts or counts per hour. The latter have been derived from the former. Captured data are often the input into a model, with derived data the output. For example, traffic count data might be an input into a transportation model with the output being predicted or simulated data (such as projected traffic counts at different times or under different conditions). In the case of a model, the traffic count data are likely to have been combined with other captured or derived data (such as type of vehicle, number of passengers, etc.) to create new derived data for input into the model. Derived data are generated for a number of reasons, including to reduce the volume of data to a manageable amount and to produce more useful and meaningful measures. Sometimes the original captured data might be processed to varying levels of derivation depending on its intended use. For example, the NASA Earth Observing System organises its data into six levels that run from unprocessed captured data, through increasing degrees of processing and analysis, to model outputs based on analyses of lower-level data (Borgman 2007; see Table 1.2).

Table 1.2 The six levels of data of NASA's Earth Observing System

Data level	Description
Level 0	Reconstructed, unprocessed instrument and payload data at full resolution, with any and all communications artefacts (e.g., synchronisation frames, communications headers, duplicate data) removed.
Level 1A	Reconstructed, unprocessed instrument data at full resolution, time-referenced, and annotated with ancillary information, including radiometric and geometric calibration coefficients and georeferencing parameters computed and appended but not applied to Level 0 data.
Level 1B	Level 1A data that have been processed to sensor units.
Level 2	Derived geophysical variables at the same resolution and location as Level 1 source data.
Level 3	Variables mapped on uniform space-time grid scales, usually with some completeness and consistency.
Level 4	Model output or results from analyses of lower-level data (e.g., variables derived from multiple measurements).

Source: Adapted from https://earthdata.nasa.gov/data/standards-and-references/processing-levels

Primary, secondary and tertiary data

Primary data are generated by a researcher and their instruments within a research design of their making. *Secondary data* are data made available to others to reuse and analyse that are generated by someone else. So one person's primary data can be another person's secondary data. *Tertiary data* are a form of derived data, such as counts, categories, and statistical results. Tertiary data are often released by statistical agencies rather than secondary data to ensure confidentiality with respect to whom the data refer. For example, the primary data of the Irish census are precluded from being released as secondary data for 100 years after generation; instead the data are released as summary counts and categorical tertiary data. Many researchers and institutions seek to generate primary data because they are tailored to their specific needs and foci, whereas these design choices are not available to those analysing secondary or tertiary data. Moreover, those using secondary and tertiary data as inputs for their own studies have to trust that the original research is valid.

In many cases researchers will combine primary data with secondary and tertiary data to produce more valuable derived data. For example, a retailer might seek to create a derived dataset that merges their primary sales data with tertiary geodemographics data (data about what kind of people live in different areas, which are derived from census and other public and commercial data) in order to determine which places to target with marketing material. Secondary and tertiary data are valuable because they enable replication studies and the building of larger, richer and more sophisticated datasets. They later produce what Crampton et al. (2012) term 'data amplification'; that is, data when combined enables far greater insights by revealing associations, relationships and patterns which remain hidden if the data remain isolated. As a consequence, the secondary and tertiary data market is a multi-billion dollar industry (see Chapter 2).

Indexical and attribute data and metadata

Data also vary in kind. *Indexical data* are those that enable identification and linking, and include unique identifiers, such as passport and social security numbers, credit card numbers, manufacturer serial numbers, digital object identifiers, IP and MAC addresses, order and shipping numbers, as well as names, addresses, and zip codes. Indexical data are important because they enable large amounts of non-indexical data to be bound together and tracked through shared identifiers, and enable discrimination, combination, disaggregation and re-aggregation, searching and other forms of processing and analysis. As discussed in Chapter 4, indexical data are becoming increasingly common and granular, escalating the relationality of datasets. *Attribute data* are data that represent aspects of a phenomenon, but are not indexical in nature. For example, with respect to a person the indexical data might be a fingerprint or DNA sequence, with associated attribute data being age, sex, height, weight, eye colour, blood group, and so on. The vast bulk of data that are generated and stored within systems are attribute data.

Metadata are data about data. Metadata can either refer to the data content or the whole dataset. Metadata about the content includes the names and descriptions of specific fields (e.g., the column headers in a spreadsheet) and data definitions. These metadata help a user of a dataset to understand its composition and how it should be used and interpreted, and facilitates the conjoining of datasets, interoperability and discoverability, and to judge their provenance and lineage. Metadata that refers to a dataset as a whole has three different forms (NISO 2004). Descriptive metadata concerns identification and discovery and includes elements such as title, author, publisher, subject, and description. Structural metadata refers to the organisation and coverage of the dataset. Administrative metadata concerns when and how the dataset was created, details of the technical aspects of the data, such as file format, and who owns and can use the data. A common metadata standard for datasets that combines these three types of metadata is the Dublin Core (http://dublincore.org/). This standard requires datasets to have 15 accompanying metadata fields: title, creator, subject, description, publisher, contributor, date, type, format, identifier, source, language, relation, coverage, and rights. Metadata are essential components of all datasets, though they are often a neglected element of data curation, especially amongst researchers who are compiling primary data for their own use rather than sharing.

DATA, INFORMATION, KNOWLEDGE, WISDOM

What unites these various kinds of data is that they form the base or bedrock of a knowledge pyramid: data precedes information, which precedes knowledge, which precedes understanding and wisdom (Adler 1986; Weinberger 2011). Each layer of the pyramid is distinguished by a process of distillation (reducing, abstracting, processing, organising, analysing, interpreting, applying) that adds organisation, meaning and value by revealing relationships and truths about the world (see Figure 1.1).

While the order of the concepts within the pyramid is generally uncontested, the nature and difference between concepts often varies between schools of thought. Information, for example, is a concept that is variously understood across scholars. For some, information is an accumulation of associated data, for others it is data plus meaning, or the signal in the noise of data, or a multifaceted construct, or tertiary data wherein primary data has been reworked into analytical form. To a physicist, data are simply zeros and ones, raw bits; they are noise. Information is when these zeros and ones are organised into distinct patterns; it is the signal (von Baeyer 2003). Airwaves and communication cables then are full of flowing information – radio and television signals, telephone conversations, internet packets – meaningful patterns of data within the wider spectrum of noise. For others, information is a broader concept. Floridi (2010: 74), for example, identifies three types of information:

Factual: information *as* reality (e.g., patterns, fingerprints, tree rings)

Instructional: information *for* reality (e.g., commands, algorithms, recipes)

Semantic: information *about* reality (e.g., train timetables, maps, biographies).

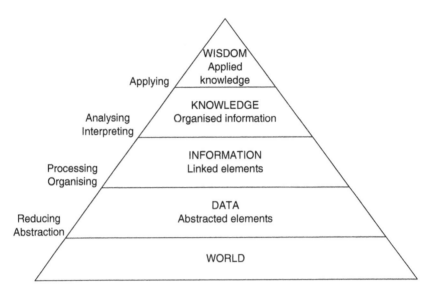

Figure 1.1 Knowledge pyramid (adapted from Adler 1986 and McCandless 2010)

The first is essentially meaningful data, what are usually termed facts. These are data that are organised and framed within a system of measurement or an external referent that inherently provides a basis to establish an initial meaning that holds some truth. Information also extends beyond data and facts through adding value that aids interpretation. Weinberger (2011: 2) thus declares: 'Information is to data what wine is to the vineyard: the delicious extract and distillate.' Such value could be gained through sorting, classifying, linking, or adding semantic content through some form of text or visualisation that informs about something and/or instructs what to do (for example, a warning light on a car's dashboard indicating that the battery is flat and needs recharging, Floridi, 2010). Case (2002; summarised in Borgman 2007: 40) argues that differences in the definition of information hinge on five issues:

> uncertainty, or whether something has to reduce uncertainty to qualify as information; physicality, or whether something has to take on a physical form such as a book, an object, or the sound waves of speech to qualify as information; structure/process, or whether some set of order or relationships is required; intentionality, or whether someone must intend that something be communicated to qualify as information; and truth, or whether something must be true to qualify as information.

Regardless of how it is conceived, Floridi (2010) notes that given that information adds meaning to data, it gains currency as a commodity. It is, however, a particular kind of commodity, possessing three main properties (which data also share):

Non-rivalrous: more than one entity can possess the same information (unlike material goods)

Non-excludable: it is easily shared and it takes effort to seek to limit such sharing (such as enforcing intellectual property rights agreements or inserting pay walls)

Zero marginal cost: once information is available, the cost of reproduction is often negligible.

While holding the properties of being non-rivalrous and non-excludable, because information is valuable many entities seek to limit and control its circulation, thus increasing its value. Much of this value is added through the processes enacted in the information life cycle (Floridi 2010):

Occurrence: discovering, designing, authoring

Transmission: networking, distributing, accessing, retrieving, transmitting

Processing and management: collecting, validating, modifying, organising, indexing, classifying, filtering, updating, sorting, storing

Usage: monitoring, modelling, analysing, explaining, planning, forecasting, decision-making, instructing, educating, learning.

It is through processing, management and usage that information is converted into the even more valuable knowledge.

As with all the concepts in the pyramid, knowledge is similarly a diversely understood concept. For some, knowledge is the 'know-how that transforms information into instructions' (Weinberger 2011: 3). For example, semantic information can be linked into recipes (first do this, then do that ...) or a conditional form of inferential procedures (if such and such is the case do this, otherwise do this) (Floridi 2010). In this framing, information is structured data and knowledge is actionable information (Weinberger 2011). In other words, 'knowledge is like the recipe that turns information into bread, while data are like the atoms that make up the flour and the yeast' (Zelany 1987, cited in Weinberger 2011). For others, knowledge is more than a set of instructions; it can be a practical skill, a way of knowing how to undertake or achieve a task, or a system of thought that coherently links together information to reveal a wider picture about a phenomenon. Creating knowledge involves applying complex cognitive processes such as perception, synthesis, extraction, association, reasoning and communication to information. Knowledge has more value than information because it provides the basis for understanding, explaining and drawing insights about the world, which can be used to formulate policy and actions. Wisdom, the pinnacle of the knowledge pyramid, is being able to sagely apply knowledge.

While not all forms of knowledge are firmly rooted in data – for example, conjecture, opinions, beliefs – data are clearly a key base material for how we make sense of the world. Data provide the basic inputs into processes such as collating, sorting, categorising, matching, profiling, and modelling that seek to create information and knowledge in order to understand, predict, regulate and control phenomena. And generating data over time and in different locales enables us to track, evaluate and compare phenomena across time, space and scale. Thus, although information and knowledge are rightly viewed as being higher order and more valuable concepts, data are nonetheless a key ingredient with significant latent value that is realised when converted to information and knowledge. Whoever then has access to high-quality and extensive data has a competitive advantage over those excluded in being able to generate under-standing and wisdom. A key rationale for the open data movement, examined in Chapter 3, is gaining access to the latent value of administrative and public sector datasets.

FRAMING DATA

So far in this chapter, data have already started to be framed conceptually in terms of discussing the ontology of data (what data are), their different forms, and how they fit within the pyramid of knowledge. There is a myriad of other ways in which data can be thought about and understood, for example from a technical perspective concerning data quality, validity, reliability, authenticity and usability, and how they can be processed, structured, shared and analysed; or an ethical perspective concerning the reasons why data are generated and the uses to which data are put; or a political or economic perspective that considers how data are normatively conceived and contested as public goods, political capital, intellectual property or a commodity, and how they are regulated and traded; or a spatial and/or temporal perspective that considers how technical, ethical, political and economic regimes concerning data production and their uses develop and mutate across space and time; or a philosophical perspective that considers the varied and contested ontologies and epistemologies of data. Many of the issues, discussed in brief in this section, are returned to throughout the book.

Technically

Across all disciplines, data are considered from a normative, technical viewpoint. What is at stake is the extent to which methods of capture and measurement generate certain, clean, and accurate data, and how such data can and should be processed, structured, shared and analysed in ways that maintain their integrity, thus ensuring that reliable and valid conclusions can be drawn from them. There are always doubts about the veracity of data because they are inherently abstracted, generalised and approximated through their production (Goodchild 2009). Considerable attention is thus directed at issues such as data representativeness, uncertainty, reliability, error, bias, and calibration within research design and implementation, with this information recorded as metadata.

Given that data are a surrogate for some aspect of a phenomenon – light representing a star, physical characteristics representing a plant, words representing a person's thoughts – *representativeness* relates to how well data capture the phenomenon they seek to represent, and how well the sample of data generated represents the overall population. With respect to the former, the key question is the extent to which we can be confident that scientific techniques accurately capture the phenomenon in question. This has been a particular problem in the social sciences and humanities and has proven difficult to resolve. For example, it is well noted that what people say they will do and what they do are often quite different, and what people do is often not what they intended. There is therefore a question over how well interview data represent human behaviour, or how well behaviour represents conscious thought. Similarly, there are concerns over the extent to which key indicators adequately capture and represent how a domain is performing. For example, to what extent do indicators such as citation counts, an h-index, and patents registered denote high-quality performance by university staff (with respect to humanities faculty they are considered very poor indicators)? The solution has been to try and develop more and more sophisticated research designs that counteract the shortcomings of different methods, or to largely ignore the shortcomings.

With respect to how well a sample represents a population, we might decide to generate detailed, longitudinal, astronomical data with respect to 50 stars in order to better understand their nature, but to what extent can we be confident that these 50 stars represent the qualities of the billions of stars that exist? Even in the age of big data, which seeks to be exhaustive rather than selective in data generation (see Chapter 4), the data are inherently a sample (not all people use social media, or shop with credit cards, and indeed many people across the world do not have access to phones or computers), meaning the data are representative of a set of people, even if that set is very large. Again, the solution has been to devise a range of sampling techniques that seek to ensure representativeness under different conditions (often dependent on the sample being random), and statistical methods that calculate the extent to which we can be confident that the sample represents the population (Kitchin and Tate 1999).

Reliability concerns the repeatability or consistency in obtaining the same finding from the administering of a research instrument. Golledge and Stimson (1997) describe three kinds of reliability: (1) quixotic reliability, where a single method of observation continually yields an unvarying measurement; (2) diachronic reliability, the stability of an observation through time; and (3) synchronic reliability, the similarity of observations within the same time period. Reliability is important because it is generally accepted that the more consistent a measure in producing data, the more confidence can be attributed to it.

Error is the difference between a measured and a real value, and can include absences (missing data), mistakes (such as miscoding or misclassification or the misapplication of a technique), and misunderstandings. *Bias* is a particular kind of error, where the data are skewed due to a consistent pattern of error. Bias is usually caused by the method, instrument or sampling technique used to generated the data having an undue influence on what data are produced, or can be introduced due to the ideological position or aspirations of the researcher often in a non-deliberate manner (Kitchin 1996). Processing techniques such as aggregation can introduce bias by reducing variance in a dataset leading to ecological fallacy errors – that is, assuming that an aggregate value accurately represents the individuals aggregated (for example, if we had two people weighing 50 kilograms and two weighing 150 kilograms their mean aggregate weight would be 100 kilograms, yet nobody in the set weighs that amount) (Kitchin and Fotheringham 1997). *Uncertainty* concerns the extent to which a researcher can be confident concerning the accuracy of the data and any analysis based on them. With respect to quantitative data it relates to the certainty of a statistical test given the data inputted, and is usually calculated as probabilities and expressed as confidence levels (Goodchild 2009). Uncertainty with respect to qualitative data is more likely to be assessed by expert judgement based on prior experience.

Underpinning the drive to tackle these concerns is a belief that such issues arise due to human frailties in research design or deficiencies in the instruments or methods used and that they can be fixed through technical solutions. That is, they can be addressed by improving the quality of procedures and equipment used, implementing regimes of standardisation that provide known benchmarks of data quality (such as those endorsed by the ISO), and finding ways to compensate for uncertainty, error and bias in the modes of analysis employed.

Ethically

Ethics is concerned with thought and practice related to value concepts such as justice, equality, fairness, honesty, respect, rights, entitlements and care. Every society operates with respect to a mix of commonsensical, informal and taken-for-granted moral values, and highly codified ethical positions enshrined in rules, principles, policies, licences and laws, subject to enforcement by state and other agencies. These ethical positions are often contested, with different groups taking contrasting views on values themselves and the extent to which ethical stances should be legislated for, and their debate is an exercise in moral philosophy. Such contestation also exists with respect to data, especially concerning what data are

generated and the means of production, how data are shared, traded and protected, and to what ends data are employed.

While some data are considered relatively benign, for example measurements
relating to the weather, other data are considered to be highly sensitive, for
example those related to individuals which can be used to produce a detailed
picture of the lives they lead and to regulate those lives. In some cases, generating
data might do harm, for example interviewing the survivors of war crimes might
cause psychological distress. Here, there are questions about the extent to which
data generation and various forms of dataveillance (surveillance enacted through
the processing and analysing of data records) and data analysis infringe on privacy and other human rights, and can be used to actively socially sort individuals (provide differential service based on their characteristics) (Graham 2005).
These concerns are exacerbated given that digital data can be easily combined,
shared and traded, and we live in an age of widespread invasive data generation
and surveillance. It is perhaps no surprise then that agencies funding academic
research and higher education institutions now routinely evaluate the ethical
dimensions of research projects as to their potential wider implications, and
nations have enacted legislation, such as data protection acts and privacy laws, to
try and prevent the misuses and abuses of data. These and related issues are discussed more fully in Chapter 10.

Politically and economically

A consideration of the ethics of data starts to reveal the ways in which data
are framed by wider political and economical concerns. What data are generated, and how they are processed, analysed and employed are contextualised
with respect to: how they are normatively conceived within a population and
employed by states, and notions of how they should be regulated and legislated for; the discourses employed within discursive regimes that support or
oppose their generation and application; decision-making about funding and
investing in data; the unfolding of capitalism and the ways in which data are
used to manage endeavours and leverage value and profit; and are traded as a
commodity with the emergence of a multi-billion-dollar data marketplace
made up of a diverse set of players (producers, aggregators, sellers, analysts, and
consumers; see Chapter 2). Those producing data have to consider public and
political opinion, ethical considerations, the regulatory environment, the
funding available, and the soundness of their investment vis-à-vis resourcing.
And those in charge of the legislative and funding arenas have to ponder and
make decisions about how to shape the landscape in which producers and
users of data operate, as well as consider their own data regimes and what they
reveal about their agendas, priorities, and modes of governance and governmentality (Lauriault 2012).

In both cases, a diverse set of politics and economic rationalities is at play, with competing voices seeking to influence opinion and the wider data terrain. The open data movement, for example, casts data as a public good that should constitute a commons and be freely accessible (with the exception of sensitive, personal data) or be accessible through fair use agreements. In contrast, business views data as a valuable commodity that, on the one hand, needs to be protected through intellectual property regimes (copyright, patents, ownership rights) and, on the other, not be so tied down by ethical concerns that they cannot be exploited for capital gain. For communities and states, data are a means by which political agendas and work can be legitimated, conducted and contested by enabling the construction of evidence-informed narratives and counter-discourses that have greater rhetorical value than anecdote or sentiment (Wilson 2011; Garvey 2013). In other words, data constitute in Foucault's (1981) terms a form of power/knowledge; a means through which people, phenomena and territory can be surveyed and regulated (Lauriault 2012). These alternative interests can often become aligned in paradoxical ways, though they may have quite different agendas, for example the support of big business for the open data movement with respect to public data (see Chapter 3). In other words, data are manifested and situated within complex and contested political economies and, at the same time, they are used to shape such debates and regimes.

Moreover, data constitute an economic resource, one that is a key component of the next phase of the knowledge economy, reshaping the mode of production to one that it is data-driven (see Chapter 7). Since the late 1980s, scholars such as Castells (1988, 1996) have argued that the latest cycle of capitalism is underpinned by the production of knowledge that creates new products and forms of labour, facilitates economic restructuring, and enhances productivity, competitiveness, efficiencies, sustainability and capital accumulation. Big data, in particular, is the latest development in deepening and advancing this cycle, providing a wealth of evidence that is being used by companies to, on the one hand, monitor and evaluate company performance in real time, reduce waste and fraud, and improve corporate strategy, planning and decision-making and, on the other, to design new commodities, identify and target new markets, implement dynamic pricing, realise untapped potential, and gain competitive advantage (Manyika et al. 2011; Zikopoulos et al. 2012). In so doing, the production and analysis of data enables companies to be run more intelligently with respect to how they are organised and operate, promoting flexibility and innovation, reducing risks, costs and operational losses, improving customer experience, and maximising return on investment and profits. By driving capital accumulation, big data facilitates new divisions of labour and the next round of uneven development. Data can thus be understood as an agent of capital interests.

Temporally and spatially

Data have both a temporality and a spatiality. What data are produced and the ways in which they are processed, analysed, stored or discarded varies across time and space; data and the assemblages surrounding them have histories and geographies. How data are processed and analysed mutates over time, affected by organisational change and improvements in enumeration and administration, new laws regarding data handling and protection, new technologies, new methods of data sorting and analysis, varying statistical geographies (such as new local area or county boundaries), and new statistical techniques. Moreover, the data assemblages operating in one jurisdiction can be quite different from another. Even within a jurisdiction, how one entity produces and manages data can vary due to institutional or personal vagaries.

Consider population censuses. A census consists of a comprehensive survey of an area and its population, usually conducted every ten years. The aim is to establish key information about who is living in a locale and their characteristics (e.g., age, gender, marital status, household composition, religion, race, social class, etc.) and aspects about their lives (their work, accommodation, etc.). To enable change to be measured censuses require continuity with respect to the questions asked and how they are administered. At the same time, in order to capture new data of interest that reflect broader changes in society, transformation is required, such as new or modified questions (see Figure 1.2: note, even when questions were maintained across censuses, how they were phrased was often quite different). Further, how the census is subsequently administered is shaped by institutional, political and economic forces and new technical developments: see Linehan (1991) for a history of the Irish census 1821–1991, and Lauriault (2012) for an analysis of the Canadian census 1871–2011. Moreover, the construction of a census is contested and negotiated as vested interests compete to include, alter or remove questions. In some cases, changes can be quite radical, such as the decision in Germany to discontinue their census in the 1980s (see Hannah 2011). As a consequence, a national census is always caught in a tension between continuity and change, but nonetheless evolves over time and has varying geographies. To date, however, there have been few histories and geographies of data assemblages (though see Alder 2002; Desrosières 1988; Hannah 2011; Hewitt 2010; Lauriault 2012; Poovey 1998; Porter 1995).

Philosophically

For some, at the ontological level data are benign. Data are simply data, essential elements that are abstracted from the world in neutral and objective ways subject to technical constraints. They 'do not have any inherent meaning, do not necessarily

[PARTICULARS FOR INDIVIDUALS ON FORM A AT EACH CENSUS

- = Not collected; Y = precoded; E = entered by Enumerator; y = reply menu given in notes

	Year of Census	1841	1851	1861	1871	1881	1891	1901	1911	1926	1936	1945	1951	1958	1961	1966	1971	1979	1981	1988	1991	
M	Month	6	3	4	4	4	4	4	3	4	4	5	4	4	4	4	4	4	4	4	4	M
D	Date	6	30	7	2	3	5	31	2	18	26	12	8	8	9	17	18	5	1	13	21	D
C	Capacity of Form–Number of Persons	20	15	15	12	15	15	15	15	10	10	10	10	11	10	10	10	10	6	8	8	C
1	Name and surname	X	X	X	X	X	X	X	X	X	X	X	X	X	X	X	X	X	X	X	X	1
2	Sex	X	X	X	X	X	X	X	X	X	X	X	X	X	X	X	X	X	X	X	X	2
3	Relationship to head of household	X	X	X	X	X	X	X	X	X	X	X	X	X	X	X	X	X	X	X	X	3
4	Age (A); (B) Years, Months; (C) Date of Birth	A	A	A	A	A	A	A	A	A	B	B	C	C	C	C	C	C	C	C	C	4
5	Marital Status (S shows separated)	X	X	X	X	X	X	X	X	X	X	X	X	X	X	X	Y	Y	Y	VS	VS	5
6	Place of birth (County, City, Country)	X	X	X	X	X	X	X	X	X	X	X	X	X	X	X	X	X	X	X	X	6
7	Absent family members (separate table)	X	X	X	X	X	-	-	-	-	-	-	-	-	-	-	-	-	-	-	-	7
8	Deaths in family members since last Census (separate table)	X	X	X	X	X	-	-	-	-	-	-	-	-	-	-	-	-	-	-	-	8
9	Literacy (Read, write); y = notes gave reply menu	↑X	↑X	X	X	X	X	Y	Y	Y	-	-	-	-	-	-	-	-	-	-	-	9
10	Occupation: ♠ pre 1926 no separate "industry"	↑X	↑X	↑X	↑X	↑X	↑X	↑X	↑X	X	X	X	X	X	X	X	X	X	X	X	X	10
11	Marriage date "D" or duration "d"; w women only	D	D	D	D	-	-	-	dw	dw	dw	Dw	-	Dw	Dw	-	Dw	-	Dw	-	-	11
12	Irish: "as addendum to literacy question; y as 9	-	*y	*y	*y	*y	*y	Y	Y	Y	Y	Y	Y	-	Y	-	Y	Y	Y	Y	Y	12
13	Incapacity (D=deaf, dumb, blind; L= Lunatic)	-	D	D	D	DL	DL	DL	DL	DL	X	X	X	X	X	X	X	-	X	X	X	13
14	Religion	-	-	X	X	X	X	X	X	X	X	X	X	X	X	X	X	-	X	X	X	14
15	Live births to present marriage for married women	-	-	-	-	-	-	-	X	X	X	X	X	X	X	-	-	-	-	-	-	15
16	Children of present marriage: still living	-	-	-	-	-	-	-	X	X	-	-	-	-	-	-	-	-	-	-	-	16
17	Orphanhood (for children)	-	-	-	-	-	-	-	X	-	-	-	-	-	-	-	-	-	-	-	-	17
18	Dependants = no. <16 for married men and all widowed	-	-	-	-	-	-	-	-	-	X	-	-	-	-	X	X	-	Y	-	-	18
19	Industry (Question "Employer and Employers' Business")	-	-	-	-	-	-	-	-	X	X	X	X	-	X	X	X	-	X	X	X	19
20	Area, viz. agric. holdings; H=household; I=individual	-	-	-	-	-	-	-	-	H	H	H	H	-	H	I	H	-	I	-	-	20
21	Period of unemployment previous year; 3 causes	-	-	-	-	-	-	-	-	-	X	X	X	-	-	-	-	-	-	-	-	21
22	Period of residence for immigrants	-	-	-	-	-	-	-	-	-	X	X	-	-	-	-	-	-	-	-	-	22
23	Home address of visitors	-	-	-	-	-	-	-	-	-	-	-	X	X	X	-	-	-	-	-	-	23
24	Employ. status–sep. ques. re employee/own account	-	-	-	-	-	-	-	-	-	-	-	-	X	X	X	X	Y	Y	Y	Y	24
25	Subsidiary occupation	-	-	-	-	-	-	-	-	-	-	-	-	-	X	-	-	-	-	-	-	25
26	Age at which fulltime education ceased	-	-	-	-	-	-	-	-	-	-	-	-	-	-	X	X	-	X	X	X	26
27	Types of school etc. attended fulltime: I - duration	-	-	-	-	-	-	-	-	-	-	-	-	-	-	Y	IV	-	IV	-	-	27
28	Scientific or technological qualifications	-	-	-	-	-	-	-	-	-	-	-	-	-	-	-	X	-	X	X	X	28
29	Usual residence now	-	-	-	-	-	-	-	-	-	-	-	-	-	-	-	X	-	X	X	X	29
30	Usual residence one year ago	-	-	-	-	-	-	-	-	-	-	-	-	-	-	-	X	-	X	X	X	30
31	Means of travel to work, school etc.	-	-	-	-	-	-	-	-	-	-	-	-	-	-	-	X	-	X	Y	Y	31
32	Distance to work, school etc.	-	-	-	-	-	-	-	-	-	-	-	-	-	-	-	X	-	X	Y	Y	32
33	Became resident within past year: Yes/No	-	-	-	-	-	-	-	-	-	-	-	-	-	-	-	-	Y	-	-	-	33
34	Address of place of work, school or college	-	-	-	-	-	-	-	-	-	-	-	-	-	-	-	-	-	X	X	X	34
35	Present status – sep. ques. re labour force status	-	-	-	-	-	-	-	-	-	-	-	-	-	-	-	-	Y	Y	Y	Y	35
36	Lived outside >-1 year; when, whence came	-	-	-	-	-	-	-	-	-	-	-	-	-	-	-	-	-	X	X	X	36
37	Highest level of education completed - [for no. 27]	-	-	-	-	-	-	-	-	-	-	-	-	-	-	-	-	-	-	-	Y	37
38	Is person farming – principal or subsidiary?	-	-	-	-	-	-	-	-	-	-	-	-	-	-	-	-	-	-	-	Y	38

Figure 1.2 Questions concerning individuals on the Irish census 1841–1991

Source: Reproduced from Linehan 1991

present any interpretations or opinions, and do not carry indicative characteristics that may reveal their importance or relevance' (Pérez-Montoro and Díaz Nafría 2010). They are pre-analytical and pre-factual. From this perspective, a sensor has no politics or agenda. It simply measures light or heat or humidity, and so on – producing readings that reflect the truth about the world unless tainted by a technical glitch. In other words, the sensor produces an objective, realist view of the world revealing things as they really are, wherein the reality of thing being measured is independent of the measuring process (Desrosières 1998). Within measurement processes in which people play a central role – in a lab or conducting a survey or interview – a form of mechanical objectivity is employed that adheres to defined rules and rigorous, systematic method to produce distant, detached, impartial and transparent data that is free of researcher bias and preferences, and is thus independent of local customs, culture, knowledge and context (Porter 1995). As such, science when practised properly has no politics or ulterior agenda and data then can be taken at face value. Indeed, the terms commonly used to detail how data are handled suggest benign technical processes: 'collected', 'entered', 'compiled', 'stored', 'processed' and 'mined' (Gitelman and Jackson 2013). It is only the uses of data that are political. In other words, it is people who corrupt data and twist them to their own ends, not science.

For others, such a view is untenable. How we conceive of data, how we measure them, and what we do with them actively frames the nature of data. For them data does not pre-exist their generation; they do not arise from nowhere. Data are produced through measuring, abstracting and generalising techniques that have been conceived to perform a task and are recorded into forms and measures that conform with standards invented by people (e.g., the metric system). They are epistemological units, made to have a representational form that enables epistemological work, and data about the same phenomena can be measured and recorded in numerous ways, each providing a different set of data that can be analysed and interpreted through varying means (Poovey 1998). How data are generated is not inevitable: protocols, organisational processes, measurement scales, categories, and standards are designed, negotiated and debated, and there is a certain messiness to data generation. Take the case of measuring the population of a country: decisions need to be taken as to who is and is not counted (e.g., to include visitors, legal and illegal aliens, those who avoided taking part either deliberately or not, etc.) and where they should be counted (e.g., where they are on census night or where they normally reside); all kinds of rules and procedures are set up, but there is still indeterminacy and variation across enumerators (Porter 1995).

Consequently, how data are ontologically defined and delimited is not a neutral, technical process, but a normative, political, and ethical one that is often contested and has consequences for subsequent analysis, interpretation and action (Bowker and Star 1999). However, once in place, data ontologies work to foreclose variability and define what will be visible and invisible within a dataset, though this process of convergence and stability is always open to resistance and reworking due to the multiplicity of actors, things and processes at work, and the contrariness of data that do not easily fit within a system (Bowker and Star 1999). Moreover, once data are produced they can sorted, spliced and diced in any number of ways into various categories. In other words, data are not independent of the thought system and the instruments underpinning their production (Bowker and Star 1999). And such thought systems are infused with philosophical assumptions and beliefs and are differentially practised. Indeed, as Borgman (2007: 38) notes, while science seeks to portray itself as universal, 'their practices are local and vary widely'. Thus, data do not simply represent the reality of the world; they are constructions about the world (Desrosières 1998; Poovey 1998).

From such a perspective 'scientific knowledge is produced – rather than innocently "discovered"' (Gitelman and Jackson 2013: 4). As such,

> [d]ata are difficult to separate from the software, equipment, documentation, and knowledge required to use them. For example, if data are produced by an instrument such as a sensor network, interpreting those data requires an understanding of the instrument – for example, what do the sensors detect, under what conditions, at what frequency of observation, and with what type of calibration? (Borgman 2007: 183)

Yet science often tries to shear data free and independent of such a contextual understanding, organising and sharing the data via databases in which the messiness of their creation is ameliorated and users are 'protected' from having to know how the data were produced and organised (Gitelman and Jackson 2013). Ribes and Jackson (2013: 165) thus argue that scientific conceptions of data as neutral and objective are fictions that 'assume or project a world where data floats free of its origins, shedding form, substance, and history, and is thereby rendered free to travel the world as an undifferentiated and universal currency'. In contrast, they assert 'data is stickier than that'.

Consequently, no data are pre-analytic, or objective and independent elements. As Gitelman and Jackson (2013: 2, following Bowker (2005)) put it, 'raw data is an oxymoron'; 'data are always already "cooked" and never entirely "raw"'. 'Data need to be imagined *as* data to exist and function as such' (Gitelman and Jackson 2013: 3). Data are both social, in that they are situated in context, and material, in that they have a form (as bits, as symbols, as numbers, etc.), stored on paper, magnetic tapes, hard disks, etc. (Wilson 2011; Gitelman and Jackson 2013). Both actively shape the constitution of data. For example, big data are reliant on the discursive, political and economic discourses that support their roll-out (see Chapter 7), and on the databases, computers, servers, and networks that enable their production, processing, sharing, analysis and storage (see Chapter 5). Such media facilitate the rotting of data, the misplacing or forgetting or deletion of data, or its erosion through bit-rot (the breakdown of storage media such as the decaying of computer tape and damaged hard drives) (Boellstorff 2013). Indeed, data are never only cooked but are also open to 'the unplanned, unexpected, and accidental', 'transformed in parahuman, complexly material, and temporally emergent ways that do not always follow a pre-ordained, algorithmic "recipe"' (Boellstorff 2013).

Given the social and material nature of data we actively remake 'our material, technological, geographical, organizational, and social worlds into the kind of environments in which data can flourish ... enter[ing] into a symbiotic relationship with data' (Ribes and Jackson 2013: 152). Thus, while '[d]ata is seen as something that is out there – something that is *about* the real' (Shah 2013, original emphasis), they are more productively understood as both a component of the real and a producer of the real. Data are not merely an abstraction and representative, they are constitutive, and their generation, analysis and interpretation has consequences. As Gitelman and Jackson (2013: 2) state: 'if data are somehow subject to us, we are also subject to data'. Data are captured from the world, but in turn do work in the world. Data are not, and can never be, benign (Shah 2013). Instead, '[d]ata ... need to be understood as framed and framing' (Gitelman and Jackson 2013: 5). In other words, there is much more to conceptualising data than science and business generally acknowledge.

THINKING CRITICALLY ABOUT DATABASES AND DATA INFRASTRUCTURES

In order to make sense of data they are usually pooled into datasets, which are often organised and held in databases (a means of structuring and storing data that can be queried in multiple ways) and data infrastructures such as archives and repositories (see Chapters 2, 3 and 5). As with conceptualising data more generally, it is then important to think critically about the nature of databases and data infrastructures, their sociotechnical production, and how they reflect rationalities about the world at the same time as they reproduce and reinforce such rationalities. Such critical reflection has been largely absent with respect to big data, open data, and the scaling of small data, with the focus to date being more technical and instrumental in nature.

The thesis adopted and developed throughout this book continues the argument set out in the last section, positing that databases and data infrastructures are not simply neutral, technical means of assembling and sharing data; they are not merely products that store captured data about the world, but are bundles of contingent and relational processes that do work in the world (Star and Ruhleder 1996; Kitchin and Dodge 2011). They are complex sociotechnical systems that are embedded within a larger institutional landscape of researchers, institutions and corporations, constituting essential tools in the production of knowledge, governance and capital.

Databases are designed and built to hold certain kinds of data and enable certain kinds of analysis, and how they are structured has profound consequences as to what queries and analysis can be performed; their formulation conditions the work that can be done on and through them (Ruppert 2012). For example, it is quite different to store data in databases rather than in a narrative form in terms of what is stored, how it is stored, and how it can be recalled and reworked (Bowker 2005). Databases create silences, adding to the inherent gaps in the data, as much as they reveal relationships between data and enable some questions to be answered; they constrain and facilitate through their ontology, producing various presences and absences of relations (Ruppert 2012; Vis 2013). Drawing on Derrida, Bowker (2005: 12) thus argues that databases and archives are jussive: they 'tell us what we can and cannot say' by defining what is remembered and what is ignored and forgotten. Such remembering/forgetting is determined by rules and practices that are political and philosophical acts. The ontologies within databases are thus neither fixed nor natural, but are created by actors with particular aims working within communities of practice, modes of governance, and technical constraints. Databases then are expressions of power/knowledge and they enact and reproduce such relations (Ruppert 2012), for example determining what someone's insurance rate is or whether they can travel between countries. Moreover, databases are dynamic entities that perform a 'constant process of differentiating' (Ruppert 2012: 129) through interactions with their associated assemblage (creators, users, software, hardware, networks, etc.).

At the same time, databases unmoor data analysis from the data by enabling complex queries and calculations without those conducting such analyses having to peruse and work the data themselves or even understand how the data have been compiled and organised (Gitelman and Jackson 2013). This unmooring is aided by techniques such as standardisation of formats and metadata and works to decontextualise and depoliticise the data contained within (Wilson 2011). Importantly, such unmooring enables the power/knowledge of the database to travel and be deployed by others shorn of its complex inner workings and history and politics of production (in the same way as a driver can utilise a car without knowing how all its complex systems are made or what they do or how they interact to shape the driving experience). Researchers can thus utilise government databases such as a census or business survey or economic indicators without knowing the politics of why and how such databases were constructed, the technical aspects of their generation, or having personal familiarity with the phenomena captured. For example, using the Irish Department of Environment's databases of unfinished estates in Ireland post the 2008 economic crash (available at http://www.housing.ie/Our-Services/Unfinished-Housing-Developments.aspx) one can interrogate, map and draw conclusions about the estates without knowing anything about the history and politics of the survey, how it was undertaken, or visiting any of estates (see Kitchin et al., 2012a, b). Such unmooring then enables databases to act as immutable mobiles (that is, stable and transferable forms of knowledge that are portable across space and time) (Latour 1989).

Data infrastructures host and link databases into a more complex sociotechnical structure. As with databases, there is nothing inherent or given about how such archiving and sharing structures are composed. Indeed, as discussed throughout the book, the design and management of data infrastructures are riddled with technical and political challenges that are tackled through messy and contested negotiations that are contextualised by various agendas and governmentalities. The solutions created in terms of standards, protocols, policies and laws inherently have normalising effects in that they seek common shared ground and to universalise practices amongst developers and users (Lauriault 2012), glossing over and ameliorating the tension between enabling interoperability and limiting customisation and constraining innovation, and denying alternative ways of structuring and ordering data (Star and Ruhleder 1996). Given these tensions, normalising processes have to constantly and recursively be reaffirmed through implementation, management and system governance (Star and Lampland, 2009). Star and Ruhleder (1996: 112) thus contend '[t]here is no absolute center from which control and standards flow; as well, no absolute periphery', with 'infrastructure [being] something that emerges for people in practice, connected to activities and structures'.

This emergence, while never fully centred is, however, not free-form and is shaped by wider structural relations. As Graham and Marvin (2001) argue, infrastructures are constitutive of 'long-term accumulations of finance, technology, know-how, and organizational and geopolitical power' (p. 12) and sustain 'sociotechnical geometries of power' (p. 11) of congealed social interests. Such accumulations include regimes of regulation that seek to delimit legally and through forms of governmentality how data are managed, analysed and shared, for example data protection laws (see Chapter 10). Starr (1987: 8) thus proposes that a data infrastructure has

> two kinds of structures – social and cognitive: Its social organization consists of the social and economic relations of individual respondents, state agencies, private firms, professions, international organizations and others involved in producing flows of data from original sources to points of analysis, distribution and use. Cognitive organization refers to the structuring of the information itself, including the boundaries of inquiry, presupposition about social reality, systems of classification, methods of measurement, and official rules for interpreting and presenting data.

As Dourish and Bell (2007) contend, databases and infrastructures then cannot be considered in purely instrumental terms as they are thoroughly cultural, economic and cognitive in nature and steeped in social significance. They thus suggest two lenses through which to understand data infrastructures. The first is a sociopolitical reading which examines them as 'crystallizations of institutional relations' (p. 416). The second perspective is an experiential reading that examines 'how they shape individual actions and experience' (p. 417). In both cases, data infrastructures are understood as relational entities. This relationality reshapes the world contingently around it, as it in turn is shaped by the world. So as we come to use and rely on databases and data infrastructures to make sense of and do work in the world, our discursive and material practices adapt and mutate in response to them (Star and Ruhleder 1996). The world is not just reflected in data, it is changed by them; 'the work of producing, preserving, and sharing data reshapes the organizational, technological, and cultural worlds around them' (Ribes and Jackson 2013: 147).

In other words, databases and data infrastructures do not simply support research, they fundamentally change the practices and organisation of research – the questions asked, how they are asked, how they are answered, how the answers are deployed, who is conducting the research and how they operate as researchers (see Chapter 8). For example, in her study of the evolution of the Canadian Census and the Atlas of Canada, Lauriault (2012) details how each has developed recursively and iteratively based on models of the world which construct ways to imagine and produce Canada. She argues that the data archives and the data themselves constitute an institutional 'extrasomatic memory system that allows for the telling of stories about the nature of Canada ... [through] maps, graphs, models and statistics which rely on sensors, data, interoperability and web mapping standards, portals, metadata and models, science, and open architectures' (p. 27). In turn, these stories modulate the underlying models and thus the data infrastructure mutates, inflecting the means through which the stories are created.

Making sense of databases and data infrastructures then requires carefully unpacking and deconstructing their always emerging, contingent, relational and contextual nature (Star and Ruhleder 1996). This means looking for what Bowker and Star (1999: 34) describe as infrastructural inversion that recognises 'the depths of interdependence of technical networks and standards, on the one hand, and the real work of politics and knowledge production on the other'. As Lauriault (2012) argues, this also requires a historical analysis that documents how databases and data infrastructures develop over time and space.

DATA ASSEMBLAGES AND THE DATA REVOLUTION

The principal argument forwarded in this chapter has been that thinking about data is not straightforward. Data do not exist independently of ideas, techniques, technologies, systems, people and contexts, regardless of them often being presented in this manner (Lauriault 2012; Ribes and Jackson 2013). Data are generated as the product of many minds working within diverse situations, framed and shaped within mileau circumstances and structures.

One way to make sense of data is to think of them as the central concern of a complex sociotechnical assemblage. This data assemblage is composed of many apparatuses and elements that are thoroughly entwined, and develop and mutate over time and space (see Table 1.3). Each apparatus and their elements frame what is possible, desirable and expected of data. Moreover, they interact with and shape each other

Table 1.3 The apparatus and elements of a data assemblage

Apparatus	Elements
Systems of thought	Modes of thinking, philosophies, theories, models, ideologies, rationalities, etc.
Forms of knowledge	Research texts, manuals, magazines, websites, experience, word of mouth, chat forums, etc.
Finance	Business models, investment, venture capital, grants, philanthropy, profit, etc.
Political economy	Policy, tax regimes, public and political opinion, ethical considerations, etc.
Governmentalities and legalities	Data standards, file formats, system requirements, protocols, regulations, laws, licensing, intellectual property regimes, etc.
Materialities and infrastructures	Paper/pens, computers, digital devices, sensors, scanners, databases, networks, servers, etc.
Practices	Techniques, ways of doing, learned behaviours, scientific conventions, etc.
Organisations and institutions	Archives, corporations, consultants, manufacturers, retailers, government agencies, universities, conferences, clubs and societies, committees and boards, communities of practice, etc.
Subjectivities and communities	Of data producers, curators, managers, analysts, scientists, politicians, users, citizens, etc.
Places	Labs, offices, field sites, data centres, server farms, business parks, etc., and their agglomerations.
Marketplace	For data, its derivatives (e.g., text, tables, graphs, maps), analysts, analytic software, interpretations, etc.

through a contingent and complex web of multifaceted relations (see Figure 1.3). And, as Ribes and Jackson (2013) contend, not only do they frame what and how data are produced and to what ends they are employed, but they are themselves organised and managed to produce such data. Data and their assemblage are thus co-determinous and mutually constituted, bound together in a set of contingent, relational and contextual discursive and material practices and relations. Every data assemblage then varies in concert with the arrangement of elements and context, but they share commonalities and echoes of each other due to overarching and overlapping apparatus and conventions that span assemblages. And as new ideas and knowledges emerge, technologies are invented, skill sets develop, and markets open, data assemblages evolve, mutate, coalesce and collapse. As a consequence, there is a huge diversity of data assemblages across domains and jurisdictions.

This book examines the emerging and evolving data assemblages producing open data, data infrastructures and big data. In so doing it advances three key arguments. First, there is a need to develop conceptual and philosophical ways to make sense of data. There has been remarkably little critical reflection and research on data in and of themselves and on the constitution and operation of the assemblages surrounding them, especially compared to the attention focused on the concepts of information and knowledge. And yet, data are a fundamental element of knowledge production. Second, there is a data revolution underway that constitutes a key moment in evolution and mutation of data assemblages. Due to the confluence of several emerging developments in computing, methodological techniques, and the political and economic realm, the volume, variety, velocity, resolution, and availability of data, and how data are being processed, analysed, stored, and employed to leverage insight and value, is being radically transformed. Third, given the various technical, ethical and scientific challenges that the data revolution raises there is an urgent need to develop a detailed understanding of the new and emerging data assemblages being created. The ten chapters that follow thus aim to provide a broad, synoptic and critical overview of these assemblages and to highlight issues that demand further attention and research.

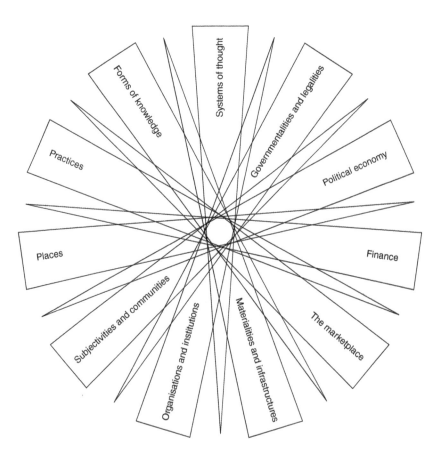

Figure 1.3 The intersecting apparatus of a data assemblage

2

SMALL DATA, DATA INFRASTRUCTURES AND DATA BROKERS

Until a couple of years ago the term 'small data' was rarely, if ever, used. Its deployment has arisen purely as the de facto oppositional term to so-called 'big data'. All data were, in effect, small data and therefore did not require labelling as such. What constitutes big data is discussed in detail in Chapter 4, but it is necessary here to highlight the distinction between small and big data, before going on to discuss how small data are being transformed through new data infrastructures and multi-billion-dollar data markets and, as discussed in the next chapter, are being opened up for sharing and reuse.

Traditionally, given the costs and difficulties of generating, processing, analysing and storing data, they have been produced in tightly controlled ways using sampling techniques that limit their scope, temporality and size (H.J. Miller 2010). While some datasets could be very large in volume, such as a national census, to make the exercise of compiling such data manageable they have been produced only every few years and are limited in scope (in the case of the census usually once every 10 years, asking 30 to 40 questions). Moreover, the resolution of small tertiary data has often been quite coarse (e.g., counties or states rather than individuals and households) and the methods used to generate them quite inflexible (for example, once a census is set and is being administered it is all but impossible to tweak the questions or add new questions or remove others because it would seriously compromise processing and analysis). In contrast, big data are characterised by being generated continuously, seeking to be exhaustive and fine-grained in scope, and flexible and scalable in their production (see Table 2.1 and Chapter 4).

Table 2.1 Comparing small and big data

	Small data	Big data
Volume	Limited to large	Very large
Exhaustivity	Samples	Entire populations
Resolution and identification	Coarse and weak to tight and strong	Tight and strong
Relationality	Weak to strong	Strong
Velocity	Slow, freeze-framed/bundled	Fast, continuous
Variety	Limited to wide	Wide
Flexibile and scalable	Low to middling	High

Whereas small data are largely oases of data within data deserts, big data produce a veritable data deluge. This has led some to question whether big data might lead to the demise of small data or whether the stature of studies based on small data might be diminished due to their limitations in size, scope and temporality. For example, Sawyer (2008) notes that academic research funding agencies are increasingly pushing their limited funding resources to data-rich areas, perhaps conflating data volume and velocity with insight, utility and value, and consigning research questions for which it is difficult to generate big data to a funding desert and a marginal position within and outside the academy. This move has been complemented by a reorientation away from fundamental research by many funding agencies towards instrumental, applied and industry-partnered research. Such a reprioritisation misunderstands both the nature of big data and the value of small data.

Big data may seek to be exhaustive, but as with all data they are both a representation and a sample. What data are captured is shaped by:

- the field of view/sampling frame (where data-capture devices are deployed and what their settings/parameters are; who uses a space or media, e.g. who belongs to Facebook or shops in Walmart, etc);

- the technology and platform used (different surveys, sensors, lens, textual prompts, layout, etc., all produce variances and biases in what data are generated);

- the context in which data are generated (unfolding events mean data are always situated with respect to circumstance);

- the data ontology employed (how the data are calibrated and classified); and

- the regulatory environment with respect to privacy, data protection and security.

Big data generally capture what is easy to ensnare – data that are openly expressed (what is typed, swiped, scanned, sensed, etc.; people's actions and behaviours; the movement of things) – as well as data that are the 'exhaust', a by-product, of the primary task/output, and auto-generated metadata. It takes these data at face value, despite the fact that they may not have been designed to answer specific questions and the data produced might be messy and dirty (see Chapter 9).

Small data may be limited in volume and velocity, but they have a long history of development, with established methodologies and modes of analysis, and a record of producing answers to scientific questions. Small data studies can be much more finely tailored to answer specific research questions and to explore in detail and in depth the varied, contextual, rational and irrational ways in which people interact and make sense of the world, and how scientific processes work (see Chapters 8 and 9). Small data can focus on specific cases and tell individual, nuanced and contextual stories. And because they are targeted, they are intensely focused on an issue and are usually much less resource-intensive: small data studies seek to mine gold from working a narrow seam, whereas big data studies seek to extract nuggets through open-pit mining scooping up and sieving huge tracts of land. Sawyer (2008) thus argues that funding needs to target answering critical questions, whether they are to be tackled using small or big data, and not simply be directed towards projects that have access to vast quantities of data in the hope that they inherently contain useful insights.

That said, more value and insight can be extracted from small data by scaling them up into larger datasets, making them accessible for reuse through digital data infrastructures that also make them amenable to forms of computational analysis, and preserving them for future generations. Consequently, like big data, considerable resources have been invested in recent years to create such data infrastructures, which are altering significantly the data landscape.

DATA HOLDINGS, DATA ARCHIVES AND DATA INFRASTRUCTURES

Data have been collected together and stored for much of recorded history. Such practices have been both informal and formal in nature. The former consists simply of gathering data and storing them, whereas the latter consists of a set of curation practices and institutional structures designed to ensure that data are preserved for future generations. The former might best be described as data holdings, whereas the latter are data archives. The two are often confused or used interchangeably, along with other terms such as backup, databank and data repository, but for professional archivists, an archive has very particular characteristics.

Archives are formal collections of data that are actively structured, curated and documented, are accompanied by appropriate metadata, and actively plan issues of preservation, access and discoverability (Lauriault et al. 2013). Archives explicitly seek to be long-term endeavours, preserving data for future reuse. Preservation, in this context, has a particular use as a set of managed activities underpinned by 'principles, policies, rules and strategies aimed at prolonging the existence of an object [data] by maintaining it in a condition suitable for use, either in its original format or in a more persistent format, while leaving intact the object's intellectual form' (InterPARES 2, 2013). An archive seeks to preserve the full record set, not simply the data; that is, all supporting documentation, metadata, and other related material that details provenance and context with respect to how the data were generated and should be treated, analysed and interpreted. The approach to preservation is mindful that technologies, protocols and best practice guidelines are subject to change and obsolescence, that data will need to be migrated across platforms and technologies as new innovations come on stream, and that without active curation data may become corrupted, lost or shorn of its contextual metadata and supporting documents (Borgman 2007; Dasish 2012). By maintaining the integrity of the data over time, the archive seeks to provide a trustworthy resource.

In some cases, data custodians may have a legal responsibility to appropriately archive data for ongoing and future reuse, and the archiving body itself may be a statutory legal authority. For example, national archives and national statistical agencies are legal entities that are entrusted to gather, generate and archive specific datasets such as personal records, national accounts, and censuses. Archives are also bound to comply with legislation relating to access, privacy, ethics, copyright and intellectual property rights, delimiting who can access the data and what they can do with them. For example, in many countries, census records can only be released in an aggregated form, with personal records restricted from release for 100 years. The commitment to access and reuse does not then necessarily adopt an open model (see Chapter 3), but rather ensures that the data are available in the future to a designated community in a form that is legally permissible (CCSDS, 2012). A designated community is usually a particular set of scientists or policy specialists who usually have quite specific data needs, functional requirements and support that mean a generic archiving solution will be of limited benefit (Lauriault et al. 2013).

Data archives then are not simply data stores or back-up systems (that preserve data in the event of short-term glitches such as media or technological failure), but are actively planned, curated and managed, staffed by dedicated and specialist personnel who add value and ensure continuity. These personnel, and the functional administrative entity responsible for the archive, are joined by three other sets of actors in the archiving process: data producers, data consumers, and management (CCSDS 2012). Producers are the creators of data or the legal entity responsible for their production; consumers are archives users, stakeholders or a designated community; and management is the body that oversees the process, providing the archive with its charter and scope but does not take an active role in day-to-day archive operations (CCSDS 2012; Lauriault et al. 2013). Together these constituencies shape how the archive is structured, works and develops over time.

In contrast, a data holding is an informal collection of data. Some producers of data might consider backup and storage systems to constitute de facto archives, but they lack the institutional apparatus, organisation, formalised policies (with respect to standards, access, reuse, intellectual property rights [IPR], ethics, etc.), and the ambition of an archive (Lauriault et al. 2013). The data maybe organised and tended, but largely without rigour or with any long-term plan concerning preservation, or any commitment to share the data or make it available for reuse. And while the data may well comply with expected data standards, such compliance may lack certification and they may lack other documentation and appropriate metadata.

Most of the data generated throughout history has been lost or destroyed because it was stored in a data holding, not an archive, or it was decided to keep the information derived from the data (such as articles and books) which were considered more valuable, storing them in libraries. In general, only the most valuable datasets were retained, such as those associated with key scientific and cultural endeavours, government records, economic transactions, and legal contracts. In the cases of specimens, art, objects and so on that might be considered to constitute particular forms of data these have mainly been curated and stored in museums and galleries along with associated metadata. The data of most scientists have been informally stored in files and boxes or on various hard drives in their offices or at home. When they retire or die most of their effects are destroyed, and along with them any data they generated. The vast bulk of data generated for doctoral theses are lost after completion, and even information derived from the research is often not published. Moreover, research funders have traditionally not required projects to retain and store data, or if they did it was only for a short time. In the case of many EU-funded projects, all project materials including data were to be retained for seven years, but after that they could be disposed of, which in many cases they duly have been, due to the cost of storage and the sense that the derived articles held more value.

With the development of digital storage solutions, which reduce the cost and space of retaining data, the wide-scale, long-term storage of routine and lower-value data has begun to occur (see Chapter 5). The first digital databases that conjoined datasets first appeared in the 1950s and 60s and organised data in either flat or hierarchical structures (Driscoll 2012). Such arrangements were, however, inefficient to search and query. Relational databases were initially developed in 1970 by Edgar Codd and structure attribute data into a set of interlinked tables, where each table shares at least one field with another table. For example, the shared field (the indexical key) between two tables, one containing personal details (such age, gender, marital status, address) and the other concerning financial payments, might be a social security number. The social security number allows the data in both tables to be linked together to be queried or produce new derived data. If the shared key was an address or a date, then the data can be placed geographically or temporally. Relational databases enabled more efficient and sophisticated organisation and querying of structured data (using SQLs – structured query languages). Alongside relational databases, the development of spreadsheets allowed large volumes of numeric data to be structured and stored and for formulae to be applied to the data to produce new derived data. In recent years, these forms of databases have been complemented by non-relational (NoSQL) databases that can handle very large volumes of unstructured data (see Chapter 5).

In instances where data are born digital (created as binary code) collections of data are easily constructed and grown, sometimes in automatic and automated ways. They are also highly vulnerable to loss due to obsolescence in software and hardware. As O'Carroll and Webb (2012) note: 'While it is possible for anyone to pick up, look at and read a page from a book written 100 years ago, the same would not be true of a floppy disk containing Word Perfect files from 20 years ago.' Analogue forms of data, in contrast, have to be digitised (e.g., scanned or re-recorded), which can be expensive and time-consuming, though the process can be automated to an extent. The overheads associated with digitisation, in terms of cost, staff time and specialist equipment, have limited its employment in many older analogue archives held by museums, libraries and private collections. While such institutions have struggled to finance their digitisation activities, both philanthropic (e.g., the Internet Archive: https://archive.org/) and commercial (e.g., Google) entities are helping to undertake such activities, using their own resources and that of 'the crowd', making them freely available to the public (see Chapter 5).

In all cases, the data within digital data holdings and archives can be easily shared and reused for a low marginal cost, though they can be restricted with respect to access and reuse by IPR policies. Moreover, they can be manipulated and analysed by exposing them to the power of computation. Procedures and calculations that would be difficult to undertake by hand or using analogue technologies (e.g., slide rules) become possible in just a few microseconds, and more and more complex models and simulations can be built and tested. Digital data holdings and archives can also be relatively easily linked together and scaled into other forms of data infrastructure.

A data infrastructure is the institutional, physical and digital means for storing, sharing and consuming data across networked technologies. Over the past two decades in particular, considerable effort has been expended on developing and promoting such infrastructures, which take a number of forms: catalogues, directories, portals, clearing houses, repositories, trusted digital repositories, and cyber-infrastructures (Lauriault et al. 2007). These terms are often used interchangeably and are confused with one another, though they are slightly different types of entity (see Table 2.2 for examples).

Catalogues, directories and portals are centralised resources detailing and linking to data holdings and archives held by individual institutions. They might provide fairly detailed inventories of the datasets held, and may act as metadata aggregators, but the site itself does not host the data (O'Carroll et al. 2013). A data repository or clearing house is a shared place for storing and accessing data holdings and archives. It might provide some data services in terms of search and retrieval, and data management and processing, but each holding or archive has been produced independently and may lack shared data formats, standards, metadata, and policies. Nevertheless, the repository seeks to ensure that each archive or holding meets a set of requirement specifications and uses audit and certification to ensure data integrity and trust amongst users (Dasish 2012). O'Carroll et al. (2013) identify two types of repositories. Single-site repositories host all the datasets in a single site, accessible through a web interface, though they may maintain back-up or mirror sites in multiple locations. Multi-site repositories host data within a federated structure that allows datasets to be accessed that are held on a number of institutional sites.

A trusted digital repository (TDR) is a certified single or multi-site repository whose mission is to provide reliable, long-term, trusted access to the data it manages (RLG and OCLC 2002). In order to qualify as a trusted repository, the RLG and OCLC (2002: 5) details that the data infrastructure must have the following attributes:

- accept responsibility for the long-term maintenance of digital resources on behalf of its depositors and for the benefit of current and future users, consumers or designated communities;

- have an organisational system that supports not only long-term viability of the preservation system, but also the digital information for which it has responsibility;

- demonstrates fiscal responsibility and sustainability;

- designs its systems in accordance with commonly accepted conventions and standards to ensure the ongoing management, access, and security of materials deposited within them;

- establishes methodologies for system evaluation that meet community expectations of trustworthiness;

- is dependable and carries out its long-term responsibilities to depositors and users openly and explicitly;

- has policies, practices, and performance that can be audited and measured.

For a repository to gain such attributes, the RLG and OCLC (2002: 13) contends it must be compliant with the Reference Model for an Open Archival Information System (OAIS) (CCSDS 2012) and have administrative responsibility, organisational viability, financial sustainability, technological and procedural suitability, system security, and procedural accountability. Together all these attributes help ensure and build trust in the data and the repository.

A cyber-infrastructure is more than a collection of trusted archives and enables the sharing of data and expensive infrastructural resources. It consists of a suite of dedicated and integrated hardware and networked technologies (including observatories and experimental facilities, sensor nets, etc.), interoperable software and middleware services and tools, shared services (relating to data management and processing), analysis tools such as data visualisations (e.g., graphing and mapping apps), and shared policies (concerning access, use, IPR, etc.) which enable data to be distributed, linked together and analysed (Cyberinfrastructure Council 2007). It also seeks to foster the development of a cultural community that supports peer-to-peer collaboration that transcends geographic and institutional boundaries (Cyberinfrastructure Council 2007). While it is sometimes used to describe the infrastructure that enables a federated repository to function, here it is used more specifically to denote a data infrastructure in which data share common technical specifications relating to formats, standards, and protocols. In other words, there are strong rules relating to data standardisation and compliance within the infrastructure. Such cyber-infrastructures include those implemented by national statistical agencies and national spatial data infrastructures, as well as large-scale scientific infrastructures related to genomes, astronomy, meteorology, etc., that require all data stored and shared to comply with defined parameters in order to maximise data interoperability and ensure data quality, fidelity and integrity that promote trust. The latter is particularly important in science, and for policy based upon it such as climate change-tracking and predictions, where data integrity is paramount to ongoing debates.

In addition to data portals, repositories and infrastructures a number of institutional organisations and structures have been created that provide advice on best practices in digital preservation, curation and sharing, validate the work and standards of various kinds of databank, lobby for their development, and coordinate various efforts (see Table 2.3). They do this through activities such as delivering training and education programmes, hosting seminars and conferences, producing handbooks and guides, and providing funding for specific initiatives. These organisations are important for creating communities of practice amongst data professionals, facilitating negotiations between bodies and scaling institutional efforts, and establishing shared guidelines and protocols. The rest of this section focuses on research data repositories and infrastructures, detailing their rationale and challenges. The private infrastructures of commercial data consolidators are discussed later in the chapter.

Table 2.2 Types and examples of data infrastructures

Type	Examples
Data holding	Informal collections of data files on a personal computer. Sometimes called a back-up system.
Data archive	The *LONI Image Data Archive* (IDA) is a secure archive of neuroimaging and related clinical data from research projects across North America and Europe. *The Archive of World Music* is held in the Loeb Music Library at Harvard University providing secure storage and access to archival field and commercial sound and video recordings of musics worldwide.
Catalogues, directories, portals, metadata aggregators	The *Australian National Data Service* enables users to browse over 40,000 datasets and over 30,000 projects that create datasets. The *Digital Public Library of America* provides access to 2.5 million metadata records from US-based libraries, archives and museums. *Europeana* is a portal and metadata aggregator for over 150 libraries, museums and multimedia libraries across Europe. The *Council of European Social Science Data Archives* (CESSDA) is a portal and metadata aggregator for 23 European social science statistical repositories that hold more 25,000 data collections.
Single-site repositories	*Data Archiving and Network Services* (DANS) is the Dutch national archive of digital research data. As well as archiving it provides training and accreditation guidelines. The *UK Data Archive* (UKDA) is a single repository of social sciences and humanities research data funded by the Economic and Social Research Council (ESRC), JISC (Joint Information Systems Committee) and the University of Essex.
Multi-site repositories (federated)	The *Digital Repository of Ireland* (DRI) is a trusted digital repository for contemporary and historical social and cultural data held by Irish institutions, providing access, preservation and discovery to data held across stakeholders. *Openaire* is a multi-site digital repository for accessing open scientific data in the European research area from 41 member organisations in 33 European countries. The *Texas Digital Library* (TDL) is a consortium of higher educational institutes that provide a shared platform and services to provide open access and preservation of data.
Cyber-infrastructures	The *Canadian Geospatial Data Infrastructure* (CGDI) provides access to standardised, consistent, accurate and interoperable spatial data across scales and sectors for Canada.

Source: Adapted and expanded from O'Carroll et al. (2013).

Table 2.3   A selection of institutions advising on, lobbying for and coordinating data preservation, curation and sharing in social sciences and humanities

The Federation of All European Academies (ALLEA)	www.allea.org
Ariadne	www.ariadne-eu.org
British and Irish Sound Archives (BISA)	www.bisa-web.org
Consortium of European Social Science Data Archives	www.cessda.org/
Coalition for Networked Information (CNI)	www.cni.org
Databib	www.databib.org
DataONE	dataone.org
Common Language Resources and Technology Infrastructure (CLARIN)	www.clarin.eu
Committee on Data for Science and Technology of the International Council for Science	www.codata.org
Digital Services Infrastructure for Social Sciences and Humanities (DASISH)	www.dasish.eu
Digital Curation Centre (DCC)	www.dcc.ac.uk
Digital Library Federation (DLF)	www.diglib.org
Digital Preservation Coalition (DPC)	www.dpconline.org
Digital Production Partnership (DPP)	www.digitalproductionpartnership.co.uk
International Federation of Television Archives (FIAT/IFTA)	www.fiatifta.org
International Association for Social Science Information Services and Technology (IASSIST)	www.iassistdata.org
IcarusNet	www.icarusweb.arhiv.hr
International Association of Sound and Audiovisual Archives	www.iasa-web.org
Inter-university Consortium for Political and Social Research (ICPSR)	www.icpsr.umich.edu/icpsrweb/ICPSR
Network of Expertise in Long-term Storage of Digital Resources (NESTOR)	www.langzeitarchivierung.de/Subsites/nestor/DE/Home/
Open Planets Foundation	www.openplanetsfoundation.org
PrestoCentre	www.PrestoCentre.eu
Research Data Alliance (RDA)	www.rd-alliance.org
Text Encoding Initiative (TEI)	www.tei-c.org

Source: Adapted from O'Carroll et al. (2013).

RATIONALE FOR RESEARCH DATA INFRASTRUCTURES

Given that building data infrastructures is a non-trivial exercise, and is expensive in terms of resources and time to create and maintain them on an ongoing basis, there have to be compelling reasons to undertake such an endeavour. Table 2.4 lists over thirty such reasons divided into three dimensions – direct/indirect, near-term/long-term, public/private – as defined by Beagrie et al. (2010). These translate approximately into scientific and financial gains, the cumulative effect of benefits, and who gains from such infrastructures.

The scientific arguments for the storing, sharing and scaling of data within data infrastructures centre on the promises of new discoveries and innovations through the combination of datasets and the crowdsourcing of minds. Individual datasets are valuable in their own right, but when combined with other datasets or examined in new ways fresh insights can be potentially discerned and new questions answered (Borgman 2007). By combining datasets, it is contended that the cumulative nature and pace of knowledge building is accelerated (Lauriault et al. 2007). Moreover, by preserving data over time it becomes possible to track trends and patterns, and the longer the record, the greater the ability to build models and simulations and have confidence in the conclusions drawn (Lauriault et al. 2007). Over time, then, the cumulative value of repositories and infrastructures increases as the data become more readily and broadly available, both in scope and temporality.

Such a sharing strategy is also more likely to spark new interdisciplinary collaborations between researchers and teams and to foster enhanced skill through having access to new kinds of data (Borgman 2007). Moreover, the sharing of data and the adoption of infrastructure standards, protocols and policies increases data quality and enables third-party derived data production and study verification, thus increasing data integrity (Lauriault et al. 2007). It also makes available high-quality data for teaching, improving pedagogical resources for the training of the next generation of researchers. In cases where scientific projects are highly dependent on expensive ICT-enabled instruments that generate vast quantities of data, as well as very large teams of researchers who may be distributed across the globe to analyse such data, data infrastructures are the only means of efficiently and effectively managing such data and projects (Borgman 2007).

The financial benefits of data infrastructures centre on the scales of economy created by sharing resources and avoiding replication, the leveraging effects of reusing costly data, the generation of wealth through new discoveries, and producing more efficient societies. Research is typically a costly undertaking, with various funding agencies collectively spending billions of dollars every year to fund research activity. Much of this activity involves unnecessary duplication of effort in terms of data generation, processing, management and analysis. Rather than a plethora of ad hoc archives, it makes more sense to establish a smaller number of dedicated infrastructures which undertake basic data standardisation and preparation, and produce significant efficiencies in effort, as well as enable broader access to data for individual researchers/institutions where entry costs to a field would normally be prohibitive (Fry et al. 2008). These also make the processes and outcomes of research projects more transparent and able to be judged as representing value for money. As well as reducing wastage, preserving and sharing the fruits of such endeavours is more likely to maximise the return on investment by enabling as much value as possible to be extracted from the data (Lauriault et al. 2007). For example, making data more widely available may produce new knowledge-based industries and the formation of spin-off companies through commercialisation of publicly funded research (Science Coalition 2013). The data within data infrastructures can also lead to more efficient modes of governance and societal management. For example, as well as supporting spatially focused research, many national spatial data infrastructures provide effective tools for territorial management and governance, enable more effective emergency preparedness and disaster response, and facilitate cross-border planning.

As the discussion so far highlights, the benefits gained from data infrastructures are potentially extensive and are not limited to either the public or private domain (Beagrie et al. 2010). Indeed, the strategy of sharing data appears to benefit all parties – researchers, institutions, funders, and public and private enterprises. Given the anticipated gains from sharing data, over the past two decades the research agencies of national governments and supranational bodies such as the European Union, along with philanthropic organisations, have invested extensively in funding a wide variety of initiatives. However, as discussed below, there is resistance to such projects, most particularly by researchers themselves, and it is clear that while there are undoubtedly benefits to the creation of data infrastructures, there are also costs.

THE CHALLENGES OF BUILDING DATA INFRASTRUCTURES

Despite the anticipated and realised benefits of data infrastructures they have not been universally welcomed, nor have they proven easy to construct and implement. There are two broad sets of issues at play – technical and social/political – that are hindering development and will continue to do so for quite some time.

Table 2.4 Benefits of data repositories/infrastructures

Direct benefits	Indirect benefits (costs avoided)
New research opportunities.	No re-creation/duplication of data.
Scholarly communication/access to data.	No loss of future research opportunities.
Re-purposing and reuse of data.	Lower future preservation costs.
Increasing research productivity.	Re-purposing data for new audiences.
Stimulating new network/collaborations.	Re-purposing methodologies.
Data available for teaching and student projects.	Use by new audiences.
Knowledge transfer to industry.	Protecting return on earlier investment.
Improves skills base.	Tools and standards have potential
Increasing productivity/ economic growth.	to increase data quality.
Verification of research/ research integrity.	Reduces ad hoc queries concerning data.
Fulfilling mandate(s).	

Near-term benefits	Long-term benefits
Value to current researcher and students.	Secures value to future researchers and students.
No data lost from researcher turnover.	Adds value over time as collection grows and develops critical mass.
Widens access where costs prohibitive for researchers/institutions.	Increases speed of research and time to realise impacts.
Short term reuse of well curated data.	Stimulates new research questions, especially relating to linked and derived data.
Secure storage for data intensive research.	
Availability of data underpinning publications.	

Private benefits	Public benefits
Benefits to sponsors/funder of research/archive.	Input for future research.
Benefits to researchers and institutions.	Motivating new research.
Fulfil grant obligations.	Catalysing new companies and high skills employment.
Increased visibility/citation.	Transparency in research funding.
Commercialising research.	

Source: Beagrie et al. 2010; Fry et al. 2008.

Creating a functioning and interoperable data infrastructure is not a trivial challenge, especially if it is a trusted system that provides different levels of access depending on user profile and assurances with regards to data provenance, integrity, fidelity and validity. It requires extensive cooperation and alignment between data generators and archive owners with respect to:

- data generation procedures;
- data formats and data standards;
- metadata and documentation;
- data preparation, cleaning and ingestion procedures;
- data quality and assurance measures;
- preservation, backup and auditing policy;
- software and hardware;
- security and data protection;
- access, licensing, use, reuse, privacy and ethics policies;
- ownership, copyright and intellectual property rights policy;
- administrative arrangements, management organisation and governance mechanisms;
- funding of the infrastructure, its services and management.

(Borgmann 2007; Data Seal of Approval 2010; O'Carroll and Webb 2012)

The infrastructure will only be a success if it has a long-term vision, there is commitment to manage and be responsible for the content on behalf of depositors and users, and all the factors listed above are effectively implemented (O'Carroll and Webb 2012).

These issues are not simply technical, but are also social and political in that they require negotiation and agreement in their design, selection and ongoing management between many parties – funders, designers, creators, managers, depositors, steering groups, stakeholders and other vested interests – within the context of various directives, regulations and laws pertaining to generating, storing and sharing data. They are therefore shaped by personal agendas and personalities, institutional values, mandates, cultures, structures, and processes, funding, governmentalities, and path dependencies (once a project has started down a particular track it is often difficult to steer it onto a radically different path) (Feenberg in Lauriault 2012; Lauriault et al. 2007). Pooling and aligning archives that have adopted different technical paths can be a painful, protracted and costly process because it requires those projects which have to make changes to retrofit their legacy data to the agreed specifications (Lauriault 2012). It is for this reason that many archiving projects adopt a repository structure rather than seeking to become a cyber-infrastructure.

Beyond the difficulties of creating the data-sharing structures is persuading data holders to share a valuable commodity. An underlying principle of academic research is open access; that is, all aspects of knowledge production should be freely available for others to inspect. This principle has never worked optimally. Academic papers are often behind pay walls and researchers are often reluctant to share data. As Borgman (2007) notes, sharing is only common in a handful of disciplines such as astronomy, genomics and geomatics which rely on large, distributed teams; in others data are shared occasionally or not at all. She concludes that '[t]he "dirty little secret" behind the promotion of data sharing is that not much sharing may be taking place' (Borgman 2012: 1059). This is because there are a number of disincentives to sharing data:

- a lack of rewards to do so;

- the effort required to prepare and archive the data;

- a lack of expertise, resources and tools to archive data;

- concerns over being able to extract value prior to others in terms of papers and patents, given the effort invested in generating the data;

- concerns over how the data will be used, especially if they relate to people, or how they might be mishandled or misinterpreted;

- worries over the data generating queries and requests that will create additional work;

- concerns over issues with the data being exposed and research findings being undermined through alternative interpretations of the same data;

- intellectual property issues;

- a fear that the data will not be used, thus archiving constituting a wasted effort. (Borgman 2007, 2012; Strasser 2013)

It is clear that ensuring data are archived for future reuse is going to take more than creating data repositories and infrastructures; it is going to require a cultural change in research practices. This change is unfolding using a carrot and stick strategy. On the one hand, incentives are starting to be used to encourage researchers to deposit data, such as promoting data citation and attribution (Borgman 2012), and building adequate funding for archiving into grant awards. On the other hand, research agencies are starting to compel researchers to deposit data, taking into account ethical and IPR issues, as a condition of research funding.

DATA BROKERS AND MARKETS

The private sector has a very different motivation for the production and reuse of data than have academics. Research data infrastructures seek to fulfil a public good by creating a data commons that facilitates and encourages data sharing and reuse. In contrast, data brokers (sometimes called data aggregators, consolidators or resellers) capture, gather together and repackage data into privately held data infrastructures for rent (for one-time use or use under licensing conditions) or re-sale on a for-profit basis. Products include lists of potential customers/clients who meet certain criteria (including details such as names, addresses, telephone numbers, e-mail addresses, as well as information such as 'gender, age, ethnicity, presence of children, income, home value, credit card ownership, credit status, buying patterns, and hobbies'; CIPPIC 2006: ii), search and background checks, a suite of derived data products, wherein brokers have added value through integration, and data analysis products that, in the main, are used to micro-target advertising and marketing campaigns, assess credit worthiness and socially sort individuals, provide tracing services, and supply detailed business analytics (CIPPIC 2006). In the case of lists, these are mostly rented and in many cases the renter does not receive the list, with a third-party service bureau preparing and sending mail on their behalf (CIPPIC 2006). Similarly, with data analytics, clients usually receive the analysis, but not the underlying data.

Data consolidation and re-sale, and associated data analysis and value-added services, are a multi-billion-dollar industry, with vast quantities of data and derived information being rented, bought and sold daily across a variety of markets – retail, financial, health, tourism, logistics, business intelligence, real estate, private security, political polling, and so on. These data concern all facets of everyday life and include public administration, communications, consumption of goods and media, travel, leisure, crime, social media interactions, and so on. Specialist data brokers have been around for a long time, collating data from media subscriptions (e.g., newspapers, magazines), mail-order retailers, polls, surveys, travel agencies, conferences, contests, product registration and warranties, payment processing companies, government records, and so on (CIPPIC 2006). In recent years, especially since the advent of the Internet, the industry has expanded rapidly, with a diversification in the data captured and consolidated, and the products and services offered, often mashing together both small and big data.

Selling data to brokers has become a significant stream of revenue for many companies. For example, retailers often sell on data concerning transactions such as credit card details, customer purchases and store loyalty programmes, customer relationship management, and subscription information.

Websites sell on clickstream data concerning how a person navigated through a website and the time spent on different pages. Likewise media companies, such as newspapers, radio and television stations, harvest the data contained within their content (e.g., news stories, adverts). Social media companies harvest the metadata and content of their users' interactions, using the data to construct consumer profiles and their own data products, or selling on the data to data brokers. For example, Facebook uses the profiles, networks and uploaded content of its billion users (their likes, comments, photos, videos, etc.) to power a set of advertising products such as Lookalike Audiences, Managed Custom Audiences, and Partner Categories, partnering with large data brokers and marketers such as Datalogix, Epsilon, Acxiom, and BlueKai in order to incorporate their non-Facebook purchasing and behaviour data (Edwards 2013).

In a variety of ways, then, individuals 'give up their personal data, wittingly or unwittingly, in various capacities: as purchasers, subscribers, registrants, members, cardholders, donors, contest entrants, survey respondents, and even mere inquirers' (CIPPIC 2006: ii). Moreover, because creating, managing and analysing data is a specialised task, many firms outsource their data requirements to data-processing and analytics companies. By offering the same kinds of data services across clients, such companies can build up extensive datasets that can be bundled and used to produce new derived data which provide more insights than any one source of data. In addition to these privately sourced data, data brokers also gather together public datasets relating to both individuals and aggregates (e.g., groups, places) such as property and census records, and rent/buy lists from charities and non-governmental organisations.

By assembling data from a variety of sources data brokers construct a vast relational data infrastructure. For example, Epsilon is reputed to own data on 300 million company loyalty card members worldwide, with a databank holding data related to 250 million consumers in the United States alone (Edwards 2013). Acxiom is reputed to have constructed a databank concerning 500 million active consumers worldwide (about 190 million individuals and 126 million households in the United States), with about 1,500 data points per person, its servers processing over 50 trillion data transactions a year, and its turnover exceeding one billion dollars (Singer 2012a). It also manages separate customer databases for, or works with, 47 of the Fortune 100 companies (Singer 2012a). Datalogix claim to store data relating to over a trillion dollars' worth of offline purchases (Edwards 2013). Other data broker and analysis companies include Alliance Data Systems, eBureau, ChoicePoint, Corelogic, Equifax, Experian, ID Analytics, Infogroup, Innovis, Intelius, Recorded Future, Seisint and TransUnion. Each company tends to specialise in different types of data and data products and services. For example, eBureau evaluates potential clients on behalf of credit card companies, lenders, insurers and educational institutions, and Intelius provides people-search services and background checks (Singer 2012a).

In general, what data brokers and analysis companies desire is a wide variety of data (both small and big), relating to as large a segment of the population as possible, that are highly relational and indexical (provide unique identification) in nature. The more data a broker can source and integrate, the more likely their products work optimally and successfully, and they gain competitive advantage over their rivals. By gathering data together and structuring them appropriately they can create derived data, individual and area profiles, and undertake predictive modelling as to what individuals might do under different circumstances and in different places. This enables the more effective identification of targets and risks amongst consumers and some indication of how such targets might behave and be nudged into a particular response (e.g., selecting and purchasing a particular item). Acxiom, for example, seeks to mesh offline, online and even mobile data in order to create a '360-degree view' on consumers, using this data to create detailed profiles and robust predictive models (Singer 2012a). Such information and models are very useful to purchasing companies because they enable them to focus their marketing and sales efforts, increasing the likelihood of a successful transaction while reducing their overheads in terms of wastage and loss through risky investments. By using such products companies thus aim to become more effective and efficient in their operations.

Interestingly, given the volumes and diversity of personal data that data brokers and analysis companies possess, and how their products are used to socially sort and target individuals and households, there has been remarkably little critical attention paid to their operations. Indeed, there is a dearth of academic and media analysis about such companies and the implications of their work and products. This is in part because the industry is relatively low-profile and secretive, not wishing to draw public attention to, and undermine public trust in, their assets and activities, which might lead to public campaigns for transparency, accountability and regulation. At present, data brokers are generally largely unregulated and are not required by law to provide individuals access to the data held about them, nor are they obliged to correct errors relating to those individuals (Singer 2012b). And yet their data and products can have a profound effect on the services and opportunities extended to individuals, such as whether a job will be offered, a credit application accepted, an insurance policy issued, or a tenancy approved, and what price goods and services might cost based on perceived risk and value to a company (Lyon 2002).

The worry of some, including Edith Ramirez (2013) the chairperson of the Federal Trade Commission (FTC) in the US, is that such firms practise a form of 'data determinism' in which individuals are not profiled and judged just on the basis of what they have done, but on the prediction of what they might do in the future using algorithms that are far from perfect, which may hold inbuilt biases relating to race, ethnicity, gender and sexuality, and yet are black-boxed and lack meaningful oversight and remediate procedures, and use data that are often low in quality and thus prone to error (also see Chapter 10). Moreover, they employ the data for purposes for which they were never generated, and certainly not for purposes that those whom the data refers to and represents might wish: those applying for a store loyalty card do not necessarily expect their data to be sold and used for purposes beyond their relationship with the store, and not in ways that may subsequently penalise them (Ramirez 2013). While some consumers welcome personalised offers from stores or targeted ads on websites, others view them as intrusive and manipulative (Singer 2012a). Further, data are hoarded as a speculative measure that they may have future value, breaking data minimisation rules that stipulate that only data of defined value should be retained (Raley 2013). Given the volume of sensitive personal records, such as names, addresses, identity numbers (e.g. social security, passport, driver's licence), and credit card numbers held by data brokers, they are a prime target for criminals intent on conducting identity theft fraud. Indeed, the FTC has pursued over 40 cases of serious data security breaches, many against data brokers, for failing to provide adequate security safeguards (Ramirez 2013).

Recently, in the wake of security breaches and revelations about the dubious sale and uses of sensitive data (Dwoskin 2013), along with the NSA PRISM disclosures about government access to commercial records (Greenwald and MacAskill 2013) and the *News of the World* phone hacking scandal and Leveson Inquiry in the UK (http://www.levesoninquiry.org.uk/), more attention is being focused on data brokers and their business practices. In late 2012, the FTC subpoenaed nine data brokers to discover more about what data and derived information they generate and collate about people and how the data are employed and sold, as well as issuing a report calling for privacy by design (see Chapter 10), simplified choice, and greater transparency (Federal Trade Commission 2012). Moreover, political pressure is being applied for tighter and more transparent regulation. In Europe, the new EU data protection directive seeks to regulate how data can be used, and provide citizens with the right to access and dispute data about them and the right to be forgotten (see Chapter 10). How successful such actions will be in reshaping the data brokerage business time will tell. In the meantime, there are many questions that need exploring concerning data brokers and markets and their implications for citizens and consumers (see Chapter 6).

CONCLUSION

Despite the rhetoric of big data advocates and the funding priorities of research agencies, small data will continue to persist as a vital component of the research landscape. Small data studies may be limited in volume, narrow in sample and variety, static, and inflexible once implemented, but they have served science well up until the present because they are specifically designed to answer tightly focused questions. Their production, along with finely honed tools of analysis, allows researchers to effectively mine narrow, tailored seams of high-quality data in order to make sense of the world. In contrast, as discussed in Chapter 8, many big data studies are seeking questions that might be answered with the data produced; the tail is wagging the dog.

Nonetheless, it is clear that much more value and insight can be gained from small data by scaling them into data infrastructures and preserving them for future generations. While data have long been collected together, stored and archived, the development of digital technologies has radically changed our ability to manage, structure, process, analyse, share and reuse data, especially those born digital. Where once small data were scarce and restricted, they are becoming more abundant and open (see Chapter 3). By scaling such data, economies of scale are achieved with respect to data services, analysis tools and pedagogic resources, and the data can be put to new uses, producing fresh discoveries. As a consequence, significant effort is now being expended to produce data infrastructures across all areas of the academy; an effort that is opening up significantly more data to their designated communities and is changing the nature of the science being conducted (see Chapter 8).

The extent to which such scaling produces value is demonstrated by the rapidly growing data brokerage and analytics sector. By gathering together large stores of small data held by public institutions and private corporations and mashing them together with big data flows, data brokers can produce various kinds of detailed individual and aggregated profiles that can be used to micro-target, assess and sort markets, providing high-value intelligence for clients. Such practices also reveal some of the issues and risks arising from scaling data, namely re-purposing, security, and criminal opportunities if data are stolen, none of which is as yet thoroughly understood, with weak regulation and courses of counteraction.

There are dozens of questions requiring attention concerning the future role and form of small data studies, the scaling of small data into various forms of data infrastructures and their implications, and the consequences of conjoining and brokering data on a for-profit basis. Yet it is clear that a critical analysis of the changes that are taking place is not keeping pace with technical and commercial developments. Indeed, there have been few critical reflections to date that think through the mechanisms and connotations of how small data are produced, scaled and used, and theorise the apparatus – databases and data infrastructures – that are being used to organise, share and analyse data. As a consequence, there is a dearth of knowledge on the emerging, complex socio-technical systems being created, with few in-depth case studies. Thus, it is clear that a lot more research and reflective thought is required to make sense of data infrastructures in all their forms.

3

OPEN AND LINKED DATA

Given the expense and resources required to produce datasets and their value in revealing information about the world, access to them has generally been restricted in some way, for example limiting access to approved users, or requiring a fee, or circumscribing how the data can be used through licensing or policy. Even when datasets have been relatively open and available, they have required specialist equipment and tools, such as computers and software, skills such as statistics and mapping know-how, and contextual knowledge concerning a field or topic, to make sense of them, much of which is beyond the capabilities of the general population. As a consequence, data and the information and knowledge derived from them have traditionally been largely closed in nature – locked inside an institution or archive. Indeed, gaining access to datasets that can help answer particular questions has been a centuries-old frustration of researchers, analysts, journalists and civil society organisations.

The open data movement seeks to radically transform this situation, both opening up data for wider reuse, but also providing easy-to-use research tools that negate the need for specialist analytic skills. The movement is built on three principles: openness, participation and collaboration (White House 2009); that through transparency, sharing and working together the value of data for society can be realised. Its aim is to democratise the ability to produce information and knowledge, rather than confining the power of data to its producers and those in a position to pay for access. In particular, attention has been focused on opening data that has been produced by state agencies (often termed public sector information – PSI) or publicly funded research (see Chapter 2), given that these have been funded by the public purse for the public's benefit, with a more limited focus on opening up data generated by private industry, which might have more proprietary value to its creators.

The open data movement has been developing for a couple of decades, in tandem with, but largely separate from, the right to information (RTI) movement concerned with making transparent key decision and policy-making by agencies (also known as freedom of information), and the open source and open science movements concerned with reconfiguring software and publishing into open and transparent forms with respect to licensing, copyright and intellectual property rights. Since the late 2000s the movement has noticeably gained prominence and traction, initially with the *Guardian* newspaper's campaign in the UK to 'Free Our Data' (www.theguardian.com/technology/free-our-data), the Organization for Economic Cooperation and Development (OECD)'s call for member governments to open up their data in 2008, the launch in 2009 by the US government of data.gov, a website designed to provide access to non-sensitive and historical datasets held by US state and federal agencies, and the development of linked data and the promotion of the 'Semantic Web' as a standard element of future Internet technologies, in which open and linked data are often discursively conjoined (Berners-Lee 2009). Since 2010 dozens of countries and international organisations (e.g., the European Union [EU] and the United Nations Development Programme [UNDP]) have followed suit, making thousands of previously restricted datasets open in nature for non-commercial and commercial use (see DataRemixed 2013). Such a shift in position has been facilitated by influential international and national lobby groups such as the Open Knowledge Foundation and the Sunlight Foundation, accompanied by the lobbying of knowledge-economy industry groups and companies, as well senior civil servants convinced by the arguments used, and dozens of local groups seeking to leverage municipal data.

While the arguments of the open data movement are presented in a commonsensical manner, using tropes such as transparency, accountability, participation, innovation and economic growth, the rapid opening up of government and scientific data has not been universally welcomed. Indeed, many of the social, political and economic consequences of opening data are presently being revealed, critiqued and debated. Moreover, somewhat paradoxically, the scope and duration of intellectual property rights has been strengthened over the past half century, meaning that the growth of the open data movement is being paralleled by a rise in proprietary rights (Pollock 2006). Resistance to providing open access to scientific data was discussed in the previous chapter, and critiques of open data are examined in the final section of this chapter. First, however, the chapter sets out the characteristics of open and linked data, the various ways in which the case is being made for opening data, and the economics associated with making data open. Although the opening up of government data is still partial, there is little doubt that a significant shift is occurring regarding how data in general are viewed and shared.

OPEN DATA

At one level, the term open data is relatively straightforward to define. For example, Pollock (2006) delineates it thus: 'data is open if anyone is free to use, reuse, and redistribute it – subject only, at most, to the requirement to attribute and/ or share-alike'. This definition, however, hints at the diverse nature of what can be meant by 'open' and how it can mean different things to different agencies in the context of intellectual property rights. Openness might refer to use or reuse, reworking, redistribution, or reselling, and might have terms and conditions with respect to each. For example, a user might be able to freely use a dataset under licence, but not to rework it for profit or to resell it, and any use might require attribution. In other words, access to the dataset is open, but not necessarily what one can do with the data accessed. In other cases, organisations retain and control access to the data themselves, but make the associated metadata freely available, or an organisation might allow some users access to the data, but these can only be re-disseminated if there has been some value added to them and there is no access to the underlying primary data.

Nevertheless, a number of organisations have sought to set out the ideal characteristics of open data. Open Definition, for example, contends that a work is open if its manner of distribution satisfies the conditions set out in Table 3.1, which provide few restrictions on access, use, reworking and redistribution, and actively promote for-profit use of open data with no financial compensation for the original creator of the data. Similarly, OpenGovData sets out nine principles of open data that extend beyond the mode of distribution to also consider the nature of the data themselves (see Table 3.2). In addition to these two sets of conditions/ principles, other agencies such as the OECD (2008) and the Australian government (Fitzgerald 2010) have proposed that open data needs to be accompanied by

Table 3.1   Open Definition's ideal characteristics of open data

Access	The work shall be available as a whole and at no more than a reasonable reproduction cost and must be available in a convenient and modifiable form.
Redistribution	The licence shall not restrict any party from selling or giving away the work either on its own or as part of a package made from works from many different sources. The licence shall not require a royalty or other fee for such sale or distribution.
Reuse	The licence must allow for modifications and derivative works and must allow them to be distributed under the terms of the original work.
Absence of technological restriction	The work must be provided in such a form that there are no technological obstacles to use or redistribution.
Attribution	The licence may require as a condition for redistribution and reuse the attribution of the contributors and creators to the work. If this condition is imposed it must not be onerous.

Integrity	The licence may require as a condition that modified versions being redistributed carry a different name from the original work.
No discrimination against persons or groups	The licence must not discriminate against any person or group of persons, ensuring access for all.
No discrimination against fields of endeavour	The licence must not restrict anyone from making use of the work in a specific field of endeavour. For example, it may not restrict the work from being used in a business.
Distribution of licence	The rights attached to the work must apply to all to whom it is redistributed without the need for execution of an additional licence by those parties.
Licence must not be specific to a package	The rights attached to the work must not depend on the work being part of a particular package.
Licence must not restrict the distribution of other works	The licence must not place restrictions on other works that are distributed along with the licensed work. For example, the licence must not insist that all derived works are open.

Source: Adapted from http://opendefinition.org/od/

Table 3.2 OpenGovData's principles of open data

Data must be complete	All data are made available, subject to statutes of privacy, security or privilege limitations.
Data must be primary	Data are published as collected at the source, with the finest possible level of granularity, not in aggregate or modified forms.
Data must be timely	Data are made available as quickly as necessary to preserve the value of the data.
Data must be accessible	Data are available to the widest range of users for the widest range of purposes.
Data must be machine-processable	Data are reasonably structured to allow automated processing of them.
Access must be non-discriminatory	Data are available to anyone, with no requirement of registration.
Data formats must be non-proprietary	Data are available in a format over which no entity has exclusive control.
Data must be licence-free	Data are not subject to any copyright, patent, trademark or trade secret regulation. Reasonable privacy, security and privilege restrictions may be allowed as governed by other statutes.
Compliance must be reviewable.	A contact person must be designated to respond to people trying to use the data or complaints about violations of the principles and another body must have the jurisdiction to determine if the principles have been applied appropriately.

Source: Adapted from http://www.opengovdata.org

asset lists and mechanisms of data discovery, to issue indications of data quality and reliability, use open data formats and standards that enhance interoperability, and provide easy-to-use data infrastructures that facilitate regular publication and promotion of new datasets, access to these datasets, as well as suites of basic and specialist tools that enhance use and analysis. Ensuring interoperability is particularly important because it allows for different datasets to be conjoined, thus building new, more complex datasets and revealing new insights (Open Knowledge Foundation 2012). There are no restrictions with regards to the focus of open data – it could concern any type of socio-economic, business, cultural (media, libraries, heritage), environmental, or scientific phenomena – but, in general, the emphasis to date has been on opening up data that has high public policy and commercial reuse value such as economic, transport and spatial data.

These idealised characteristics largely regard open data as a product, rather than as a service. In contrast, Gurstein (2013) has argued that open data need to be rethought as a service process – as an interaction and relationship between data supplier and end-user. For him, it is not enough that data are simply made available by organisations for reuse. Instead, the opening of data should be more service orientated, taking into account the needs and expectation of end-users. Such a reconceptualisation suggests a different approach to data management and end-users is required by those who produce open data, one that potentially has resourcing implications. For him, this kind of approach would require end-users to be involved in the ongoing planning, development and management of open data projects, as well as the use of metrics to evaluate the success of such projects in enhancing the public good. This would necessitate capacity building programmes aimed at up-skilling users to be able to manage, process and analyse data appropriately and effectively. Given that by their nature open data generate no or little income to fund such service arrangements, nor indeed the costs of opening data, while it is easy to agree that open data should be delivered as a service, in practice it might be an aspiration unless effective funding models are developed (as discussed more fully below).

LINKED DATA

The idea of linked data is to transform the Internet from a 'web of documents' to a 'web of data' through the creation of a semantic web (Berners-Lee 2009; P. Miller, 2010), or what Goddard and Byrne (2010) term a 'machine-readable web'. Such a vision recognises that all of the information shared on the Web contains a rich diversity of data – names, addresses, product details, facts, figures, and so on. However, these data are not necessarily formally identified as such, nor are they formally structured in such a way as to be easily harvested and used. Indeed, most Web documents are largely unstructured in nature. By encoding and structuring documents using unique identifiers and a mark-up language it is possible to make visible the data they contain, enabling others to automatically incorporate, process and understand them and to link them with other related data (P. Miller, 2010).

In order to make the semantic web work as linked data, Berners-Lee (2009) argues that documents published on the Internet need to conform to four 'expectations of behaviour'. First, objects and resources need to be identified within each document using a mark-up language such as XML (Extensible Markup Language) and unambiguously named using URIs (Uniform Resource Identifiers). Second, the inherent structure of the Web should be used to connect documents and information (e.g., using HTTP – Hypertext Transfer Protocol – and URIs so that names can be looked up). Third, discovering information about a named object or resource should be made easy (e.g., when someone looks up a URI, useful information should be presented by using RDF standards). The Resource Description Framework (RDF) is a document that details and describes the nature of URIs within a domain and each URI should resolve to this document (Goddard and Byrne 2010). Using these standards ensures a common framework for harvesting data across the Internet, rather than a plethora of incompatible approaches being adopted (Dietrich 2012). Fourth, links should be provided to related objects and resources, if known, so that users can discover more things.

These 'expectations of behaviour' enable documents to be machine-read and processed so that the nature of entities can be identified (e.g., United States is a country, Barack Obama is a person), concepts can be disambiguated (e.g., Mars the chocolate bar, Mars the planet; or Barack Obama as the author of a document vs. Barack Obama as the subject of a document), and to establish associations and relationships within the data (e.g., Barack Obama is the President of the United States) (Goddard and Byrne 2010). In such a way, it becomes possible for Web documents to be machine-read so that software does not just understand the content but can also derive new information and knowledge by reasoning about that content (Goddard and Byrne 2010).

When documents are published in this way, information on the Internet can be rendered and repackaged as data and can be linked in an infinite number of ways depending on purpose. However, as P. Miller (2010) notes, 'linked data may be open, and open data may be linked, but it is equally possible for linked data to carry licensing or other restrictions that prevent it being considered open', or for open data to be made available in ways that do not easily enable linking. In general, any linked documents that are not on an intranet or behind a pay wall are also open in nature. For Berners-Lee (2009), open and linked data should ideally be synonymous and he sets out five levels of such data, each with progressively more utility and value (see Table 3.3). His aspiration is for what he terms five-star (level five) data – a fully operational semantic Web. It should be noted that for many organisations, just getting to levels above one is considered an achievement, with level five some way off without skilled labour, additional resources and new tools.

Table 3.3 Five levels of open and linked data

Level	Form	Benefits	Costs
1	Non-machine-readable	Data are available.	Data are locked in document and is difficult to release.
2	Machine-readable but using proprietary format (e.g., Excel)	Data can be analysed with proprietary software; data can be exported in other formats.	Depends on propriety software to access and use.
3	Machine-readable using non-proprietary format (eg., CSV)	Data can be analysed in any software package.	Are data on the Web, not data in the Web, and are not linked in nature and so exist in isolation.
4	Machine-readable, using non-proprietary format and URIs and RDF	Data can be accessed from anywhere on Web, be easily linked to and combined with other data, and plugged into existing tools and libraries.	Can increase data preparation time and data management and curation.
5	Machine-readable, using non-proprietary format and URIs and RDF, and linking to other data and metadata	As level 4, but data become more discoverable and users have full access to data schema/ontology.	Needs active data management to maintain inward and outward links.

Source: Adapted from http://5stardata.info/ by Michael Hausenblas.

THE CASE FOR OPEN DATA

While some countries, such as the United States, have a long tradition of making some public sector data freely available, especially high–utility data such as census, mapping and weather data, in others access has generally been mediated through a cost recovery model that releases data for a fee and under licence. In the UK, for example, government documents are under Crown copyright and high–utility data are controlled by trading funds (e.g., map data within Ordnance Survey, weather data within the Met Office) which act as monopolies, controlling access to key datasets (Arthur and Cross 2006; Pollock 2006). Over the past couple of decades a range of interconnected arguments has been assembled to make the case for recasting the role of such trading funds and to open up public sector data. In broad terms these contentions can be divided into five forms, all of which are seen as being of benefit to both the data holder and end-user.

First, since much data held within public and non-governmental bodies concerns the operations of those bodies, they provide a means through which to measure the success of their various programmes and activities. Opening these data to public scrutiny thus makes the workings and decision-making of an organisation transparent and can be used to assess accountability and value for money (Janssen 2012; Gordon 2013). Such transparency and accountability have become increasingly important in public discourse in an age of austerity and limited resources, and in the context of ongoing debates about procurement, wastage and fecklessness within public services.

Second, enabling end-users to access an organisation's data, it is argued, allows them to become more informed about an issue, which facilitates choice and decision-making with respect to public services, and encourages active and informed participation in the public realm (Janssen 2012; Yiu 2012). Moreover, it promotes active citizenship and political involvement in shaping how local governance is performed and organised (Huijboom and Van der Broek 2011). These, in turn, foster social innovation, enhance community relations, and elevate the standard of public debate (Yiu 2012). Consequently, open data enable and promote participatory democracy.

Third, opening up data about an organisation and its performance encourages the body to utilise such data to improve operational efficiencies and productivity through evidence-informed monitoring and decision-making. Moreover, units within the institution gain access to and can utilise data from across the entire organisation, leading to new insight and knowledge and greater joined-up thinking and efficiencies (Northcutt 2012; Verwayen et al. 2011). Further, they can gain valuable feedback and advice from external agencies utilising, analysing and interpreting the data, increasing the quality, fidelity and utility of the data. These internal and external analyses lead to enhanced organisational governance and the governance of society more broadly, for example tackling fraud and other crimes by creating more effective services (Huijboom and Van der Broek 2011). They also enable the ongoing monitoring and assessment of the impact of new policies and programmes (Open Knowledge Foundation 2012).

Fourth, providing open data enables brand enrichment. Making data freely available raises the profile of an organisation, marks it as innovative, entrepreneurial and serving its public mission, increases connections and interactions with customers and end-users, and drives traffic to an organisation's services (Verwayen et al. 2011). In turn, this builds trust and reputation, creating a virtuous loop.

Fifth, while some publicly created and held datasets have marginal economic value, for example that related to cultural heritage, much has great commercial value. Publicly generated data can be used to add value to existing business data, create new applications and services and thus new markets, and improve business knowledge and decision-making (Janssen 2012; Yiu 2012). Not unsurprisingly, therefore, industry interests have been keen advocates of opening up publicly generated data for commercial reuse, especially data that have long been known to hold and create value such as that administered by public sector trading funds (e.g., map data). Restricting access to public data, which is generated in the public interest, it is argued, stifles innovation and creates a dead weight loss to the economy; that is, it limits use to those who can afford it, pricing others out of the market (Pollock 2006; Yiu 2012). Thus, public investment in generating data is being under-utilised and many opportunities to add value to private sector activities are being lost (Yiu 2012). Further, the general lifting effect on the wider economy of opening up the value of public data is being missed (Northcutt 2012).

The balance of how these five arguments are mobilised across jurisdictions and context varies; however, collectively they constitute a powerful discursive regime that has been remarkably successful in persuading organisations to open up their data, not least because they dovetail with general processes of neoliberalism that promote the marketisation of public services (Bates 2012). Indeed, the arguments for opening data are mostly driven by political and business interests aimed at holding public institutions and non-governmental organisations to account and gaining access to a valuable commodity, rather than seeking to challenge the notion of intellectual property per se (Verwayen et al. 2011).

In contrast, and unsurprisingly in this context, the arguments and calls for businesses to make their data freely available for wider reuse are much less well developed and promoted. However, many of the same arguments for opening public sector data hold for business data, or at least selective elements of such data. Opening data has the potential to enable companies to benefit from the analysis and insights generated by other end-users, combine data with other datasets that enrich them in productive ways, foster collaboration with partners and suppliers that creates efficiencies in logistics and new products, and build a relationship with customers that helps expand the customer base and enhances a company's profile and reputation (Deloitte 2012). Moreover, it may aid the development of public–private partnerships. Here, an open innovation approach, which has been successful with regard to open software, is adopted, working on the principle that sharing resources will generate more commercial value than jealously hoarding and guarding them. In cases where private companies have received public monies to aid research and development, a case can be made that any data produced from such endeavours should be either fully or selectively made open as a means of producing a public good for such investment.

THE ECONOMICS OF OPEN DATA

There are a number of factors that are acting as brake on the opening up of data. Some of these relate to concerns with respect to warranty and liability issues, concerns over privacy and security, potential embarrassment over data quality or extent, and technical proficiency to build suitable Application Programming Interfaces (APIs) and manage infrastructure. By far the most significant concern, however, is financial. Data might be non-rivalrous in nature, meaning that it can be distributed for marginal cost, in theory at least, but the initial copy needs to be paid for along with ongoing data management and customer service (Pollock 2006). As such, open data might well be a free resource for end-users, but its production and curation is certainly not without significant cost (especially with respect to appropriate technologies and skilled staffing). In many cases, such data has also been a major source of revenue for organisations and, in the case of companies, competitive advantage. A key question, therefore, centres on how open data projects are funded sustainably in the absence of a direct revenue stream. There are two sides to this funding conundrum. On the one hand there is the funding required by the state to produce data and to make it open. On the other hand there is the funding to keep citizen-led initiatives going, which are reliant on volunteer labour and grants, and business models that will enable companies using open data to flourish.

The funding of government data services varies between countries and agencies. In many cases, taxes pay for the generation and processing of data. In some jurisdictions and cases, however, data services are complicated by four factors. First, they have been contracted out to third parties to manage and run on behalf of the state, where the third party adds proprietary value or makes the data available at a fee. This has recently happened with the forthcoming Irish postcodes that are going to be managed by a company on behalf of the state and will fund the operation by selling/licensing the data. Second, third-party resellers are actively lobbying to stop data being made open as it destroys their business model. Third, some state agencies operate as trading funds. They do not receive all of their funding from tax revenue, but raise a substantial portion of their income from the sale of data. Ordnance Survey Ireland, for example, operates in this way with less than half of its income coming directly from the state in the form of a subvention. Admittedly some of the payments it receives come from other state agencies, but they also come from private enterprise and individual purchases. Making all of its data available for free undermines its ability to operate and fund ongoing services. Fourth, making data open is not simply a case of publishing them in the form held by the state. Much of the data needs to be repurposed and curated to enable them to be made open (e.g., anonymised, aggregated) and new systems put in place to enable this to happen. This is not a trivial exercise and in a time of austerity and cutbacks it means reallocating funding to pay for this work, which is also needed for essential services. These four complications mean that declarations that all state data has already been paid for via taxes and should be freely available are often not as simple as desired. With respect to citizen-led initiatives, these too have costs with respect to staffing, equipment and services if they are to be sustainable as long-term endeavours. How to secure such resources beyond voluntary labour and gifts is a difficult challenge and, at present, such organisations are largely reliant on philanthropic donations and state funding, neither of which holds guarantees of renewal. And yet, the consequences of reductions or fluctuations in the financial base of open data services are likely to be a decline in data quality, responsiveness, innovation, and general performance (Pollock 2009).

It is generally argued by open data advocates that securing a stable financial base for open data within and outside the state is best achieved by direct government subvention of the costs. Proponents of this approach argue that the increased public expenditure is offset in four ways. First, enabling direct access to the data can reduce some of the producers' transaction costs, such as staffing required for marketing, sales, communicating with customers, and monitoring compliance with licence arrangements (Pollock 2006). Second, the open model can leverage free additional labour and innovation from the crowd of users that adds significant value to the dataset and for the organisation in terms of data quality, analysis and derived knowledge, new products and innovations, and new relationships and partnerships (de Vries et al. 2011; Houghton 2011). Third, open data will produce diverse consumer surplus value, generating significant public goods which are worth the investment of public expenditure (Pollock 2009). Fourth, open data will lead to new innovative products that will create new markets, which in turn will produce additional corporate revenue and tax receipts. These tax receipts will be in excess of additional government costs of opening the data. In other words, zero or marginal cost approaches are more advantageous over the long term than cost-recovery strategies (European Commission 2012).

Indeed, it is believed that opening data has the potential to create several tens of billions of euros annually in the EU alone (Open Knowledge Foundation 2012). The examples used to support such an argument are the US's decision to make publicly generated GPS and weather data freely available (Pollock 2006; de Vries et al. 2011). Both underpin multi-billion-dollar industries that generate sizeable tax revenues and employ large numbers of workers. *The Economist* (2013) estimates that 3 million jobs in the US depend on GPS. If one compares the use of public weather data in US and Europe, there is a vast difference in their use and the generation of additional value, with Pollock (2006) noting that while the 'two economies are of roughly the same size, the US commercial weather industry is over ten times larger than Europe's while the nascent weather risk management industry is over a hundred times larger'. In other words, where public data has been made openly available for free or marginal cost, it has been utilised in ways that produce significant additional value. Markets for open data are both high-end (a small base of customers paying substantial fees for high additional value; e.g., highly targeted weather forecasts) and low-end (large volumes of users for low additional value where the service is free, supported by advertising revenue; e.g., traffic apps) (de Vries et al. 2011). The potential effect of opening public sector data in Europe is illustrated by a study of 21 open data projects in 10 countries which found that moving to zero or marginal cost operations increased the number of users by between 1,000 and 10,000 per cent, attracting many new types of users, in particular SMEs (de Vries et al. 2011). That said, while there will be some large wins, Eaves (2013) notes that the majority of finance created will be from a long tail of savings and efficiencies and modest increased turnover.

Despite such arguments, the jury is still out on whether opening up all public sector data is economically viable and sustainable, especially in the short term. It is certainly the case that open data that can be commercialised, leading to high- and low-end products that can generate income streams and employment. However, de Vries et al. (2011) reported that the average apps developer made only $3,000 per year from apps sales, with 80 per cent of paid Android apps being downloaded fewer than 100 times. In addition, they noted that even successful apps, such as MyCityWay which has been downloaded 40 million times, do not yet generate profits. Instead, venture capitalists are investing in projects with potential while a sustainable business model is sought. It may well be that it will take time for new innovations and markets to develop; for example, industries underpinned by GPS took many years to blossom and mature after the decision to make the data openly available was taken in 1984. It might also be the case that some data has much wider value but weak economic value, and will always have to be subvented if it is to remain open in nature.

In the absence of the state underwriting all the associated costs of opening its data, other potential funding solutions are being examined, notably various business models. Ferro and Osella (2013) detail eight different models that are, or might be, used to fund open data initiatives (see Table 3.4). These different models are not mutually exclusive. Other semi-open models are to make the data free for non-commercial reuse, but to charge for-profit reusers, or to enter into public–private partnerships with the public sector providing the data and private companies providing finance and value-added services for access and reuse rights (OECD 2008). Another model is to build a consortium that collectively owns the data, pools labour, resources and tools, and facilitates capacity-building, but charges a membership fee to consortium members to cover shared value-added services. Which model, or combination of models, is adopted depends on which group is designated to pick up the cost for the production and maintenance of the data – users, updaters/resellers or government – and whether an organisation is seeking to recover full costs or marginal costs, or even make more than full costs which can be reinvested back into the service (Pollock 2009; Ferro and Osella 2013).

Table 3.4 Models of open data funding

Model	Description
Premium product/ service	Offers end-users a high-end product or a service that adds value to data (e.g., derived data, tools or analysis) for payment, either as fixed payment, recurrent fees or pay-per-use, without using monopoly rights. This enables the data producer to gain first-mover advantages in the marketing and the sale of complementary goods.
Freemium product/ service	Offers end-users a graded set of options, including a free of charge option that includes basic elements (e.g., limited features or sampled dataset), with more advanced, value-adding options being charged a fee. Opens up the product/service to a wider, low-end market and more casual use, while retaining paid, high-end product/service for more specialised users.
Open source	Offers end-users data products/services for free, cross-subsidised by other core funding or other products/services.
Infrastructural razor and blades	An initial inexpensive or free trial is offered for products/services (razor) that encourages take-up and continued paid use (blades). It might be that access is free through APIs, but that computational usage is charged on a pay-as-you-go model, with the latter cross-subsidising the former.
Demand-oriented platform	Offers value-added services by cleaning, refining, standardising and linking data, providing a standard set of analytic tools, and making accessible through a one-stop shop with users charged on a freemium or premium pricing (essentially scales up options 1 and 2 to gain efficiencies).
Supply-oriented platform	Developers are given free access to data to create services and products which they can sell to the public sector body, who can then make them available to others through freemium model.
Free with advertising	Products/services are provided for free, but users receive advertising when using the product/service (revenue-generating) or the products/services are provided by different companies and branded as such to encourage use of their other products/services (cross-subsidisation).
White-label development	A customised product/service is created for a client and branded for their use, with that client paying a one-off fee or subscription that includes maintenance and update costs.

Source: Compiled from Ferro and Osella (2013).

CONCERNS WITH RESPECT TO OPENING DATA

With the exception of how to sustainably fund open data initiatives, and the possible losses for companies which have built business models on reselling public sector data (de Vries et al. 2011), there seem at first consideration to be few downsides to opening up public data for reuse, and many upsides. However, a number of counter-critiques have recently started to emerge that contend that the open data movement is not politically or economically benign, that some elements are disingenuous in their aims and, moreover, that there are a number of pernicious effects that can result from opening data that can disenfranchise some citizens. These critiques do not suggest abandoning the move towards opening data, but contend that open data initiatives need to be much more mindful of how data are made available, how they are being used, and how they are being funded. Critiques can be divided into three broad classes: open data facilitates the neoliberalisation and marketisation of public services; it promotes a politics of the benign and empowers the empowered; and it lacks sustainability, utility and usability.

Neoliberalisation and marketisation of public services

Jo Bates (2012) argues that 'open initiatives such as OGD [open government data] emerge into a historical process, not a neutral terrain'. As with all political initiatives, the politics of open data are not simply commonsensical or neutral, but rather are underpinned by political and economic ideology. The open data movement is diverse and made up of a range of constituencies with different agendas and aims, and is not driven by any one party. However, Bates makes the case that the open data movement in the UK had little political traction until big business started to actively campaign for open data, and open government initiatives started to fit into programmes of forced austerity and the marketisation of public services. For her, political parties and business have appropriated the open data movement on 'behalf of dominant capitalist interests under the guise of a "Transparency Agenda"' (Bates 2012).

   In other words, the real agenda of business is to get access to expensively produced data for no cost, and thus to a heavily subsidised infrastructural support from which they can leverage profit, while at the same time removing the public sector from the marketplace and weakening its position as the producer of such data. Indeed, because the income from data services has disappeared (in cases where it was being funded by fees not the taxpayer), and thus the funds to support in-house production and management, public sector bodies are more likely to be forced to outsource such services to the private sector on a competitive basis or cede data production to the private sector which they then have to procure

(Gurstein 2013). Here, data services and data derived from freely available public data have to be purchased by the data creator, at the same time as the data literacy of the organisation is hollowed out. Moreover, because open data often concern a body's own activities, especially when supplemented by key performance indicators, they facilitate public sector reform and reorganisation that promote a neoliberal, New Public Management ethos and private sector interests (McClean 2011; Longo 2011). Such processes, Bates (2013) argues, are part of a deliberate political strategy to open up the 'provision of almost all public services to competition from private and third sector providers', with open data about public services enabling 'service users to make informed choices *within a market* for public services based on data-driven applications produced by a range of commercial and non-commercial developers' (2013, original emphasis). In such cases, the transparency agenda promoted by politicians and businesses is merely a rhetorical device. If either party was genuinely interested in transparency and open government then it would be equally supportive of the right to information movement and the work of whistle-blowers (Janssen 2012) and also of loosening the shackles of intellectual property rights more broadly (Shah 2013). Instead, governments and businesses are generally resistant to both.

Politics of the benign and empowering the empowered

A related argument is that much of the open data movement is driven from a technical and economic perspective, and focuses largely on gaining access to the data, not on the politics of the data themselves, what that data reveal, or how they are used and for whose interests (Shah 2013). In other words, the movement largely seeks to present an image of being politically benign and commonsensical, promoting a belief that opening up data is inherently a good thing in and of itself. For others, making data accessible is just one element with respect to the notion of openness. Just as important is what the data consist of and how they can create a more just and equitable society. If open data merely serve the interests of capital by opening public data, but keeping proprietary data locked behind pay walls and protected by intellectual property regimes, and further empower those who are already empowered and disenfranchise others, then they have failed to make society more democratic and open (Gurstein 2011; Shah 2013).

Implicit in most discussions on open data is the notion that the data are neutral and objective in nature and that everyone has the potential to access and use such data (Gurstein 2011; Johnson 2013). However, this are not the case. With respect to open data themselves, as Johnson (2013) contends, a high degree of social privilege and social values is embedded in public sector data with respect to what data are generated, relating to whom and what (especially within domains that function as disciplinary systems, such as social welfare and law enforcement), whose interests are represented within the dataset and whose interests are excluded. Thus, value structures are inherent in datasets and these subsequently shape analysis and interpretation and may work to propagate injustices and reinforce dominant interests.

Citizens have differential access to the hardware and software required to download and process open datasets, as well as varying levels of skills required to analyse, contextualise and interpret the data (Gurstein 2011). And even if some groups have the ability to make compelling sense of the data, they do not necessarily have the contacts needed to gain a public voice and influence a debate, or the political skill to take on a well-resourced and savvy opponent. Thus, the democratic potential of open data has been overly optimistic, with most users those with high degrees of technical knowledge and an established political profile (McClean 2011). Indeed, open data can work to further empower the empowered and to reproduce and deepen power imbalances (Gurstein 2011). An oft-cited example of the latter is the digitisation of land records in Karnataka, India, where an open data project, which was promoted as a 'pro-poor' initiative, worked to actively disenfranchise the poor by enabling those with financial resources and skills to access previously restricted data and to re-appropriate their lands (Gurstein 2011; Slee 2012; Donovan 2012). Far from aiding all citizens, in this case open data facilitated a change in land rights and a transfer of wealth from poor to rich. In other words, opening data does not mean an inherent process of democratisation. Indeed, open data can function as a tool of disciplinary power (Johnson 2013).

Here, it is important to be mindful that government data is generated for the purposes of governance. They consist of two broad types: those related to the activities of the state and those concerning citizens, places and business. The former concern how the state operates and, when made transparent, can be used to evaluate performance and accountability. Few would argue against such data being made publicly available, though the politics of such an unveiling needs to be appreciated, especially if the measures used have the counter-effect of skewing service provision to game the evaluation data (conforming to Campbell's Law, see Chapter 7), in turn negatively impacting what services are being delivered and making the lives of those people receiving the services worse. The latter consist of highly sensitive personal and institutional records. They were not created with the intention of being shared. Indeed, citizens expect them to be protected by privacy and data protection laws. Even when anonymised and aggregated, data can be quite sensitive and political. Consider, for example, social welfare and health data aggregated to relatively refined spatial units (e.g., neighbourhood level). Such data have utility for directing targeted interventions aimed at addressing social disadvantage. They also make useful inputs into data analytics that seek to socially sort and profile citizens with respect to credit and insurance risk, and can be used to create area profiles that stigmatise a locale and reduce inward investment (see Chapter 10). In other words, the data can be repurposed in various ways which have differential outcomes, and there are legitimate reasons to be cautious with respect to what government data are released and to resist the rather simplistic mantra used by some open data advocates of 'they're our data, we've paid for them, and we should have access to them'.

Sustainability, utility and usability

To date, attention has been largely focused on the supply-side of accessing data and creating open data initiatives, and there has been insufficient attention paid to the sustainability of initiatives and how data are being utilised and employed. In a study of a number of different open data projects, Helbig et al. (2012) reported that many are too technically focused, amounting to 'little more than websites linked to miscellaneous data files, with no attention to the usability, quality of the content, or consequences of its use'. The result is a set of open data sites that operate more as data holdings or data dumps, lacking the qualities expected in a well-organised and run data infrastructure, such as clean, high-quality, validated and interoperable data that comply with data standards and have appropriate metadata and full record sets (associated documentation); preservation, backup and auditing policies; reuse, privacy and ethics policies; administrative arrangements, management organisation and governance mechanisms; and financial stability and a long-term plan of development and sustainability (see Chapter 2). Many sites also lack appropriate tools and contextual materials to support data analysis. Moreover, the datasets released are often low-hanging fruit, consisting of those that are easy to release and contain non-sensitive data that has relatively low utility. In contrast, data that might be more difficult and demanding to make open, due to issues of sensitivity or because they require more management work to comply with data protection laws, often remain closed (Chignard 2013).

Part of the issue is that many open data sites have been rough and ready responses to an emerging phenomenon. They have been built by enthusiasts and organisations who have little experience of data archiving or the contextual use of the data being opened. They have been supported and promoted by hackathons and data dives, which reproduce many of these issues. As McKeon (2013) and Porway (2013) contend, these events, which invite coders and other interested parties to build apps using open data, can be of little benefit. While they do focus attention on the data and are good for networking, those doing the coding often have little deep contextual knowledge with regard to what the data refer to, or belong to a particular demographic that is not reflective of wider society (e.g., young, educated and tech-orientated), and believe that deep structural problems can be resolved by technological solutions. They are 'built by a micro-community of casual volunteers, not by people with a deep stake in seeing the project succeed' (McKeon 2013). Further, hackathon-created solutions often remain at version 1.0, with little post-event follow-up, maintenance or development. Porway's (2013) answer to building solutions that might enact appropriate change is to try and match those who understand the data and problem (working in a sector) with those who can code, build and sustain apps, and McKeon (2013) suggests pre-planning meetings and post-event mentorship aimed at making the outcome sustainable and creating a longer-term community. In other words, there is a need to match existing expertise with developer expertise. The same need is required with open data sites, learning from those who have been in the archiving and data-sharing business for a long time, including archivists, scientists and geomaticians.

As a consequence of these various teething issues, rather than creating a virtuous cycle, where the release of more and more datasets, in more formats, produces growing use and therefore the release of more data, as assumed by the open data movement, many sites, as noted by Helbig et al. (2012), have low and declining traffic because they do not encourage use or facilitate users, and are limited by other factors such as data management practices, agency effort and internal politics. After an initial spark of interest, data use drops quite markedly as the limitations of the data are revealed and users struggle to work out how the data might be profitably analysed and used. McClean (2011), for example, notes that analysis arising from open data has had limited impact on political debates, and concludes with respect to COINS (Combined Online Information System; government financial data in the UK), that after

> a brief flurry of media interest in mid-2010, in the immediate aftermath of the release ... reports explicitly mentioning COINS are now extremely rare and those members of the press who were most interested obtaining access to it report that it has not proved particularly useful as a driver of journalism.

Where data are released periodically (e.g., quarterly or annually), usage tends to be cyclical and often tied to specific projects such as consultancy reports rather than having a more consistent pattern of use which one might expect for data that is real-time in nature or has high economic worth. In such cases, Helbig et al. (2012) observed that a set of negative or balancing feedback loops slowed the supply of data and use, thus further decreasing usage. Thus, after some initial 'quick wins', the danger is that any virtuous cycle shifts from being positive to negative, and the rationale for central government funding of such initiatives is undermined and in due course cut. The key to avoiding the creation of such a negative cycle is to ensure that any initiative focuses as much on the demand-side as the supply-side, providing users with interoperable data and analytic tools and other services that facilitate use and add value to the data, rather than simply linking to files.

CONCLUSION

At one level, the case for open and linked data is commonsensical – open data create transparency and accountability; participation, choice and social innovation; efficiency, productivity and enhanced governance; economic innovation and wealth creation. Linked data convert information across the Internet into a semantic web from which data can be machine-read and linked together. Open and linked data thus hold much promise and value as a venture. However, the case for open and linked data is more complex, and their economic underpinnings are not at all straightforward. Open and linked data might seem to have marginal costs, but their production and the technical and institutional apparatus needed to facilitate and maintain them has real cost in terms of labour, equipment, and resources. Indeed, open data are far from free data, but as yet no established model has been devised to sustainably fund open data initiatives beyond government subvention, and the benefits of open data in terms of producing additional consumer surplus value and new commercial ventures, innovative products, and costs being offset by additional tax revenue are largely hypothetical or only beginning to materialise. Moreover, the potential negative consequences of opening data have not been fully explored.

Much more critical attention then needs to be paid to how open data projects are developing as complex sociotechnical systems with diverse stakeholders and agendas. To date, efforts have concentrated on the political and technical work of establishing open data projects, and not enough on studying these discursive and material moves and their consequences. As a result, we lack detailed case studies of open data projects in action, the assemblages surrounding and shaping them, and the messy, contingent and relational ways in which they unfold. It is only through such studies that a more complete picture of open and linked data will emerge, one that reveals both the positives and negatives of such projects, and which will provide answers to more normative questions concerning how they should be implemented and address issues of sustainability, usability, and their inherent politics.

4

BIG DATA

Francis Diebold (2012) traces the etymology of the term 'big data' to the mid-1990s, first used by John Mashey, retired former Chief Scientist at Silicon Graphics, to refer to handling and analysis of massive datasets. Initially, the term had little traction. In 2008 very few people were using the term 'big data', either in the academy or industry. Five years later it had become a buzzword, commonly used in business circles and the popular media, with regular commentaries in broadsheet newspapers, such as the *New York Times* and *Financial Times*, and feature pieces and sections in popular and science magazines such as *The Economist*, *Time*, *Nature*, and *Science*. Such was its prevalence and associated boosterism that Gartner's had already declared by January 2013 that it had moved along the hype cycle from 'peak of inflated expectation' to 'trough of disillusionment' (Sicular 2013), with some evangelists already declaring 'big data' dead as a meaningful term, having become too wide-ranging and woolly in definition (e.g., de Goes 2013), some early adopters struggling to convert investment into return, and others voicing scepticism as to its potential benefits. Nonetheless, business, government and research funders have largely remained firm in their conviction that big data is set to rise back up the hype cycle's 'slope of enlightenment' to the 'plateau of productivity', and, what's more, it is set to alter fundamentally how science and business are conducted (Sicular 2013; see Chapters 7 and 8).

As discussed in Chapter 2, across government, industry and academia there have long been very large datasets from which information has been extracted in order to provide insights and knowledge. Governmental departments and agencies routinely generate huge quantities of data. For example, in 2013 the National Archives and Records Administration (NARA) in the US was storing some 4.5 million cubic feet of physical documents from US executive branch agencies, courts, Congress and presidents (just 5 per cent of the federal government's records) to which it adds 30,000 linear feet of new records annually (Ellis 2013), as well as holding more than 500 terabytes of digital data. Likewise, businesses have collated data about their operations, markets and customers, and vast databases of scientific data have been assembled and curated since the start of modern science. So, what is meant by the term 'big data', given these data volumes in previous eras?

Like many terms used to refer to the rapidly evolving use of technologies and practices, there is no agreed academic or industry definition of big data. The most common makes reference to the 3Vs: volume, velocity and variety (Laney 2001; Zikopoulos et al. 2012). Big data are:

- huge in *volume*, consisting of terabytes or petabytes of data;

- high in *velocity*, being created in or near real-time;

- diverse in *variety* in type, being structured and unstructured in nature, and often temporally and spatially referenced.

Prior to big data, databases were constrained across these three attributes: it was only possible to have two at any one time (large and fast; varied and fast; large and varied) (Croll 2012). With enhanced computational power, new database design and distributed storage (see Chapter 5), all three have become simultaneously achievable enabling new forms of analysis and providing very detailed views of large systems in flux. Beyond the 3Vs, the emerging literature denotes a number of other key characteristics, with big data being:

- *exhaustive* in scope, striving to capture entire populations or systems (n = all), or at least much larger sample sizes than would be employed in traditional, small data studies;

- fine-grained in *resolution*, aiming to be as detailed as possible, and uniquely *indexical* in identification;

- *relational* in nature, containing common fields that enable the conjoining of different datasets;

- *flexible*, holding the traits of extensionality (can add new fields easily) and *scalable* (can expand in size rapidly)

(boyd and Crawford 2012; Dodge and Kitchin 2005; Marz and Warren 2012; Mayer-Schonberger and Cukier 2013).

Given the drive to digitise and scale traditional small data into digital infrastructures that are voluminous and varied (such as national archives, censuses and collections of cultural and social heritage; see Chapter 2) it is velocity and these additional characteristics that set big data apart and make them a disruptive innovation (Christensen's 1997) one that radically changes the nature of data and what can be done with them (see Table 2.1). For example, a national household survey has large volume, strong resolution and relationality, but lacks velocity (once a year), variety (usually *c.*30 structured questions), exhaustivity (a sample of perhaps one in twenty households), and flexibility (the fields are fixed, typically across surveys, to enable time-seried analysis). In this chapter, the seven characteristics of big data are elaborated and the next chapter discusses the enablers and sources of big data.

VOLUME

The last decade has witnessed an explosion in the amount of data that are being generated and processed on a daily basis. As *Wired* magazine put it in the title of their 2008 special issue: we are entering 'The Petabyte Age' (in fact, we have already entered the zettabyte age; 2^{70} bytes). Several studies have sought to estimate and track the volumes involved (e.g., Hilbert and López 2009; Gantz and Reinsel 2011; Short et al. 2011). They employ different methodologies and definitions, but all are unanimous that the rate of growth has been staggering in scale. Moreover, it is set to grow exponentially for the foreseeable future. The simplest way to illustrate this growth is to give some examples of the global estimates of data volumes and some estimates relating to specific entities. To provide a frame of reference, Table 4.1 details a summary of how data volume is measured.

Table 4.1 Measurements of digital data

Unit	Size	What it means
Bit (b)	1 or 0	Short for 'binary digit', after the binary code (1 or 0) computers use to store and process data
Byte (B)	8 bits	Enough information to create an English letter or number in computer code
Kilobyte (KB)	1,000, or 2^{10} bytes	From 'thousand' in Greek. One page of typed text is 2KB
Megabyte (MB)	1,000KB; 2^{20} bytes	From 'large' in Greek. The complete works of Shakespeare total 5MB. A typical pop song is about 4MB
Gigabyte (GB)	1,000MB; 2^{30} bytes	From 'giant' in Greek. A two-hour film can be compressed into 1–2GB
Terabyte (TB)	1,000GB; 2^{40} bytes	From 'monster' in Greek. All of the catalogued books in America's Library of Congress total 15TB
Petabyte (PB)	1,000TB; 2^{50} bytes	All the letters delivered by America's postal service in 2010 amounted to around 5PB of data
Exabyte (EB)	1,000PB; 2^{60} bytes	Equivalent to 10 billion copies of *The Economist*
Zettabyte (ZB)	1,000EB; 2^{70} bytes	The total amount of information in existence in 2010 was forecast to be around 1.2ZB

(Continued)

Table 4.1   (Continued)

Unit	Size	What it means
Yottabyte (YB)	1,000ZB; 2^{80} bytes	Currently too big to imagine
	The prefixes are set by an intergovernmental group, the International Bureau of Weights and Measures. Yotta and Zetta were added in 1991; terms for larger amounts have yet to be established.	

Source: The Economist (2010).

Zikopoulos et al. (2012) detail that in 2000, *c.*800,000 petabytes of data were stored in the world. According to Short et al. (2011: 7), in their annual report – *How Much Information?* – by '2008, the world's servers processed 9.57 zettabytes of information ...This was 12 gigabytes of information daily for the average worker, or about 3 terabytes of information per worker per year. The world's companies on average processed 63 terabytes of information annually' excluding non-computer sources. By 2010, MGI (cited in Manyika et al. 2011: 3) 'estimated that enterprises globally stored more than 7 exabytes of new data on disk drives ... while consumers stored more than 6 exabytes of new data on devices such as PCs and notebooks'. They further estimated that in '2009, nearly all sectors in the US economy had at least an average of 200 terabytes of stored data ... per company with more than 1,000 employees. Many sectors had more than 1 petabyte in mean stored data per company.' In 2013, EU commissioner for Digital Agenda, Neelie Kroes, stated that 1.7 million billion bytes of data per minute were being generated globally (Rial 2013).

Based on their review of data volume growth, Manyika et al. (2011) projected a 40 per cent rise in data generated globally per year. Gantz and Reinsel (2011) estimated that the 'amount of information created and replicated on the Internet will surpass 1.8 zettabytes (1.8 trillion gigabytes)' in 2011 stored in '500 quadrillion files'. This they reported represented a growth by 'a factor of 9 in just five years', with growth at that time projected to 'more than doubl[e] every two years'. As a result, they predicted that in the decade following their report,

> the number of servers (virtual and physical) worldwide will grow by a factor of 10, the amount of information managed by enterprise datacenters will grow by a factor of 50, and the number of files the datacenter will have to deal with will grow by a factor of 75, at least.

Such is the phenomenal growth in data production, IBM (2012) contended that '90% of the data in the world today has been created in the last two years alone' and Zikopoulos et al. (2012) expect data volumes to reach 35 zettabytes by 2020.

We can get a sense of why this digital data explosion is occurring by considering some specific examples. TechAmerica estimates that each day 114 billion e-mails and 24 billion text messages are sent, and 12 billion phone calls made globally (Strohm and Homan 2013). According to CISCO, in 2013 there were estimated to be 10 billion objects (devices and sensors) making up the Internet of things, each of which is producing data in varying quantities, with this figure set to rise to 50 billion by 2020 (Farber 2013). With respect to online activity, in 2012 Google was processing 3 billion search queries daily, each one of which it stored (Mayer-Schonberger and Cukier 2013) and about 24 petabytes of data every day (Davenport et al. 2012). In 2011, Facebook's active users spent more than 9.3 billion hours a month on the site (Manyika et al. 2011), and by 2012 Facebook reported that it was processing 2.5 billion pieces of content (links, stores, photos, news, etc.), 2.7 billion 'Like' actions and 300 million photo uploads per day (Constine 2012). In 2012, over 400 millions tweets a day were produced, growing at a rate of 200 per cent a year, each tweet having 33 discrete items of metadata (Mayer-Schonberger and Cukier 2013). Much of these data are unstructured in nature. A similar explosion in structured data has taken place. For example, with respect to retail data concerning stock and sales, collected through logistics chains and checkouts, Walmart was generating more than 2.5 petabytes of data relating to more than 1 million customer transactions every hour in 2012 ('equivalent to 167 times the information contained in all the books in the Library of Congress'; Open Data Center Alliance 2012: 6), and the UK supermarket Tesco was generating more than 1.5 billion new items of data every month in 2011 (Manyika et al. 2011).

Likewise, governments and public bodies are generating vast quantities of data about their own citizens and other nations. For example, transit bodies have started to monitor the constant flow of people through transport systems, for example, collating the time and location of the use of pre-paid travel cards such as the Oyster Card in London. Many forms of tax payment, or applications for government services, are now conducted online. In 2009, the US Government produced 848 petabytes of data (TechAmerica Foundation 2012). The 16 intelligence agencies that make up US security, along with the branches of the US military, screen, store and analyse massive amounts of data hourly, with thousands of analysts employed to sift and interpret the results. To get a sense of the scale of some military intelligence projects, the ARGUS-IS project, unveiled by DARPA and the US Army in 2013, is 'a 1.8-gigapixel video surveillance platform that can resolve details as small as six inches from an altitude of 20,000 feet (6km)' (Anthony 2013). It collects '1.8 billion pixels, at 12 fps [frames per second], generat[ing] on the order of 600 gigabits per second. This equates to around 6 petabytes ... of video data per day.' Using a supercomputer, analysis is undertaken in near real-time and the system can simultaneously track up to 65 moving objects within its field of vision. This is just one project in an arsenal of similar and related intelligence projects.

Similarly, with respect to scientific projects, a personal human genome sequence consists of about 100 gigabytes of data (Vanacek 2012): multiply that across thousands of individuals and the database soon scales into terabytes and petabytes of data. When the Sloan Digital Sky Survey began operation in 2000, its telescope in New Mexico generated more observational data in the first couple of months than had previously been collected in the history of astronomy up to that point (Cukier 2010). In 2010, its archive was 140 TB of data, an amount soon to be collected every five days by the Large Synoptic Survey Telescope due to become operational in Chile in 2016 (Cukier 2010). Even more voluminous, the Large Hadron Collider at CERN, Europe's particle-physics laboratory, generates 40 terabytes every second (*The Economist* 2010). In this, and other cases, the data generated are so vast that they neither get analysed nor stored, consisting instead of transient data. Indeed, the capacity to store all these data does not exist because, although storage is expanding rapidly, it is not keeping pace with data generation (Gantz et al. 2007; Manyika et al. 2011).

EXHAUSTIVITY

With small data studies a process of sampling is used in order to produce a representative set of data from the total population of all potential data at a particular time and place. Such sampling is employed because the total population might be very large and it is unfeasible in terms of time and resources to harvest all data. In contrast, big data projects strive towards capturing entire populations (n = all), or at least much larger sample sizes than would traditionally be employed in small data studies (Mayer-Schonberger and Cukier 2013). On the one hand, this is a by-product of the technologies that are employed to generate data, along with the huge growth in the ability to store data (see Chapter 5), and on the other a conviction that 'more is better' and will provide greater representativeness and validity in the analysis.

In open systems like large scientific projects, such as measuring climatic data for weather reporting and meteorological modelling, or collecting astronomical data using a powerful telescope, the drive is towards much larger sets of data, with increased sample sizes across as many variables as possible. For example, in astronomy this means not just collecting light data, but data from across the electromagnetic spectrum, in as high a resolution as possible, for as much of the sky as possible. In the case of closed systems, such as Facebook or buying goods from an online store such as Amazon or sending e-mails, it is possible to record all the interactions and transactions that occur, as well as the level of inaction. And in these cases, that is indeed the case. Every posting, 'like', uploaded photo, link to another website, direct message, game played, periods of absence, etc., is recorded by Facebook for all of its billion or so users. Similarly, Amazon records not only every purchase and purchaser details, but also all the links clicked on and all the goods viewed on its site, as well as items placed in the shopping basket but not purchased. All e-mails are recorded by the servers on which a client e-mail is hosted, storing the whole e-mail and all associated metadata (e.g., who the e-mail was sent to or received from, the time/date, subject, attachments). Even if the

e-mail is downloaded locally and deleted it is still retained on the server, with
most institutions and companies keeping such data for a number of years.

Like other forms of data, spatial data has grown enormously in recent years, from
real-time remote sensing and radar imagery, to large crowdsourced projects such
as OpenStreetMap, to digital spatial trails created by GPS receivers being embedded in devices. The first two seek to be spatially exhaustive, capturing the terrain
of the entire planet, mapping the infrastructure of whole countries and providing
a creative commons licensed mapping dataset. The third provides the ability to
track and trace movement across space over time; to construct individual time–
space trails that can be aggregated to provide time–space models of behaviour
across whole cities and regions. Together they enable detailed modelling of places
and mobility, comparison across space, marketing to be targeted at particular communities, new location-based services, and data that share spatial referents to be
mashed-up to create new datasets and applications that can be searched spatially
(e.g., combining data about an area to create neighbourhood profiles).

Given advances in storage capacity (see Chapter 5), it seems we have reached
the stage where in many cases it is easier to record everything, than to sort, sift
and sample the data, recording only that which is potentially useful (and who is
to know what might prove to be useful in the future?). As Zikopoulos et al.
(2012) note: 'it's little wonder we're drowning in data. If we can track and record
something, we typically do.' Indeed, Dumbill (2012: 7) suggests that an underlying principle of big data is 'when you can, keep everything'. This is driven by a
belief that the more data there are available, the better the chance of making a
valid and penetrating insight, and 'the better … [the] chances of finding the "generators" for a new theory' (John Seely Brown, cited in Bollier 2010: 8). The
strategy of seeking exhaustivity, however, contributes enormously to the data
deluge, the challenge of seeing the trees from the forest, and raises a host of
ethical questions concerning the scope of the data being generated and retained,
and the uses to which they are being put or could be put (see Chapter 10). It
also raises fundamental epistemological questions (Floridi 2012). For example,
given its exhaustivity, Callebaut (2012) asks whether big data analytics is post-
reductivist science. Such questions are examined in more detail in Chapter 8.

RESOLUTION AND INDEXICALITY

In addition to data exhaustivity, big data are becoming much more fine-grained in
their resolution, together with a move towards strong indexicality (unique labelling
and identification) (Dodge and Kitchin 2005). An example of enhanced resolution
are remote sensing images. In the late 1980s, the highest resolution images of the
Earth's surface available to most non-government researchers were those taken by
Landsat satellites, where each pixel relates to a 30 × 30 metre parcel of land. Much
of the imagery now available on Google Earth has a resolution of 2.5 × 2.5 metres,

enabling much more detail to be viewed and analysed. Similarly, with respect to the output of census data, the resolution of the tertiary data has increased in many jurisdictions. In the Irish case, until recently census data were published for electoral divisions (ED) (3,409 areas with an average population of *c.*1,350, with the population per ED being much higher in cities and towns and lower in rural areas). In 2011, the census data were released for a new statistical geography called Small Areas, of which there were 18,488. These new units typically report the data for 80–150 households (Gleeson et al. 2009). The Small Areas enable analysis of the census to be conducted at neighbourhood or street level, rather than quite large areas, and for areas with roughly equal population numbers to be compared, providing a much more granular understanding of the Irish population and economy. Even more fine-grained in resolution, many data brokers are now collating large volumes of data relating to individuals and households that enables companies to individually target goods and services (see Chapter 2).

The increase in the resolution of data has been accompanied by the identification of people, products, transactions and territories becoming more indexical in nature (see Chapter 5). For example, most items for sale in a supermarket presently have a barcode. This barcode identifies the product, but not the individual item – all bottles of the same brand and range of shampoo share the same barcode – meaning that they cannot be individually discriminated. In contrast, a bottle of shampoo tagged with a RFID chip is uniquely identifiable because each chip has a unique ID code which can be read at a distance by a radio transponder. Consequently, each bottle can be tracked from the place of manufacture through the supply chain into a store and a customer's basket, creating a detailed audit trail. In other words, it has become possible to minutely trace the circulation of individual things across time and space, including those who handle each thing along its path. Similarly, information, especially that in a digital form, is being identified uniquely through digital rights management codes, for example DOIs (digital object identifiers) which can be assigned to creative works available across the Internet (e.g., reports, journals, photos, audio and video files). A DOI is a permanent ID with associated metadata, such as a URL that links to the location of the file. The use of unique identifiers enhances relationality and the ability to interconnect and join data together and provides the practical means for sorting, collating, monitoring, matching, and profiling entities (Lyon 2003a; Dodge and Kitchin 2005; Graham 2005; see also Chapter 10).

RELATIONALITY

Relationality concerns the extent to which different sets of data can be conjoined and how those conjoins can be used to answer new questions. Relationality is at the heart of relational databases (see Chapters 2 and 5), and it is the ability to create data that are highly relational that drives the vast data marketplace and the profits of data brokers and profiling companies (see Chapter 2). It is the high degree of relationality that makes censuses so useful for understanding a nation's population and how it is changing over time and space. Small data studies vary in the extent of their relationality, with those involving structured data tending to have higher degrees of interconnection than unstructured ones. That said, some form of relationality must exist between data for overarching interpretations and conclusions to be drawn from them.

Although big data often do not use a relational database structure (see Chapter 5), a core feature of their nature is strong relationality. As boyd and Crawford (2011: 2) detail, 'Big Data is fundamentally networked. Its value comes from the patterns that can be derived by making connections between pieces of data, about an individual, about individuals in relation to others, about groups of people, or simply about the structure of information itself.' And unlike relational databases, it is equally proficient at handling non-numeric, unstructured data as structured data, and in binding the two together and leveraging value from intersections. It thus becomes possible to interlink diverse sets of data – personal, transactional, interactional, social, financial, spatial, temporal, and so on – and to analyse them on an individual and collective basis for relationships and patterns.

An example of the power of such relationality is evident in President Obama's election campaigns in 2008 and 2012 that made extensive use of big data. As detailed by Issenberg (2012), Obama's team sought to quantify and track all aspects of their campaigns in 2008 and 2012, devising a whole series of metrics that were continuously recorded and mined for useful information, patterns and trends. This included the rigorous monitoring of their own actions, such as placing ads across different media, undertaking mail shots, ringing up potential voters, knocking on doors and canvassing areas, organising meetings and rallies, tracking who they had spoken to and what they had said or committed to. They supplemented this information with hundreds of randomised, large-scale experiments designed to test the effectiveness of different ways of persuading people to vote for Obama or donate funds. Obama's team combined all the information they generated with respect to voters with registration data, census and other government data, polling surveys, and data bought from a whole range of suppliers, including data brokers, credit ratings agencies, and cable TV companies. The result was a set of massive databases about every voter in the country consisting of a minimum of 80 variables (Crovitz 2012), and often many more, relating to a potential voter's demographic characteristics, their voting history, every instance in which they had been approached by the Obama campaign and their reaction, their social and economic history, their patterns of behaviour and consumption, and expressed views and opinions, with the databases updated daily during the campaign as new data was produced or bought. In cases where Obama's analysts did not know the political affiliation of a voter, and they could not access this through direct contact, they employed a sophisticated algorithm to use what variables they did have to predict a person's likely voting preference (Issenberg 2012). The result was billions of pieces of interconnected data that were used to individually profile voters, assess if they were likely to vote and how, and how they might react to different policies and stories. The interlinking of data in Obama's campaign created what Crampton et al. (2012) term an 'information amplifier effect', wherein the sum of data is more than the parts.

VELOCITY

A fundamental difference between small and big data is the dynamic nature of data generation. Small data usually consist of studies that are freeze-framed at a particular time and space. Even in longitudinal studies, the data are captured at discrete times (e.g., every few months or years). For example, censuses are generally conducted every five or ten years. In contrast, big data are generated on a much more continuous basis, in many cases in real-time or near to real-time. Rather than a sporadic trickle of data, laboriously harvested or processed, data are flowing at speed. Therefore, there is a move from dealing with batch processing to streaming data (Zikopoulos et al. 2012). On the one hand, this contributes to the issue of data volume by producing data more quickly, on the other it makes the entire data cycle much more dynamic, raising issues of how to manage a data system that is always in flux.

Velocity occurs because repeated observations are continuously made over time and/or space (Jacobs 2009) with many systems operating in perpetual, always-on mode (Dodge and Kitchin 2005). For example, websites continuously record logs that track all visits and the activity undertaken on the site; medical equipment constantly monitors vital signs, recording how a body is responding to treatment and triggering an alarm if a threshold is crossed; mobile phone companies track the location, use and identity of devices accessing their networks every few seconds; weather sensor networks monitor atmospheric indicators every few minutes and transmit their findings to a central database for incorporation into weather forecasts; transponders along a city's road and rail routes record the identity of buses and trains as they pass, enabling the public transit authority to know where all of its vehicles are at any time and to calculate the estimated arrival time at different stops; a retailer monitors the sales of thousands of different products by thousands of customers, using the data to know when to restock shelves and order from suppliers; people communicate with each other through social media sites in a never-ending flow of exchanges and interconnections; a telescope continually monitors the heavens measuring fluctuations in radio waves in order to understand the nature of the universe. In all these cases, there is a persistent stream of data requiring continual management and analysis.

Transferring and managing large volumes of dynamically produced data is a technical challenge as capacity issues can quickly create bottlenecks. For example, just as YouTube videos might freeze because the bandwidth is not sufficient to keep up with the data streaming speed required, the same effect can operate with respect to capturing and processing data, with systems unable to keep up with the flow. Solutions to the problem include increasing bandwidth capacity, data sorting and compression techniques that reduce the volume of data to be processed, and efficiency improvements in processing algorithms and data-management techniques. Analysing such streaming data is also a challenge because at no point does the system rest, and in cases such as the financial markets micro-second analysis of trades can be extremely valuable. Here, sophisticated algorithms, alongside visualisations that display dynamic data in flux, are employed to track and evaluate the system.

VARIETY

Both small and big data can be varied in their nature, being structured, unstructured or semi-structured, consisting of numbers, text, images, video, audio and other kinds of data. In big data these different kinds of data are more likely to be combined and linked, conjoining structured and unstructured data. For example, Facebook posts consist of text that is often linked to photos, or video files, or other websites, and they attract comments by other Facebook users; or a company could combine its financial data concerning sales with customer surveys that express product sentiment. Small data, in contrast, are more discrete and linked, if at all, through key identifiers and common fields. A key advance with regards to big data is how they differ from earlier forms of digital data management, which was extremely proficient at processing and storing numeric data using relational databases, and which enabled various kinds of statistical analysis. It was, however, much weaker at handling non-numeric data formats, other than to store them as flat or compressed files. As the Open Data Center Alliance (2012: 7) notes, '[p]reviously, unstructured data was either ignored or, at best, used inefficiently'. However, advances in distributed computing and database design using NoSQL structures (see Chapter 5), and in data mining and knowledge discovery techniques (see Chapter 6), have hugely increased the capacity to manage, process and extract information from unstructured data. Indeed, it is widely suggested that approximately 80 per cent of all big data is unstructured in nature, though as Grimes (2011) details, this figure has become a truism with little evidential support.

FLEXIBILITY

With small data projects, given the logistics, expense and need for representativeness in a small sample size, the research design and data management can be relatively inflexible once the fieldwork and analysis get underway. For example, it is essential that every person captured by the census fills in exactly the same form to ensure that the data are comparable across the whole population. Once the forms are printed, additional fields cannot be added, meaning that the data that can be extracted across these forms is fixed. Similarly, the relational databases in which the data are held tend to have a fixed form and are limited in scale. Likewise, in scientific experiments and environmental studies to enable comparison and replication, the research design is usually inflexible once initiated. In studies that use interviews or ethnographies, however, it is possible for the researcher to be more flexible in their approach, to have free-form questions and to adapt to unfolding situations. The coding, management and analysis of such data can also be relatively flexible, but this is partly due to the limited size and scope of the dataset.

In contrast, big data systems are designed to be flexible in nature, holding the traits of extensionality (can add new fields easily) and scalability (can expand rapidly) regardless of volume (Marz and Warren 2012). The use of NoSQL databases means that changeable data can be managed at high velocity, adapting to new fields (see Chapter 5). This means that it is possible to adapt data generation on a rolling basis and to perform adaptive testing. For example, Google, Facebook and other online platforms constantly tweak their design, capturing data about how users respond to these changes (e.g., monitoring click-throughs), analysing the results and using these to make further tweaks designed to encourage certain actions. Because the volumes of people using these sites are vast, their sample sizes are enormous, meaning they can make changes without fear of losing representativeness. For example, to return to Barack Obama's election campaign, his team ran rolling experiments on how effective different tweaks to BarackObama.com were for increasing engagement, volunteering and donations. One test evaluated the effects of changing the 'sign up' button to 'learn more', 'join us now', 'sign up now': over the course of 300,000 visits it became clear that 'join us now' led to a 20 per cent increase in people registering with the site (Issenberg 2012).

Such large-volume sites also have to be scalable, able to cope with surges in demand and data generation, where the amount of traffic would usually collapse a traditional relational database held on a single server. For example, the amount of tweets that Twitter has to deal with can fluctuate markedly, with tens of thousands being posted every few seconds during large events, such as the opening ceremony of the Olympic games or during the Superbowl final. The solution to this has been to configure a hardware system composed of distributed parts where data can be stored in databases split across many servers, enabling storage to scale as needed. Moreover, in some systems, such as Twitter, flexibility can be set by users deciding whether to include data or not. For example, in many mobile and social media apps users decide whether to include their location, and also other key metadata such those relating to identity (Gorman 2013).

CONCLUSION

Big data is a recent phenomena, and given its rapid implementation and deployment there are ongoing debates as to what constitutes big data and its associated characteristics. Some definitions, such as that big data are any dataset too large to fit in an Excel spreadsheet or be stored on a single machine (Strom 2012), are quite trite and unhelpful, reducing big data to merely volume. It is becoming clear that big data have a number of inherent characteristics that make them qualitatively different to previous forms of data. In this chapter it has been argued that big data have seven essential characteristics: volume, velocity, variety, exhaustivity, resolution/indexicality, relationality, and flexibility/scalability that distinguish them from small data (see Table 2.1).

This is an initial first-level pass at providing an ontological assessment of the nature of big data. More work is needed to assess big data generated from multiple sources to establish if there are varieties in the nature of big data. For example, it may be the case that some data hold five or six of these character-istics, but do not fulfil or are weaker in one or two. For example, a dataset may lack variety (be very structured) or volume (small, but exhaustive with n = all) or are weaker in velocity (the data are generated regularly but every month rather than continuously) or lack indexicality (it is anonymised or aggregated), yet hold the other properties. Such data are clearly not small data as discussed in Chapter 2, but are not big data as understood in a narrow sense of holding all seven characteristics. They nevertheless can be considered a form of big data. In other words, there is a need to produce a taxonomy of big data based on strong empirical evidence with case examples that would help us think through more fully the nature of such data. This needs to be accompanied by an examination of other characteristics, such as data quality, veracity, fidelity, and provenance (see Chapter 9).

The seven characteristics of big data also raise questions as to the implica-tions of a deluge of such data. What does it mean for society, government and business to gain access to very large, exhaustive, dynamic, fine-grained, indexical, varied, relational, flexible and scalable data? To what extent can such data provide penetrating insights into the human condition or help address some of the most pressing social, political, economic and environmental issues facing the planet? Or, rather than serve the public good, will such data be used predominately to further private interests? Or serve the interests of the state? How will such data change the epistemology of science across all domains (arts and humanities, social sciences, physical and life sciences, engineering)? Chapters 7, 8 and 10 discuss these issues in detail, providing a critical reflection on the implications and consequences of big data.

5

ENABLERS AND SOURCES OF BIG DATA

The rapid growth of big data has arisen due to the simultaneous development of a number of enabling technologies, infrastructures, techniques and processes, and their rapid embedding into everyday business and social practices and spaces. This new knowledge infrastructure includes the widespread roll-out of a diverse set of information and communication technologies, especially fixed and mobile Internet; the embedding of software into all kinds of objects, machines and systems, transforming them from 'dumb' to 'smart', as well as the creation of purely digital devices and systems; the development of ubiquitous computing and the ability to access networks and computation in many environments and on the move; advances in database design and systems of information management; distributed and forever storage of data at affordable costs; and new forms of data analytics designed to cope with data abundance as opposed to data scarcity.

As well as enabling the accessing, sharing and storage of data, the new knowledge infrastructure is often the means by which much big data are generated. Indeed, it is undoubtedly the case that we are presently living in societies that increasingly utilise and are structured by data-intensive and data-producing technologies. Personal practices of communication, consumption, production, travel and home life are becoming ever more mediated by digital devices that produce valuable exhaust data. Further, the places in which we live are now augmented, monitored and regulated by dense assemblages of data-enabled infrastructures and technologies, such as traffic and building management systems, surveillance and policing systems, government databases, customer management and logistic chains, and financial and payment systems. In this chapter, the enablers and sources of big data are discussed in detail.

THE ENABLERS OF BIG DATA

Big data are the outcome of the development and convergence of a range of technological advances in computing since the end of the Second World War.

These include the production of mainframe computers in the 1950s and 60s; the nascent Internet in the 1970s and 80s that linked such computers together; the wide-scale roll-out of personal computers in the 1980s and 90s; the massive growth of the Internet in the 1990s and the development of Web-based industries, alongside a huge growth in mobile phones and digital devices such as games consoles and digital cameras; the development of mobile, distributed and cloud computing and Web 2.0 in the 2000s; the roll-out of ubiquitous and pervasive computing in the 2010s. Throughout this period a number of transformative effects took place: computational power grew exponentially; devices were networked together; more and more aspects and processes of everyday life became mediated by digital systems; data became ever more indexical and machine-readable; and data storage expanded and became distributed.

Computation

While the initial mainframe digital computers of the 1950s and 60s provided computation that was more efficient than that provided by people or the analogue devices they used (such as abacus, mechanical calculators, punch-card calculators, analogue computers, etc.), their processing power was limited, and thus the kinds of operations they performed constrained, and they were large and expensive. For example, the ENIAC (Electronic Numerical Integrator and Computer) developed in the mid-1940s could add or subtract 5,000 times a second, but its high-speed memory was limited to 20 words (c.80 bytes), and the machine weighed 30 tons, containing over 18,000 vacuum tubes, 1,500 relays, and hundreds of thousands of resistors, capacitors, and inductors, using 200 kilowatts of electric power (Najmi 2004). In 1965, Gordon Moore of Intel predicted that the number of transistors on integrated circuits would double every 18 months for the next decade, thus massively increasing computational power (what became known as Moore's Law). This prediction proved prescient and as technical improvements were made to components and in the design of computers (moving from vacuum tubes to transistors to integrated circuits to microprocessors), computational power grew at approximately 50 per cent per year between 1940 and 2001 (Nordhaus 2002). Alongside this growth in computation its cost fell dramatically, with one estimate suggesting that there was a quadrillion-fold (1,000,000,000,000,000) fall in the cost of computation during the twentieth century (CRA 2003).

Such rises in power and falls in cost have continued in the new millennium, but importantly have also become portable with the wide-scale roll-out of a plethora of mobile computational devices such as laptops, tablets, smartphones, satnavs, and so on. The average smartphone is 'ten times more powerful than the Cray-1 supercomputer installed at Los Alamos National Laboratory in 1976' (Townsend 2013: xiii), using a fraction of the power, and has more computational power, storage and applications than many desktop computers from only a decade previously, yet in devices a fraction of the size. For example, many smartphones have 1.5 to 2 GHz microprocessors and 16 to 32 gigabytes of memory. Such processing power and memory enable very large amounts of data to be processed quickly, to be stored locally and, because they are networked, shared.

Networking

Equally as important as the exponential growth of computation power for processing digital data is the networking together of computers that facilitates the transfer and sharing of data. The first Internet connection between two computers took place in November 1969, linking a node in UCLA (University of California Los Angeles) to one in Stanford (Salus 1995). The network grew slowly, with 13 nodes in January 1971, 23 in April 1972, 62 in June 1974 and 111 by March 1977, and was limited to ARPA contractors (Advanced Research Projects Agency of US Department of Defense) (Hart et al. 1992; O'Neill 1995). The Internet works by breaking down data and instructions into packets of equal size for posting through the system, with each packet labelled with an identifier and the address of its intended recipient. Each packet is passed from one node to another until it arrives at the intended destination where it is reassembled. To enable machines and networks that run at different clock speeds and use different-sized packets to connect, the TCP/IP network protocol (Transmission Control Protocol/Internet Protocol) was adopted in 1973 (O'Neill 1995) and is still used today. This protocol also assured net neutrality, wherein all data are treated equally without discrimination or differential charging (Wu 2011).

By the late 1970s, local area networks had been created, other networks had been established internationally and connected to the fledgling Internet, as well as independent hobbyist and corporate networks, and it had become possible to send packets via satellite communication. As well as the transfer of data and files, e-mail had been established, as had as bulletin boards (Kitchin 1998). During the 1980s the infrastructure grew, with new institutional and corporate players widening participation, along with the development of intranets (private networks). In 1992, the World Wide Web was invented by Tim Berners-Lee at CERN, Geneva, producing a much more user-friendly way of accessing and using the Internet. Throughout the 1990s and 2000s, new networking technologies were developed such as near field and proximate communication with Bluetooth, local WiFi coverage, and national GSM/3G networks. According to George Gilder's (2000) 'law of telecosm', the world's supply of bandwidth (its capacity to transfer data) doubles roughly every six months, with much of the additional capacity provided through wireless networks. As a consequence of these developments, the linking of computational devices through the Internet has become increasingly easier, faster and more widely available.

Pervasive and ubiquitous computing

Accompanying the expansion in the accessibility and bandwidth of ICT networks has been the diversification and expansion in digital-enabled devices
which either directly or indirectly (uploaded to another device first) connect to
the Internet to exchange data, instructions or receive software updates. In some
cases, new digital technologies are replacing previous forms of analogue data
collection, for example, analogue phone systems being replaced by mobile and
smartphones, analogue surveillance cameras recording on video tape being
replaced by digital cameras capturing digital images, or music captured on tape
or vinyl being replaced by digital audio files, or paper forms being replaced by
online ones. Here, devices and systems that were relatively 'dumb' have been
made 'smart' in some way, usually through the use of associated software (Dodge
and Kitchin 2005). Here, 'smart' generally means a device has programmed
awareness of its own use and an ability to make autonomous, automatic and
automated decisions from a suite of defined choices through the deployment of
algorithms on produced data (see Dodge and Kitchin 2007a). A good example
of a previously 'dumb' technological assemblage that has increasingly become
'smart' is a car. The modern car is loaded with digital devices, sensors and actuators that monitor and regulate its various systems and mediate the driving
experience (Thrift 2004). Stored data from such devices can be transmitted via
telematic networks to companies or downloaded by an engineer to perform a
diagnostic analysis (Dodge and Kitchin 2007a). In other cases, devices have no
analogue equivalent, with the data being wholly new in form, such as those
generated by new types of digital technologies, scans and sensors (for example,
in the health field such as magnetic resonance imaging [MRI] scanners). In addition to becoming 'smart', systems are often set to gather as much data as possible,
seeking to be exhaustive rather than selective. Here, data that may be tangential
or unnecessary for an operation or service provision, such as personal details or
location, are harvested. Default settings of devices or software/website contracts
are often set so that people have to choose to opt out of data-generation regimes,
with associated penalties if they choose to do so, such as the degradation of service, additional costs, or service denial.

Such has been the growth in digital devices in the home, on the street, in
workplaces, across transport networks, and elsewhere, that a number of commentators posit that we have entered an age of 'everyware' (Greenfield 2006).
That is, an era of pervasive and ubiquitous computing where computation is
distributed and available everywhere, with multiple computational devices
operating for every person (Lucas et al. 2012). Pervasive computing is the adding of computational power and access to ICT networks to everyday fixed
objects and environments to make them interactive and 'smart' (Dourish 2001).
In contrast, ubiquitous computing is computation power that moves with the

person regardless of environment; digital devices that people carry such as smartphones and satnavs that rely on accessing ICT networks to deliver services. If the mantra of pervasive computing is computation 'in everything', then the mantra of ubiquitous computing is computation 'in every place', with pervasive computing exhibiting processes of divergence (software being embedded into more and more devices) and ubiquitous computing exhibiting convergence (single digital devices undertaking more and more tasks) (Kitchin and Dodge 2011). While pervasive computing needs to be situationally aware to be successfully implemented, ubiquitous computing requires continuous context and location awareness.

Indexical and machine-readable identification

Over the past half century, more and more phenomena in the world have become uniquely identifiable and more easily captured as data, due to new labelling and digital technologies, radically increasing their resolution and relationality and thus the level of granularity in their analysis, as well as enabling more datasets to be interconnected (see Chapter 4). For example, each digital device that contributes to pervasive and ubiquitous computing is uniquely indexical, assigned an exclusive identification code that enables it to be tracked and traced. Moreover, all the elements of the Internet of things – a vast constellation of networked devices, actuators, sensors – are similarly indexical producing data that can be uniquely attributable (Gershenfeld et al. 2004). Further, the unique identifiers that have long been associated with people, such as passports, health cards, social insurance records, have been complemented by new digital and biometric identification systems that connect them to digital databases and verify their identity (Dodge and Kitchin 2005). These include usernames and passwords, chip-and-pin or magnetic swipe cards, and digital readings of fingerprints, irises and DNA. In each case, these identifiers act as a digital handshake, though they vary in their level of rigour and trust. Usernames and passwords, for example, can be easily stolen or faked, whereas DNA is uniquely inherent to each person and fulfils the first four criteria of Clarke's (1994b) list of desirable characteristics for effective human identification: universality of coverage (everyone should have one); uniqueness (each person should have only one, and no two people should have the same one); permanence (should not change, nor be changeable); and indispensability (a natural characteristic that cannot be removed). These comply with his other seven traits: collectability; storability; exclusivity; precision; simplicity; cost and convenience; and acceptability.

Similarly, spatial identification codes are systems that locate people, places and objects across the globe, and include latitude and longitude, grid references, and administrative units such as postcodes (zipcodes). These systems vary in their scale and resolution (granularity) and have been becoming ever more fine-scaled

and common. For example, administrative data are tagged to individual properties or land parcels rather than neighbourhoods; any device with a GPS receiver
records location to within a few metres; and national mapping systems have
started to assign a large number of human-created and natural objects in a landscape unique territorial identifiers. Other such unique identifiers are increasingly
common for products (see Chapter 4), transactions (e.g., purchases) and interactions (e.g., e-mail and phone conversations).

As well as being more indexical, identification codes have also become
increasingly machine-readable (Dodge and Kitchin 2005). For example, a barcode contains an identification code that when scanned by a laser reader is
linked to an information system where additional metadata are held that describe
the object (e.g. product type/model, date and place of manufacture, price, etc.).
RFID chips can be sensed at a distance by a transponder and identified. Vehicles
can be recognised by automatic number plate recognition software, and new
algorithmic techniques have been developed to recognise and identify faces and
gait (how people walk). Elements of the world have thus become open to being
automatically captured and identified, massively expanding the amount and
resolution of data generated with regard to a system, enabling new forms of
regulation and governance (Dodge and Kitchin 2007a) and systems to function
in more automated ways (Kitchin and Dodge 2011). The trend is for more and
more phenomena and practices to become uniquely identifiable and machine-
readable, thus further increasing resolution, relationality and automation.

Data storage

Over the past two decades there has been a dramatic shift in the ability to long-
term store vast quantities of data. Initially, digital data were stored in an analogue
form using punchcards, before switching to magnetic tape and hard disks. These
were complemented by mobile digital storage mediums: floppy disks, followed
by CDs, DVDs and flash/external drives. Hard-disk technologies, in particular,
have relentlessly pushed up the capacity to store digital data, with significant
growth in bits stored per square inch, while the cost per gigabyte has fallen dramatically (by an estimated factor of 10 million to one from 1956 to 2000
[Gilheany 2000] and has continued to plummet), making digital storage much
cheaper and less space-intensive than analogue forms (e.g., paper or film)
(Grochowski and Halem 2003). Costs have now become so cheap that it is possible to store enormous amounts of data for negligible cost, with the deletion of
old files virtually unnecessary. As a result, transactions undertaken today (for
example, a message sent to an e-mail list or Facebook page, paying in a store with
a credit card, speaking to a friend on the telephone) may well be logged and kept
beyond the death of the person, with the potential to be recalled and analysed
at any point in the future.

Consequently, as discussed in the previous chapter, the growth in the volume of stored data in absolute and relative terms has been prodigious, especially since 2000. For example, Hilbert and López (2009) estimated that only 25 per cent of data was stored in digital form in 2000, with the remainder being held in analogue forms such as books, magazines, photos and magnetic tapes. By 2007, digital data constituted 94 per cent of stored data. Since then, the relative share of digital data has continued to grow, especially with the development of distributed storage and services through cloud computing and data centres. Cloud computing takes two forms that often work cooperatively: utility clouds and data clouds (Farber et al. 2011). Utility clouds provide IT capabilities as location-independent, on-demand services accessible via the Internet, including 'infrastructure as a service' (IaaS) such as storage, servers and networks, 'platform as a service' (PaaS) comprising an execution environment for the development of custom applications and databases, and 'software as a service' (SaaS) that enables users to access their applications and to process data remotely (Farber et al. 2011; Hancke et al. 2012). Data clouds enable massive volumes of data, that might be generated across an enterprise, to be linked, stored and processed remotely, drawing on the computational power of hundreds of machines, and analysed via utility services (Farber et al. 2011). Individuals and companies can thus utilise storage and computing capacity without the need to make large capital investments, as well as being able to avail themselves of such resources from anywhere there is network access (Bryant et al. 2008).

Likewise, there has been a transformation in how data are curated and structured when stored. As data volumes, velocity and variety have increased, relational databases have struggled to cope. They are designed for highly organised, clean, structured and stable data. In their stead, a new database form, 'NoSQL' has been rolled out enabling the storage of big data. NoSQL databases tend to be less complex in form than relational databases, but they can cope with both structured and unstructured data, are rapidly extensible, can deal with truly enormous, dynamic sets of data, and are flexible in how they are organised, enabling bespoke data structures (Driscoll 2012; Marz and Warren 2012). NoSQL databases tend to store raw rather than derived data that is structured according to a predetermined relationship (Driscoll 2012). For example, they would store raw pageview information rather than a derived pageview count, a strategy that is more robust in that it reduces potential faults in the database, but would not be attempted with a relational database as it would grow quickly to an unworkable size (Marz and Warren 2012). In NoSQL databases data are typically distributed and replicated across many machines rather than centralised into one location (thus solving the problem of very large datasets being too big to fit on single machines) and queries are divided up and run in parallel over multiple nodes and then combined (thus speeding up computation) (Dumbill 2012). Such a strategy is summarised by the MapReduce technique pioneered by Google wherein data and queries are mapped onto multiple servers and the partial results are then reduced together (Dumbill 2012). An open-source and widely used example of such a NoSQL system that implements the MapReduce approach is Hadoop, first developed by Yahoo! The compromise of such an approach is a more limited data model, a diminished degree of relationality in the dataset, and a reduced ability to explore using a query language (Driscoll 2012). This means that NoSQL databases are ideal for the efficient storage and quick retrieval of vast quantities of data, but are less useful for examining the relationships between data elements (Open Data Center Alliance 2012).

SOURCES OF BIG DATA

The radical expansion and integration of computation, networking, digital devices and data storage has provided a robust platform for the explosion in big data, as well as being the means by which big data are generated, processed, shared and analysed. Such data production can be broadly divided into three categories. Directed data are generated by traditional forms of surveillance, wherein the gaze of the technology is focused on a person or place by a human operator. In the case of automated data, data are generated as an inherent, automatic function of the device or system, whereas volunteered data are traded or gifted by people to a system.

Directed data

Organised and structured surveillance, wherein one group of people (e.g., law enforcement officials, teachers, doctors, welfare officials, bureaucrats, bosses) observe others (e.g., citizens, pupils, patients, workers) in person or through a technological lens (e.g., surveys such as a census, government forms, tax receipts, inspections, CCTV cameras), has long been a feature of societies, an essential component of state and corporate governance (Lyon 2007). Such a form of governmentality (the interlocking rationale, apparatus, institutions, roles and procedures of governance) enables centralised control and regulation across a broad spectrum of domains and helps to maintain order, produce good government, effective administration, profitable business, and sustainable and stable communities, both through the active disciplining of subjects but also their self-disciplining (that is, people modify their behaviour to conform to expectations and rules). Such systems are complemented with methods of individual identification, such as fingerprinting, photographs, national insurance or social security numbers, passports and driver licences, that make it easier to track and trace people. Surveillance has also been extended to animals and environments, and the use and movement of objects.

Until recently all surveillance was inherently partial and analogue in nature and produced varying levels of recorded data, ranging from observations that were unrecorded to detailed logs or continuous recordings, sometimes applied to samples and in a few cases entire populations. The data recorded were selective, captured through reporting or self-reporting to paper or on tape or film, at a particular place and time. The data tended to be highly structured in nature, limited to a set of predefined fields. Records were bulky and expensive to store, meaning that only a limited amount of data, much of them either a sample or derived, would not be kept long term. Even in cases where surveillance might be continuous, such as CCTV, the footage might be time-lapsed to extend the time each tape covered and the tapes would generally be re-recorded over after a certain duration (often seven days or a month). The data produced by the various forms of surveillance employed had to be analysed by a human interpreter unless they were subsequently digitised. While the amount of data produced by such surveillance could be voluminous, and might have one or two of the characteristics associated with big data such as indexicality, relationality, exhaustivity or velocity, they never possessed the full suite of the qualities associated with big data.

While many surveillance and governance systems continue to be partial and analogue, more recently there has been a move to replace and extend them with digital equivalents so that they now produce big data. For example, fixed analogue CCTV systems are being replaced by digital and movable equivalents where the field of view can be altered, constraints on storage have been lessened, and human interpretation can be supplemented with algorithmic analyses, such as facial and gait recognition, and it is possible to link such data to other databases. Here, the gaze of the camera, and interpretation and analysis, is largely directed by a human operator, aided by software. For example, in a police operations room several cameras might be monitored and controlled, linked to a log of live incidents in order to efficiently and reactively direct appropriate resources to particular locations. Similarly, at immigration passport control passenger details are collected and checked against various security and border control databases in real-time, and new data are generated such as photographs, fingerprints or iris scans. Many local governments use management systems to real-time log citizen engagement with their services and to monitor whether staff have dealt with any issues within certain time frames, with managers overseeing the system to redirect resources.

Other kinds of more irregular, directed big data generation might consist of digital aerial photography via planes or drones, or spatial video, LIDAR (light detection and ranging), thermal or other kinds of electromagnetic scans of environments that enable the mobile and real-time 2D and 3D mapping of landscapes that are spatially indexical through GPS. Such video and scans produce vast quantities of high-velocity and varied data. For example, each LIDAR scan

can generate a million data points, with a spatial resolution down to centimetres, and a number of scans per second are possible. Placing a LIDAR scanner on a vehicle and driving it around, or flying it over, an area produces data that can create a highly detailed three-dimensional representation of a landscape.

Automated data

While directed data extends traditional surveillance and governance regimes, automated data generation radically transforms how data are generated and employed, and has enabled the creation of new regimes of regulation and auto-mated management (Dodge and Kitchin 2007a, Kitchin and Dodge 2011; see Chapter 10). Within automated systems data are generated automatically by a range of digital technologies with little human oversight. Moreover, such data are often automatically and autonomously processed, analysed and acted upon by algorithms to produce a certain outcome designed to regulate a phenome-non. There are several ways in which automated data are being generated, some of which are a by-product of a system rather than its primary purpose.

Automated surveillance

↳ eg . SPEED RADAR

As surveillance technologies have become digital in nature and networked together it has become possible to automate various aspects of monitoring sys-tems, and to add new techniques, to more effectively and efficiently track and trace the usage of different systems and places. An example of a manual form of surveillance that is increasingly becoming automated is smart metering. Here, automatic meter reading (AMR) technology is used to monitor and communi-cate utility usage without the need for manual reading (Hancke et al. 2013). Moreover, it can do these tasks on a continuous basis enabling a supplier to track usage in real-time, which has utility in matching demand with supply and in finding faults/leakage in a system. It also offers a means to undertake automated billing, reducing staff overheads. In many cases, it is also possible for the con-sumer to monitor their own use of a utility, such as electricity, gas or water, for example by using a phone app that can connect to the meter via near-field com-munication (e.g., Bluetooth), and thus alter their consumption accordingly.

Likewise, traffic management systems are augmenting their ability to regulate and discipline drivers by utilising automatic number plate recognition (ANPR) technology (Dodge and Kitchin 2007a). Here, algorithms scan the feed from digital cameras to detect licence plates. On the one hand, such information can be used to track vehicles as they cross a city and provide inputs into intelligent transportation systems (ITS), and on the other to cross-reference details to a database of vehicle owners in order to administer fines and penalties for traffic violations. For example, in relation to the latter, the licence plate details of all vehicles entering the congestion charge zone in London are scanned and

London

matched to a database of those that have paid the congestion charge. Those who
have not paid within a 24-hour period are automatically fined through a process
of automated management (the system has the autonomy to issue fines free of
human oversight). The system can similarly be used in conjunction with speed
cameras to issue tickets to speeding drivers.

In other cases, automated surveillance has been facilitated by the use of
machine-readable identification codes to enrol what were anonymous activities
into the net of surveillance. For example, anonymous paper tickets used to travel
on a transport system are increasingly being replaced with 'smart cards' that have
to be scanned to enter and exit stations and vehicles. At the point of scanning a
log is generated and thus all movements of smart card holders can be tracked. In
the case of London Transport the use of Oyster cards means that it is possible to
trace the individual journeys across the bus and rail system of 2 million passengers
a day (Batty et al. 2012). Similarly, various forms of public service provision that
were casually monitored, such as rubbish collection, can now be automatically
surveilled through the use of RFID chips attached to bins that are scanned at the
point of collection. By using scales attached to collection vehicles it then becomes
possible to measure waste disposal and to charge individual households on a volume basis rather than a flat fee. It also becomes possible to gain a detailed understanding of the patterns of waste disposal within an area and to re-plan collection
routes and times.

Digital devices

As noted, there has been an explosion in the number of digital devices in use in
the world which help to facilitate, augment and manage many aspects of everyday
life. These devices do not simply process digital data and instructions, but actively
produce digital data either as a primary function or as exhaust, or as both. Examples
of the former include cameras, videos, telescopes, GPS units, various forms of
medical equipment such as keyhole cameras, ultrasound scanners, digital ther-
mometers, etc. The latter include mobile phones and cable and satellite receiver
boxes that generate data concerning how they are being used (e.g., time, location,
person called/channel watched), with the associated data being captured as logs
that are transmitted to third parties (such as device manufacturers and service providers). Examples that produce both primary and exhaust data include smartphones that can be used to record notes, capture pictures, write e-mail and
comments to social media, and so on, as well logging the use of various apps. Such
devices constitute a new breed of objects, what have been termed logjects (Kitchin
and Dodge 2011) – objects that track and trace the history of their own use. In
many cases, the location of these devices can also be recorded. Mobile and smartphones can be traced through space by triangulation across phone masts, and also
via a built-in GPS receiver, as well monitoring speed and direction via gyroscopes,

accelerometers and compasses (as can tablets, satnavs and other devices). Moreover, many of these devices can autonomously interact with each other and share data. As complex devices multiply across tasks and places, more and more data, rich with indexical metadata, are produced, enabling more sophisticated analysis and new data-driven strategies and products.

Sensed data

A particular kind of digital device are sensors and actuators. These can be embedded in or placed on different structures to measure specific outputs such as levels of light, humidity, temperature, gas, chemicals, electrical resistivity, acoustics, air pressure, movement, speed, and so on. Sensors and actuators are small, generally inexpensive and can create a continuous stream of data. They can be passive and read by scanners, or can be active, broadcasting data at regular intervals over local or wide area networks, or they might have near-field communication (NFC) capabilities that enable two-way communication (Hancke et al. 2013). Placed on a bridge, sensors can measure and communicate corrosion rates (by measuring electrical resistivity) and stress on build materials using acoustic emission sensors (to detect propagation of sound waves) and magneto-strictive sensors (to detect changes in magnetic induction), thus lessening the need for costly manual inspection (Hancke et al. 2013). Similarly, within a water system sensors can measure water quality, pressure and flow, enabling real-time management and maintenance of the pipes. On vehicles, they can monitor workload, stress and terrain. Hitachi uses such sensors to monitor their complex, expensive heavy construction vehicles, and UPS do the same with their fleet of vans and trucks so that they can be serviced to run efficiently and before they break down (Plumridge 2012; Mayer-Schonberger and Cukier 2013). By attaching an RFID to products it becomes possible to track and trace the movement of individual units from factory or farm to consumer, reducing theft and wastage. Likewise, toll tags contain RFID chips that communicate with transponders at toll-booth barriers, leading to quicker throughput of vehicles and automatic payment, as well as measuring vehicle flow or parking space availability for traffic management. RFID chips attached to buses and trains communicate with transponders along their routes making it possible to track the location of vehicles in real-time.

By distributing many sensors and linking up the data produced by them, a dense sensor network can be created, enabling the monitoring of different conditions across a system or place. Examples of such sensor networks have been rolled out in Santander in Spain as part of their SmartSantander project: 12,000 sensors, consisting of 5 types, have been strategically distributed across the city to measure noise, temperature, ambient light levels, carbon monoxide concentration, and the availability and location of parking spaces (Bielsa 2013). The sensors are linked together through wireless communication and employ

Over-the-Air-Programming (OTAP), enabling them to be programmed and upgraded remotely (Bielsa 2013). The PlanIT Valley development in Portugal, presently under construction and designed for up to 225,000 inhabitants, aims to create a built environment laced with over 100 million embedded sensors that will produce data to monitor a diverse range of infrastructures and environments (Marchetti 2012). Sensors are thus seen a key component of smart city developments.

Scan data

In addition to digital devices and sensors which actively produce data and are part of the Internet of things, other objects can be digitally tracked and traced through machine-readable identification codes. The use of barcodes extends beyond retail to include manufactured goods and official forms, and many large organisations and industrial sectors have developed their own particular form of barcode and protocols for allocating numbers (Dodge and Kitchin 2005). 2D barcodes encode data both horizontally and vertically in a block of speckled dots and can be used to uniquely identify an object. Some mail services use such 2D barcodes to enable the tracking and tracing of individual letters and parcels. Similarly, magnetic strips on credit and loyalty cards and pass cards for swiping through doors also contain unique identification concerning the card owner that are read when swiped. These are being superseded by electronic chips whose details can be verified using a pin code. Each time a barcode, magnetic strip or chip is scanned, data concerning its use is generated, including where and when it was used and for what purpose. Given that in many cases such scans are for purchasing items, they provide an important means of generating high-resolution transaction information.

Interaction data

While some Internet users perceive the medium to be a fairly anonymous terrain, just about all interactions across ICT networks generate interaction data. In fact, data generation is inherently built into many forms of ICT-facilitated communication and use. For example, Internet service providers track the sites that individual user accounts and machines connect to, and many websites, especially corporate sites, utilise cookies to generate clickstream data, tracking how a user navigates through a website and what features are clicked on. In general, such data are used to monitor how a website performs, conduct market research and track employee productivity, though the data can be sold on to third parties. Such clickstream data are automatically generated unless the user instructs their browser to not accept cookies (and this might impair the use of a site). Similarly, all ICT-based financial trades, whether personal electronic banking, withdrawing money from an ATM, or trading in shares, are allocated unique identification codes and the transactions recorded. All e-mails contain headers that uniquely identify the e-mail, including information on the sender and recipient, and the machines and servers used. Likewise, all phone calls are tagged with the recipient, time and duration of call, and, if a mobile phone, the location. As a consequence, vast quantities of data are routinely generated concerning interactions across ICT networks

Volunteered data

PROSUMPTION (PRODUCTION/CONSUMPTION)

In contrast to surveillance that is either directed at people or things by individuals and agencies, or are captured automatically as an inherent feature of a device or system, much big data are actively volunteered by people. In such cases, individuals generate and input data and labour either to avail themselves of a service (such as social media) or to take part in a collective project (such OpenStreetMap or Wikipedia). Such labour has been called prosumption as the modes of production and consumption have been partially collapsed onto one another, with individuals assuming a role in the production of the service or product they are consuming (Ritzer and Jurgenson 2010). For example, the content of a social media site is simultaneously produced and consumed by individual users inputting comments, uploading photos and videos, and engaging in discussion and the exchange of sentiment ('liking' or 'disliking' something). Through their collective efforts, prosumers create, add value to, and extract value from the products or services they engage with, drawing on what Benkler (2006) terms the 'wealth of networks'. In the main, prosumers do this additional work for little or no recompense, either getting enjoyment from the task, or a sense of empowerment, or they save money/time as the cost of the service is reduced and often becomes more flexible in nature (such as online banking or checking-in to a flight from home). In return, the service provider or retailer receives unwaged labour, along with expertise, opinions and knowledge and gains efficiencies and potentially valuable information by getting 'closer' to the customers/clients or being able to monetise their data (Ritzer and Jurgenson 2010; Dodge and Kitchin 2013). Some forms of prosumption are more akin to self-service and are restricted in nature, with prosumers undertaking work that previously was undertaken by employees, while others are more open and interactional. Here, five are discussed in brief: transactions, social media, sousveillance, crowdsourcing and citizen science.

Transactions

Online purchasing requires the purchaser to enter personal data with respect to payment, address and other required metadata, partially as a process of verification and exchange but also to learn more about the consumer. Similarly, filling out online government forms requires a citizen to volunteer information to the site. Here, there is an exchange of data for a service that extends beyond a cash payment. Other additional data can be tied to the transactions, such as click-stream data and loyalty card information, enabling a rudimentary profile to be built up over time or to be linked to other data sources such as geodemographic data. Interactions in such exchanges are usually fairly limited, restricted to choosing what items to purchase, and many fields are compulsory to finalise the process. After the exchange, users might be asked for further data, either rating the performance of the site and customer service, or by rating/reviewing the item purchased. Such review data adds value to the site by suggesting how to tweak the design and by providing valuable feedback to other consumers about the quality and performance of products. On sites such as tripadvisor.com, where prosumers can rate and review hotels and other travel services, such volunteered data drives traffic to the site, generates advertising and referral revenue, and can have a marked influence on the choices of other travellers. It also provides useful data about the individual who volunteered the review, such as their lifestyle choices and travel spending that can be monetised by selling these on to third parties.

Social media

Prior to 2003 the Internet was largely a broadcast medium through which people could source information or purchase goods. There were bulletin boards and mailing lists through which people could converse, but they were text-based only and specifically themed as opposed to being open, general fora. And while individuals could produce other forms of content such as web pages, it required skill to create such pages and the purchasing of a domain name. These pages were largely static and in the main had to be manually edited to be updated. From 2004 onwards, however, the nature of the Internet started to change and to become much more interactive, participatory and dynamic. This shift has been referred to as the transfer from Web 1.0 to Web 2.0 (O'Reilly 2005). Rather than web content largely being provided by specialists and web designers, it became possible for anybody to create content that could be dynamically updated. Moreover, such content could be accessed and interacted with from a variety of platforms such as smartphones and tablets. Instead of simply browsing information or being constrained to relatively narrow discussions, it became possible for people to easily and actively participate in the production of the online world, designing and editing content, and contributing freely to services that share material with others. Whereas Web 1.0 was considered a read medium, Web 2.0 is a read+write medium, in which people add value to sites as they use them.

Web 2.0 sites and services tend to focus on many-to-many publishing, social communication, and providing richer, contextualised information. Examples include social-networking services (e.g., Facebook, Twitter), photo and video sharing sites (e.g., flickr and YouTube), blogging, and mashups (using open Application Programming Interfaces [APIs] to merge data from different sources to create new applications, e.g., Foursquare, Yelp). These sites are all reliant on active participation by a public willing to share information about their lives and undertake work such as writing, editing, extending, remixing, posting, sharing, tagging, communicating, and so on (Beer and Burrows 2007). In so doing, not only do they volunteer labour, but much data about themselves, including user profiles, photos, locations, opinions, preferences and values, and their network of social contacts. Since these sites are owned by newly founded corporate enter- prises, data are being traded into privately owned hands who then seek to pro- duce new models of capital accumulation by extracting value from them (see Chapters 2 and 7).

Sousveillance

Sousveillance is the self-monitoring and management of one's personal health and life through intimate digital technologies (e.g., fitness equipment, wearable computing) that record data concerning an individual (Mann et al. 2003). In contrast to surveillance, in which an individual is monitored from an external position by another entity, sousveillance is consciously employed and controlled by an individual for personal fulfilment, providing an interior, first-person per- spective on their lives. Over the past decade, a sousveillance movement has developed of people who actively monitor and record their personal data (also known as the quantified self movement). In general, individuals are monitoring aspects of health and fitness, capturing data consumption (e.g., food/calorie intake), physical states (e.g., blood pressure, pulse) emotional states (e.g., mood, arousal) and performance (e.g., miles walked/run/cycled, hours slept and types of sleep), with a number of companies providing associated self-monitoring technologies and services. For example, activity and sleep monitors include Fitbit, Nike+ Fuelband and Jawbone that synchronise generated data with tracker apps that allow the user to monitor and analyse their personal data. The data generated are not necessarily shared with a wider public, though they can be, but they are shared with the service-providing companies, providing them with a rich seam of personalised data.

   Such technologies are in an initial phase of development and there are visions for much more comprehensive life-logs that would create a unified, digital record of an individual's experiences, captured multimodally through digital sen- sors and stored permanently as a personal multimedia archive (Mann et al. 2003), with a number of research prototypes being developed. Life-logs aim to create a continuous, searchable, analysable record of the past that includes every action, every event, every conversation, every location visited, every material expression of an individual's life, as well as physiological conditions inside the body and external conditions (e.g., orientation, temperature, levels of pollution) (Dodge and Kitchin 2007b) – 'the totality of information that flows through a human life' (Johnson 2003: 85). Clearly the production of such life-logs raise a number of questions concerning privacy, the ownership of the data produced, and how such data are used (Dodge and Kitchin 2007b).

Crowdsourcing

Crowdsourcing is the collective generation of media, ideas and data undertaken voluntarily by many people to solve a particular task. While social media content can be said to be crowdsourced in the sense that it is sourced from a large number of people, its purpose is diffuse and lacking in focus. Instead, crowdsourcing focuses on the collective production of information and on creating solutions to particular issues by drawing on the energy, knowledge, skills and consensual and collective action of a crowd of people (Howe 2008). Howe (2008) argues that there are four developments that support the growth of crowdsourcing: a renaissance of amateurism (often at professional standards), the emergence of the open source software movement, the increasing availability of the tools of production outside of firms, and the rise of vibrant online communities organised according to people's interests. Together these enable distributed and democratised pooling of ideas, tools, and materials. There are three main types of crowdsourcing operating at present: those that collectively produce a solution (e.g., OpenStreetMap, Wikipedia); those that use crowd to evaluate multiple solutions/products (e.g., Amazon, Tripadvisor reviews); and those that seek single or multiple solutions from a crowd (e.g., InnoCentive, hackathons).

With respect to the first, the generation of information (an open source map, a freely editable/accessible encyclopaedia) becomes a collaborative, peer-produced act, with participants given rights and facilities to edit, refine and extend the contributions of others (Benkler 2006). By operating across the Internet anyone with access can contribute, vastly widening the potential pool of expertise and the scope of projects for little cost, and ensuring that different perspectives and techniques are brought to bear on the project (Weinberger 2011). Indeed, producing a detailed map of the world or a vast encyclopaedia with only a handful of professionals is a difficult and costly task, and simply too daunting for small groups of volunteers. But given many thousands of participants the task can be subdivided and solved. The pay-off for contributors is to produce open source data free from copyright and expensive licensing (as with national mapping agency data) (Dodge and Kitchin 2013). Similarly, by enabling consumers to review the products they buy, Amazon and other online retailers can utilise the power of the crowd to source and share opinion about those products. The benefit to contributors is the sharing of opinion as to the relative merits of goods and services.

A particular form of crowdsourcing used by some companies to source expertise or ideas is to use contests to incentivise the crowd to forward solutions for a reward (Weinberger 2011). Rather than go to tender amongst a limited pool of potential experts, companies such as Innocentive and TopCoder open the problem up to anybody who is interested, typically offering $10,000–100,000, and sometimes considerably more, for solutions to client problems. Here, a solution is sourced from a crowd, but this crowd does not work together collectively. The benefit for companies is a choice of solutions and for contributors financial payment if their solution is chosen. Similarly open data app contests held by municipalities seek to more modestly reward useful and interesting apps. Such contests can take the form of hackathons in which people work together in teams to develop solutions and apps, usually over the course of a day or weekend. The benefit to the municipality is its data being used for the public good and for citizens kudos and civil participation.

Citizen science

Citizen science is a particular form of crowdsourcing wherein 'communities or networks of citizens ... act as observers in some domain of science' (Goodchild 2007: 218). Here, people generate, prepare and process empirical observations and detailed measurements of phenomena for free, which are, crucially, of real value as data points for 'proper' science. Citizen scientists are particularly useful in observational terms because they can be geographically distributed and embedded in place through time (using professional research assistants to gather such field measurements is difficult to coordinate and costly). Examples include amateur meteorological measurements made from back garden weather stations, and hobbyist astronomers who meticulously observe the night sky. Citizen science became well established through the twentieth century as a support to mainstream science, but remains a minority activity dependent on a fair degree of skill and knowledge or specialised equipment (such as a good-quality telescope), and above all a considerable amount of motivation and ongoing commitment.

Bonney et al. (2009; cited in Miller-Rushing et al. 2012) classify forms of citizen science into three classes.

- *Contributory*: generally designed by scientists and for which members of the public primarily contribute data.

- *Collaborative*: generally designed by scientists for which members of the public contribute data but may also help to refine project design, analyse data, or disseminate findings.

- *Co-created*: designed by scientists and members of the public working together and for which at least some of the public participants are actively involved in most or all steps of the scientific process; also includes research wholly conceived and implemented by amateur (non-professional) scientists.

Typically, the level of expertise and the type of participation varies by class, with only those citizen scientists with the most advanced skills taking part in co-created projects. Participation can take a number of forms, including:

- *Distributed computing*: a participant lends the computing power of their PC to a project, allowing data to be processed using its resources (contributory).

- *Transcription/conversion/digitisation*: converting one data form into another, for example handwritten documents into digital text (contributory).

- *Observational measurement*: scientists generate the data, but use citizen scientists to undertake measurements using specific, supplied tools (contributory).

- *Data collection*: citizen scientists collect data which they then share with the scientists (contributory).

- *Observational analysis*: rather than simply generating or measuring data, citizen scientists undertake some of the analysis, including providing some interpretation of what the findings might mean (collaborative).

- *Research design and operation*: citizen scientists take an active part in designing and running of the project, as well as disseminating the findings and conclusions (co-created)

(Open Scientist 2013).

CONCLUSION

This chapter has charted the enablers and sources of big data. It has been argued that the production of big data has been facilitated by the confluence of five technological innovations from the start of the new millennium onwards – growing computational power, dense internetworking, pervasive and ubiquitous computing, indexical and machine-readable identification, and massive distributed storage. In combination these developments have led to a diverse set of social–technical systems that produce big data. The chapter has provided a preliminary tracing out of these systems, dividing them into three broad classes: directed, automated and volunteered forms of data production. Such a tracing, however, should be viewed as an initial step in trying to map an unfolding landscape. What is presently required is a detailed set of empirical studies that examine in depth the various ways in which big data are being generated, processed and used. Such studies need to chart the genealogy of the confluence of enabling technologies and unpack the data assemblage that has been created and how it operates in practice to produce particular forms of big data (see Chapters 1 and 11). This includes deconstructing the elements of its associated discursive regime (see Chapter 7). In so doing, deeper insights will be gained into each socio-technical system and its various processes, orderings and politics, and the diverse work it conducts in the world.

An accompanying set of studies needs to examine what happens when social–technical systems are linked together to create new, larger systems in which significant data amplification effects occur. The technologies underpinning big data, and the data themselves through their relationality, are ripe for such scalings. Indeed, complex socio-technical assemblages, such as a large retailer like Walmart, are increasingly interconnecting various systems (e.g., supply chain management, enterprise resource planning, customer relationship management, store management, and security systems) that generate forms of directed, automated and volunteered data to create complex and sophisticated data-driven organisations that have diverse consequences for suppliers, employees, and consumers. Similarly, smart city control and operations centres attempt to draw various kinds of data generated by various sources into a single hub where they are combined and analysed in real-time, significantly changing how urban locales are managed and governed (see Chapter 7). Such re-scalings and reorderings raise many social, political, ethical and normative questions concerning the kinds of systems and places we want to live within, and we have barely begun to ask and answer such questions (see Chapter 10).

RE-SCALINGS of SOCio-TECHNICAL SYSTEMS

6

DATA ANALYTICS

Data are not useful in and of themselves. They only have utility if meaning and value can be extracted from them. In other words, it is what is done with data that is important, not simply that they are generated. The whole of science is based on realising meaning and value from data. Making sense of scaled small data and big data poses new challenges. In the case of scaled small data, the challenge is linking together varied datasets to gain new insights and opening up the data to new analytical approaches being used in big data. With respect to big data, the challenge is coping with its abundance and exhaustivity (including sizeable amounts of data with low utility and value), timeliness and dynamism, messiness and uncertainty, high relationality, semi-structured or unstructured nature, and the fact that much of big data is generated with no specific question in mind or is a by-product of another activity. Indeed, until recently, data analysis techniques have primarily been designed to extract insights from scarce, static, clean and poorly relational datasets, scientifically sampled and adhering to strict assumptions (such as independence, stationarity, and normality), and generated and analysed with a specific question in mind (H.J. Miller 2010).

The tools for linking diverse datasets together and analysing big data were poorly developed until recently because they have been too computationally challenging to implement. It is only in the last 40 years or so that very large datasets have been routinely analysed, and even then these were dedicated initiatives that could afford the necessary resources. Without highly powered computation becoming widespread and accessible, making sense of the data deluge would be very costly or difficult and time-consuming. Of course, there is somewhat of a circular argument at play here: without the development of ubiquitous computing such big data would not be generated in the first place. Nevertheless, as Hastie et al. (2009: xi) note, given 'the advent of computers and the information age, statistical problems have exploded both in size and complexity'.

The solution to the challenges of handling and analysing scaled small data and big data has been a new suite of information management and storage techniques (see Chapter 5) and the development of big data analytics. These new techniques and analytics have been in development since the start of computing, building on established statistical tests, models and visualisation methods, but also creating new approaches rooted in research around artificial intelligence and expert systems that have sought to produce machine learning that can computationally and automatically mine and detect patterns and build predictive models. Such analytics are ideally suited to handling and extracting information from large, connected datasets and big data and they have become a significant area of research investment in order to rapidly extend and produce new data handling, statistical and modelling algorithms, and visualisation techniques (National Science Foundation 2012). These analytics, as applied in business and science, seek to answer four basic sets of questions (Minelli et al. 2013):

- *Description*: what and when did something happen? How often does it happen?

- *Explanation*: why did it happen? What is its impact?

- *Prediction*: what is likely to happen next? What if we did this or that?

- *Prescription*: what is the optimal answer or outcome? How is that achieved?

The answers to these questions are derived from four broad classes of analytics: data mining and pattern recognition; data visualisation and visual analytics; statistical analysis; and prediction, simulation, and optimisation. Each of these is discussed in brief, but first the pre-analytics phase and machine learning are introduced as they are central to all four.

PRE-ANALYTICS

All data analytics require the data to be analysed to be pre-prepared; that is readied and checked. H.J. Miller (2010) and Han et al. (2011) set out four such processes with respect to scaled and big data that are usually undertaken in sequence, though they do not have to be executed in any particular order and maybe undertaken iteratively:

- *Data selection*: determining a subset of the variables that have most utility, and potentially a sampling frame for those variables. Not all variables generated will be of interest, nor necessarily all data points, and their inclusion in models can create redundancy and inefficiency.

- *Data pre-processing*: cleaning the selected data to remove noise, errors or biases, or handle missing fields or inconsistencies, and structuring the data for input into analysis.

- *Data reduction and projection*: diminishing the dimensionality of the data through transformations (e.g., smoothing, attribute construction, aggregation, normalisation, concept hierarchy, and statistical techniques such as regression and principal components analysis) to equivalent but more efficient representations.

- *Data enrichment*: combining the selected data with other data (e.g., census data, market data) in order to leverage greater insights.

Each of these steps is designed to increase, on the one hand, the quality of the data being used in the analysis, and, on the other, with the exception of data enrichment, to decrease the volume of data the analytic has to handle. The first is designed to strengthen the validity and veracity of the conclusions drawn given the inherent messiness and uncertainty of big data (see Chapter 9). The second is to increase operational efficiency given data volumes and velocity and computational loads. Undertaking these tasks can be difficult when conducting real-time analytics, especially in terms of trying to clean data. Consequently, much big data analysis beyond indicator visualisation is not conducted in real-time, but rather undertakes the analysis on a very large sample of cleaned, reduced and enriched time-series data. Where real-time analytics are desired, pre-analytics are usually applied to a sample in advance in order to establish the nature of the data and how they might be handled to select, reduce and clean on the fly.

Data enrichment is a high-value task because it produces an amplification effect (Crampton et al. 2012) that enables insights to be gained that cannot be produced from a single dataset. As discussed in Chapter 2, along with data reuse, it is a key rationale for creating data infrastructures. The challenge is to create ways to link together data that have been generated for different purposes and may have varying metadata, data standards, units, measures, categories and scales, synchronicity and file formats, and to do so minimising the creation of potential ecological fallacies. This is no simple task, but computational methods make it easier through the use of algorithms that can search, match, combine, repackage (through various kinds of transformations) and reformat data. The resulting, new combined dataset can then be mined and analysed using the four broad classes of analytics discussed below.

Pre-analytical work can be extremely tedious and time-consuming, but it is nonetheless vital and cannot be ignored. Given the explosion in various kinds of new data infrastructures and big data it has become a fertile area of research as data scientists seek the most productive, efficient and effective ways to undertake, and especially to automate, such work.

MACHINE LEARNING

The analysis of very large numbers of data records can only be undertaken in a timely fashion by computer algorithms. While much of the analysis of big data can proceed as with small data analysis, with analysts making decisions concerning how the investigation is performed by such algorithms, the goal of much research is to develop automated processes that can assess and learn from the data and their analysis. Such automated processes are termed machine learning and constitute a branch of artificial intelligence. Machine learning seeks to iteratively evolve an understanding of a dataset; to automatically learn to recognise complex patterns and construct models that explain and predict such patterns and optimise outcomes (Han et al. 2011).

Machine learning generally consists of two broad types: supervised (using training data) and unsupervised (using self-organisation). In supervised learning, a model is trained to match inputs to certain known outputs. For example, the model might be trained to match handwritten postcodes with typed equivalents, or to predict a certain outcome. It is 'supervised' in the sense that the training data are present to guide the learning process (Hastie et al. 2009). In contrast, in unsupervised learning the model seeks to teach itself to spot patterns and find structure in data without the use of training data. In general, this is achieved through identifying clusters and relationships between the data where the characteristics of similarity or associations were not known in advance. For example, the model might learn how to segment customers into self-similar groups and to predict purchases amongst those groups (Han et al. 2011). In both cases, the model is created through a learning process shaped by learning rules and weightings that direct how the model is built in relation to the data (Hastie et al. 2009). The process of building the model starts with a simple construction and then tweaks it repeatedly using the learning rules, as if applying 'genetic mutations', until it evolves into a robust model (Siegel 2013: 122). Two variations on supervised and unsupervised learning are semi-supervised learning which involves the use of both training and unlabelled data, and active learning that lets users play an active role in directing the learning model (Han et al. 2011).

Machine learning is being employed to undertake all four types of big data analytics, though it is not the sole method through which such analytics are practised. In many cases they are undertaken more directly by a researcher. Even within machine learning, the analyst remains important for judging and guiding the process and assessing intermediate results. As H.J. Miller (2010) notes, machine learning is not simply an automated, pushbutton science, but rather demands domain expertise and thoughtful reflection; skills that human minds still do better than computers. While significant progress has been made in developing machine-learning techniques, it is still an emerging science and much research needs to be undertaken to improve the effectiveness and robustness of the models produced.

Each broad class of analytic is now discussed in turn, though it should be noted that they are often used in combination. For example, data mining and pattern recognition might provide the basis for prediction or optimisation, or statistics might be used in data mining to detect patterns or in calculating a prediction, or visualisation might be used in data mining or to communicate outputs from simulations, and so on.

DATA MINING AND PATTERN RECOGNITION

Data mining is the process of extracting data and patterns from large datasets (Manyika et al. 2011). It is premised on the notion that all massive datasets hold meaningful information that is non-random, valid, novel, useful and ultimately understandable (Han et al. 2011). As such, it uses supervised and unsupervised machine learning to detect, classify and segment meaningful relationships, associations and trends between variables. It does this using a series of different techniques including natural language processing, neural networks, decision

Table 6.1 Data mining tasks and techniques

Data mining task	Description	Techniques
Segmentation or clustering	Determine a set of implicit groups that describes the data	• Cluster analysis
Classification	Predict the class label that a set of data belongs to based on some training datasets	• Bayesian classification • Decision tree induction • Artificial neural networks • Support vector machine
Association	Find relationships among data objects; predict the value of some attribute based on the value of other attributes	• Association rules • Bayesian networks
Deviations	Find data items that exhibit unusual deviations from expectations	• Cluster analysis • Outlier detection • Evolution analysis
Trends	Lines and curves summarizing the database, often over time	• Regression • Sequence pattern extraction
Generalisations	Compact descriptions of the data	• Summary rules • Attribute-orientated induction

Source: Miller and Han (2009: 7).

trees, and statistical (non-parametric and parametric) methods. The selection of method varies between the type of data (structured, unstructured or semi-structured) and the purpose of the analysis (see Table 6.1).

Most of the techniques listed in Table 6.1 relate to structured data as found in relational databases. For example, segmentation models might be applied to a retail database of customers and their purchases to segment them into different profiles based on their characteristics and patterns of behaviour in order to offer each group different services/offers. In social network analysis, connections between individuals are analysed to understand the social dynamics between members and how information might flow between them. In detecting associations, a variety of regression models might be used to compute correlations between variables and thus reveal hidden patterns that can then be leveraged into commercial gain (for example, identifying what goods are bought with each other and reorganising a store to promote purchasing) (see Chapter 7).

Unstructured data in the form of language, images and sounds raise particular data mining challenges. Natural language-processing techniques seek to analyse human language as expressed through the written and spoken word. They use semantics and taxonomies to recognise patterns and extract information from documents. Examples would include entity extraction that automatically extracts metadata from text by searching for particular types of text and phrasing, such as person names, locations, dates, specialised terms and product terminology, and entity relation extraction that automatically identifies the relationships between semantic entities, linking them together (e.g., person name to birth date or location, or an opinion to an item) (McCreary 2009). A typical application of such techniques is sentiment analysis which seeks to determine the general nature and strength of opinions about an issue, for example, what people are saying about a product on social media. By using placemark metadata it is also possible to track where such sentiment is expressed (Graham et al. 2013) and to mine the dissemination of information within social media, for example, how widely Web addresses are favourited and shared between multiple users (Ohlhorst 2013). Such information is useful for companies, such as ad agencies, marketers and financial services, seeking to leverage emerging trends and reach in a very timely fashion (e.g., to place ads on suitable stories; to buy/sell shares ahead of wider market reaction).

Images are structured for storage and display, but not for content and search (Ohlhorst 2013). Detecting, classifying and extracting patterns within them, such as facial or place recognition, is not straightforward, but is being tackled through photogrammetric, remote-sensing, image-processing and machine vision techniques, including object recognition and template matching using training sets, clustering methods, and neural networking. The problem of image mining becomes compounded when trying to extract, compare and index patterns from across a massive number of images (Zhang et al. 2001). While still an emerging area, image mining has become more advanced in recent years. For example,

ImageVision (http://imagevision.com/) claims to be able to categorise 50,400 minutes of video per hour, per server, using machine-learning algorithms to detect certain features such as nudity and company logos.

DATA VISUALISATION AND VISUAL ANALYTICS

It is commonly stated that a picture tells a thousand words. As such, the visual register has long been used to summarise and describe datasets through statistical charts and graphs, diagrams, spatialisations, maps, and animations. These visual methods effectively reveal and communicate the structure, pattern and trends of variables and their interconnections. Given the enormous volumes and velocity of big data, it is then no surprise that visualisation has proven a popular way for making sense of data and communicating that sense.

Visualisations created within the digital realm can be used to navigate and query data, enabling users to gain an overview of the entire dataset, zoom in on items of interest, filter out uninteresting data, select an item or group of data and get details, view relationships among items, and extract sub-collections of the details when needed (Shneiderman 1996). In so doing they enable the characteristics and structure of datasets to be explored. Moreover, they can be used to make visible and comprehensible complex datasets and models that are difficult to conceptualise in the abstract (such as atomic, cosmic and three-dimensional phenomena), and plot tens of thousands of data points to reveal structure, clusters, gaps, and outliers that might otherwise remain hidden (Shneiderman 1996). For example, making sense of the millions of tweets on Twitter is not easy. One can get a rough idea of stories or themes that seem to be trending, but it is very difficult to gain a synoptic overview, and how the trend varies between people and places. A solution is to map georeferenced tweets filtered by sentiment, an approach undertaken by the floatingsheep.org collective. They have created dozens of maps about specific topics and tweeting trends, including that in Figure 6.1 which shows the geographical distribution of homophobic tweets in the United States from June 2012–April 2013. They have also mapped Wikipedia content and Google placemarks.

Visualisations are also commonly used as a means to monitor the real-time dynamics of a phenomenon, enabling several variables to be tracked over time and space, and in comparison to one another, and to identify change. Dashboards of visualised dynamic data are often on display on computer monitors in modern control rooms, summarising graphically a system in flux for human operators, with time-series graphs and charts, or maps of unfolding events (see Lake 2013, for a comparison of 24 dashboards). For example, data from across a transport system can provide a real-time map of traffic flows and accident reports; or the location of flights as they pass over a territory (see Figure 6.2), or weather

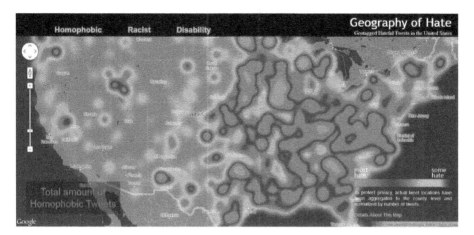

Figure 6.1   The geography of homophobic tweets in the United States

Source: http://users.humboldt.edu/mstephens/hate/hate_map.html#

Figure 6.2   Real-time flight locations

Source: http://www.flightradar24.com/

radar data can provide a real-time map of rainfall and an animation of the last few hours. Such visual data aids not only traffic management controllers or weather forecasters, but also citizens who can access and monitor unfolding situations using a computer or smartphone, altering their behaviour to avoid particular routes or dressing appropriately. An example of a prototype public city dashboard that brings together a range of real-time data about the weather, air pollution, public transport delays, public bike availability, river level, electricity demand, the stock market, twitter trends, and traffic camera feeds is displayed in Figure 6.3.

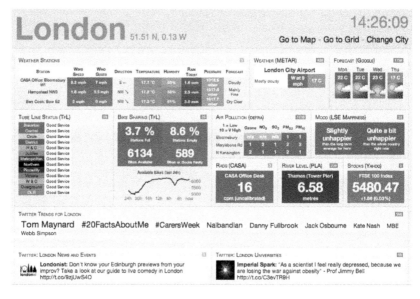

Figure 6.3   CASA's London City Dashboard

Source: http://citydashboard.org/london/

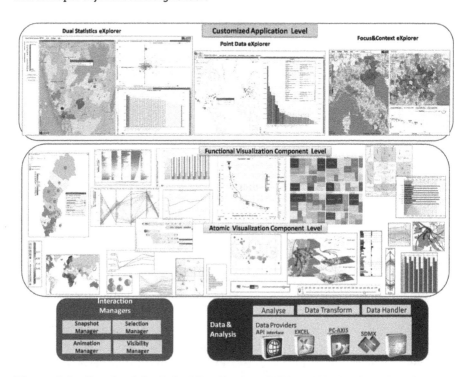

Figure 6.4   Geovisual Analytics Visualization (GAV) toolkit developed by the National Center for Visual Analytics, Linköping University

Source: http://ncva.itn.liu.se/tools?l=en

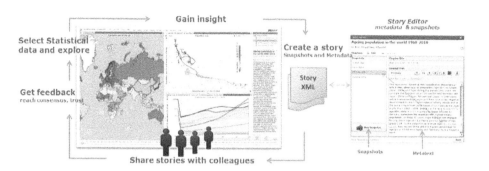

Figure 6.5 Using GAV for collaborative storytelling

Source: http://ncva.itn.liu.se/tools?l=en

Visualisations can also be used as a form of analytical reasoning. Here, the visualisation is not simply describing or displaying the data, but is being used as an analytical tool. Termed visual analytics, this approach is often guided by a combination of humans and algorithms which work in concert to extract information, build visual models and explanation, and to guide further statistical analysis (Keim et al. 2010). Visual analytics has become a significant new area of research, extending the field of information visualisation by integrating elements of data mining, statistics and cognition science (Thomas and Cook 2006). Several different types of visual graphics are commonly used and these are generally interactive and allow the user to play with and manipulate the images in order to explore and reveal patterns and connections. In addition, the panels displayed to the user are generally interlinked so that interactions in one panel are replicated in the others, enabling aspects of the data to be examined from more than one perspective simultaneously. For example, Figure 6.4 shows the kinds of visual analytics available within the Geovisual Analytics Visualization (GAV) toolkit, developed by the National Center for Visual Analytics at Linköping University in Sweden. As well as providing a suite of analytical tools, GAV enables collaborative data exploration and analysis, the building of applications, mashing with mapping applications such as Google Maps, and to construct and share narrative storytelling. The last creates a social element to the toolkit, enabling colleagues and others to share sense-making interpretations concerning the visualisations (see Figure 6.5).

STATISTICAL ANALYSIS

There is a long history of statistical techniques being applied to quantitative data in order to make sense of them. Descriptive statistics detail the characteristics and distribution of data points and their levels of error and uncertainty. It includes time-series analysis that charts how data changes over time, graph theory that mathematically studies the organisation of network structures, and spatial statistics that describe geometry and patterns of clustering, dispersion and diffusion. Inferential statistics seek to explain, not simply describe, the patterns and relationships that may exist within a dataset, and to test the strength and significance of associations between variables. They include parametric statistics which are employed to assess hypotheses using interval and ratio level data, such as correlation and regression; non-parametric statistics used for testing hypotheses using nominal or ordinal-level data; and probabilistic statistics that determine the probability of a condition occurring, such as Bayesian statistics. The armoury of descriptive and inferential statistics that have traditionally been used to analyse small data are also being applied to big data, though as discussed in Chapter 9 this is not always straightforward because many of these techniques were developed to draw insights from relatively scarce rather than exhaustive data. Nonetheless, the techniques do provide a means of making sense of massive amounts of data. And the volume of data ensures that the data can be segmented in multiple ways without groups becoming too small that differences between the control and treatment groups cannot meaningfully be calculated. Statistics are routinely used in aiding data mining, prediction and optimisation (see Table 6.1).

PREDICTION, SIMULATION AND OPTIMISATION

A key way in which value is leveraged from data is to use them to try and predict what would happen under different conditions. For example, a company might want to predict how customers would react to a particular product or campaign, or local government needs to predict how a transport infrastructure might function if a critical element is closed, or a scientist seeks to predict when a landslide might occur and under what conditions. Such information is very useful for organisations in terms of being able to plan for different contingencies, and businesses in terms of producing an uplift effect that grows profits (see Chapter 7). In all cases, models are built utilising existing knowledge about how a system works, which process data to estimate a potential outcome under different scenarios. As with data mining, there are many different methods that can be used to produce predictive models. Each has its strengths and weaknesses, producing less error and more accurate predictions depending on the type of problem and data (Seni and Elder 2010). However, it is often difficult to prejudge which type of model, and its various versions, will perform best on any given dataset. A solution to this issue has been to use an ensemble approach that takes advantage of the huge amount of computational power now available to analysts (Siegel 2013). Rather than selecting a single approach and building a handful of models, an ensemble approach builds multiple models using a variety of techniques to predict the same phenomena. Then, instead of selecting the results (estimates) from the best performing model, the estimates from all models are combined to produce a single, overall answer. Aggregating the results leads to a more robust outcome as the process compensates for the weaknesses in each model. For example, an ensemble approach to predicting customer behaviour might construct a series of regression, neural network, nearest neighbour, and decision tree models. Each model might be better at predicting certain kinds of consumers than others, but by combining the model outputs those variances are smoothed out, giving a more robust prediction (Franks 2012; Siegel 2013). By using an ensemble approach literally hundreds of different algorithms can be applied to a dataset, thus ensuring that the best predictive model possible is produced.

Simulations are models that seek to model real-world processes and systems. The aim is to determine how a system functions and how it might behave under different scenarios, and to statistically evaluate their performance with a view to improving their efficiency and effectiveness (Robinson 2003). A popular example is the computer game SimCity which simulates how a city will grow and develop under the conditions of the players choosing, based on an underlying model of known urban processes. Likewise, weather forecasts are based on simulations of how the weather will develop given prevalent conditions and scientific knowledge. There are many different kinds of simulation models, many of which utilise machine learning in order to automatically refine the model and to deal with emergent properties such as unforeseen events. SimCity is an agent-based model (Batty 2007). The model consists of an environment where individual features such as buildings and roads are assigned certain characteristics. This environment is then populated with agents that are ascribed particular qualities. When the model is run, the agents seek to solve a task, reacting to the environment and other agents in relation to their ascribed characteristics. In turn, as the agents undertake their tasks, they change the environment, in this case the city they inhabit, producing a complex, emergent system. The model thus works from the bottom up, with wider spatial and temporal patterns emerging from the interactions of individual agents with the environment. Such urban simulation models are used outside of gaming to model land-use and transportation planning and to develop contingency disaster plans (Batty 2007).

Optimisation is concerned with determining an optimal course of action to improve performance (usually reducing cost or increasing outputs/turnover). It can be calculated by utilising and evaluating predictive and simulation models, or can be developed through other kinds of algorithms or statistical testing. For example, genetic algorithms, a particular kind of machine learning, uses ideas from natural selection, such as inheritance, mutation, selection and crossover, to develop and evolve candidate solutions to a problem (Mitchell 1996). Another biologically inspired approach is neural networking that seeks to mimic how the human brain works, utilising highly interconnected processing elements, to calculate, evaluate and solve a problem (Picton 2000). A/B testing can be used on a rolling basis to assess and tweak a system, comparing a control group with a variety of test groups in order to determine what treatments (e.g., text, layouts, images, or colours used on a website) improve a given objective (e.g., donation rates).

CONCLUSION

The aim of this chapter has been to provide a broad overview of the emerging set of techniques and data analytics that are being utilised to process, analyse and apply scaled small data and big data. Such methods have been in gestation for a number of years, but are becoming more widespread and accessible as they evolve and mature, and the computation required becomes more widely available. The scale and velocity of big data nevertheless pose serious pre-analytical and analytical challenges because many traditional techniques and algorithms are not designed to scale to billions of observations, nor cope with highly dynamic datasets (Batty et al. 2012). It is thus clear that further research is required to adapt, hone and extend existing techniques and to invent new methods that can make sense of and extract value from big data and data infrastructures. Moreover, both new and old generations of scientists and business analysts need to become familiar with new data sources and their characteristics, and learn a new set of skills if they want to be able to examine and leverage the insights of the data deluge, including structured and unstructured data handling, and basic coding, data mining, visualisation, modelling and simulation (see Chapter 9).

These challenges are not simply technical and human-resource based. Analytics are reflective of a particular way of seeing and making sense of the world; they are the manifestation of a particular epistemology. As discussed in Chapter 8, scaled and big data and their associated analytics raise fundamental questions concerning the organisation and practices of science (Floridi 2012), with many suggesting that they are ushering in a new scientific paradigm. As a consequence, tackling the data deluge requires not just new thinking about analytic methods, but careful thinking with respect to the philosophy of science (Leonelli 2012). A significant part of that task requires critical reflection on the wider framing of analytics and the mechanics of specific approaches and techniques; to think through how new analytics produce particular kinds of knowledges and views of the world, and in turn to unpack how these new knowledges do work in the world, including modulating the very things they refer to (Beer and Burrows 2013; Ruppert 2013, see Chapter 11). In other words, both technical and philosophical research is urgently required with respect to emerging analytics in order to make sense with scaled and big data and to make sense of scaled and big data.

7

THE GOVERNMENTAL AND BUSINESS RATIONALE FOR BIG DATA

The data revolution is not unfolding in a non-ideological, passive manner. Like all revolutions, it is being driven by a powerful set of arguments, forwarded by passionate believers in the benefits of new ways of knowing and acting in the world and an alliance of vested interests who gain from its unfolding. While the arguments used can be quite diverse, and can often consist of diverging views, taken as a whole they constitute what Foucault (1977) termed a discursive regime: a set of interlocking discourses that justifies and sustains new developments and naturalises and reproduces their use. A discursive regime provides the rationale for adopting new ideas and technologies, and legitimates their development and implementation. The discourses utilised within the regime seek to promote and make their message seem like common sense, to persuade people and institutions to their logic, and to believe and act in relation to this logic (Dodge and Kitchin 2005). They work to produce certain 'atmospheres' 'in which the oxygen of certain kinds of thought and practice seems natural and desirable' (Amin and Thrift 2013: 5), and which instil a particular kind of affective response (Anderson 2009). Such discourses and atmospheres seek then to remake the world in a particular vision, reshaping 'issues, actors, stakes and interests that populate the political field' and economic landscape (Barnett 2013: 4).

As discussed in Chapters 2 and 3, the overlapping discursive regimes seeking to drive the development of data infrastructures and open data employ discourses such as sharing, reuse, open access, open government, transparency, accountability, social entrepreneurship, and economies of scale. As was illustrated in these cases, a discursive regime can be driven by a range of interested parties, who may well use the same arguments but have different agendas (e.g., civil society organisations and big business using discourses of transparency and accountability to open up government data, but one for civic reasons, the other to remonetise the data). Discursive regimes then are not solely driven from the top by states or businesses, but are diffused and enacted through many micro-channels (Foucault 1977, 1978). Neither are they unproblematically accepted by a populace, with citizens and institutions easily seduced by their logic. Rather, the discourses are open to challenge, resistance, rupture, subversion, denial, transgression, and the forwarding of alternative visions. In both cases, those promoting and opposing the adoption of new visions draw on a temporal register that stretches from the past, through the present, to the future, using evidence from previous rounds of social and economic change, along with challenges of the present day and speculations about how things might be in years to come under different scenarios, to bolster their arguments (Kinsley 2011, 2012). The discursive terrain then is always being negotiated as the struggle over ideas and ways of organising, acting and regulating societies, now and in the future, is played out.

In this chapter, the governmental and business rationale for big data are examined. Rather than organising the chapter with respect to the various discourses that are commonly employed to promote the adoption of big data (e.g., insight and wisdom, productivity, competitiveness, efficiency, effectiveness, utility, sustainability, securitisation), the discussion is structured around particular modes of social organisation and activities. Discourses are most powerful when they are mobilised and directed at particular tasks and issues. What is interesting in the case of big data is that its discursive regime is being targeted at all sectors – social, political, economic, environmental; its promise is to offer a radically new way of understanding and managing all aspects of human life. Here, that promise is discussed with respect to four major tasks: governing people, managing organisations, leveraging value and producing capital, and creating better places. These are illustrative, rather than comprehensive, and there are many other potential applications, including health and well-being, social and human development, and tackling social and ecological issues (see Mayer-Schonberger and Cukier 2013; Siegel 2013; Smolan and Erwitt 2012). The debate as to how big data might be reshaping research is explored in the next chapter and some of the counter-arguments to the roll-out of big data are discussed in Chapter 10.

GOVERNING PEOPLE

The state is a prime generator and user of data. Since the Enlightenment it has sought to create more systematic ways of, on the one hand, managing and governing populations, and on the other of delivering services to citizens. One of the key ways it has sought to effectively and efficiently perform these roles is through the auditing and quantification of society – creating a detailed knowledge of its jurisdiction through the development of widespread administrative systems, supported by a diverse technological apparatus, that measure and track indexical and attribute data about individuals, companies, institutions and other elements (see Alonso and Starr 1987; Barnes and Hannah 2001; Desrosières 1998; Kitchin and Dodge 2011; Porter 1995). Across all state institutions data generation, management, storage and analysis are fundamental tasks, used to assess the liabilities and entitlements of sovereign and non-sovereign subjects, and to detect non-compliance, evasion and fraud with respect to established norms and legal obligations (Rose 1996). For example, in government departments, especially those related to finance, trade and social welfare, all citizens and enti-ties are identified and monitored, their records updated, their profiles mapped and data analysed to spot issues and trends, payments are tracked, and services and disciplining administered. In schools, registration is taken, coursework and exam marks calculated and recorded, and pupils are rewarded and punished according to performance and behaviour. In the health sector, the condition of patients is measured, recorded and acted upon and the performance of health facilities calculated and evaluated. Other state agencies specialise in data genera-tion, management, analysis and dissemination that have wide utility for govern-mental business. For example, statistical agencies, mapping bodies and the intelligence services undertake continual programmes of generating data through measurement regimes such as surveying and surveillance.

To aid their calculative practices, states have sought on the one hand to justify and rationalise their systems and processes to subjects, and on the other to implement ever more sophisticated and refined means of administration (McNay 1994; Miller 2001). The former include discourses around efficient government and value for money, citizenship and empowerment, fairness and anti-crime, security and safety, that appeal to the notion that common problems and issues are being addressed through shared logic and principles. These are countered by those who would like states to have less oversight and fewer pow-ers vis-à-vis personal freedoms and the oversight and regulation of social and economic systems, or to be more transparent, open and productive in the prac-tices of government, including making the data that they hold more freely available (see Chapter 3).

The latter includes the implementation of ever more sophisticated systems, technologies and infrastructures designed to effectively capture and process data, including more robust systems of identification (signatures, photographs, finger-prints, social security and passport numbers, tax codes, licence and account num-bers, biometric information, usernames and passwords, postcodes, and so on), that can increasingly be operated in a timely fashion and at a distance (e.g., across networks) (Dodge and Kitchin 2005). Hannah (1997: 178) thus argues that a more effective mode of governmentality is always in the making, consisting of 'a complex constellation of group control ... (through censuses, bureaucracies, poli-cies, and so forth), an archipelago of disciplinary institutions (schools, workplaces) and an otherwise anonymous territory dotted with millions of staging points (ATM's, surveillance cameras, application forms)'.

In one sense then, big data are nothing new to states – they have long dealt with vast quantities of data in administering jurisdictions, a portion of which have been processed or acted upon in or near real-time as agencies interacted with subjects. Nevertheless, big data are viewed as the latest set of technologies that can both expand and improve state work by extending the timeliness and expansiveness of calculative practices. In some cases, the discursive drive towards big data solutions is being pushed by vendors seeking to sell the state services, in other cases, the state is actively taking the lead. At present, there are two main discursive strategies being used to encourage big data use. The first concerns the improvements to public administration and cost savings through enhanced 'operational efficiency, a reduction in the cost of errors and fraud in benefit administration, and an increase in tax receipts by narrowing the tax gap ... improved allocation of funding into programs, higher-quality services, increased public sector accountability, [and] a better-informed citizenry', with suggestions that big data solutions could be worth $150 billion to Europe's public sector administration in operational efficiency (Manyika et al. 2011: 61, 62). These arguments are discussed further with respect to managing organisations and making better places below.

The second concerns state security and the tackling of crime. All states are involved in surveillance for the purposes of security, safety and crime prevention and apprehension through policing and wider intelligence-gathering. How these activities are implemented has developed in line with new technologies – wiretaps and radio intercepts, closed circuit television, aerial photography and satellite imagery, Internet monitoring – and their roll-out has often been justified by key events (e.g., the cold war, terrorist incidents) (Innes 2001). In more recent times, 9/11 and the subsequent 'war on terror' has provided the rationalisation for a step change in widespread state-led surveillance and securitisation (Amoore 2006). It has been clear for some time that big data analytics have been a key component in these enhanced activities, especially with respect to border control and immigration screening (Kitchin and Dodge 2006; Clements 2013). The June 2013 revelations concerning the US National Security Agency's PRISM programme exposed the extent to which dataveillance and big data practices and analytics are being used to gather and process data with respect to everyday communications (telephone calls, text messages, e-mails, Internet use) of all citizens, rather than just foreign citizens and powers or specific targets (Greenwald and MacAskill 2013; Risen and Lichtblau 2013). This was the latest in a series of revelations concerning the US state secretly spying on its own citizens (Solove 2007; Bamford 2009). Indeed, it is clear that intelligence agencies, and their military–industrial contractors, are at the forefront of developing the next generation of big data tools for making sense of truly enormous amounts of high-velocity data, and have invested heavily in talent, technologies and facilities (e.g., a US$1.7 billion data center in Utah for processing and storing state-intercepted big data) (Carroll 2013). While states seek to rationalise such widespread surveillance on its subjects through discourses of safety and security, the fact that they have implemented much of their apparatus secretly and without due process works to undermine the ideals of a democracy founded on transparency and trust (Clements 2013). The public outcry at such practices and their flagrant disregard for rights such as privacy is, however, unlikely in the short term to slow or reconfigure the adoption of big data in this facet of governance, nor to deflect the discourses used to justify them.

MANAGING ORGANISATIONS

Just as states and their many branches of government (departments, local authorities, agencies, the military, health care providers, etc.) have changed over time, adopting new management practices and technologies to reshape how they are organised and operate, so too have businesses and other institutional entities, such as NGOs, voluntary and community bodies, charities, political parties, and so on. Data related to their core functions are a key aspect of how these organisations understand themselves and their constituencies, and make decisions about their present and future operations. Data provide the evidence for the generation of knowledge which is employed to manage the organisation more effectively, efficiently, competitively and productively, and to identify new products and markets (see next section).

Over the past 60 years information systems have thus become essential support infrastructures for all organisations of any size, enabling them to track and manage complex assemblages of people (staff, members, supporters, donors, customers), components, commodities and infrastructures across time and space, and enabling them to scale their operations from the local to the global (Castells 1996; Dicken 2003). Information systems allow an organisation to be run more intelligently, producing significant cost savings in their operational base. Three such data-driven information system that have been widely adopted are Enterprise Resource Planning (ERP), Supply-chain Management (SCM), and Customer Relationship Management (CRM). These systems facilitate greater coordination and control within an organisation, and with other organisations and customers. ERP, for example, standardises and combines an organisation's multiple databases and systems (relating to purchasing, warehousing, inventory, transport, marketing, accounting, personnel management and rostering, project management, customer relations) into one all-encompassing system that ensures that data and processes are automatically and seamlessly available from one part of a business to another (Dery et al. 2006;

Grant et al. 2006). SCM is used to organise as efficiently as possible the procurement, movement, management and storage of materials from suppliers through a company and on to customers (Chopra and Meindl 2012). CRM seeks to build a personalised relationship with customers by capturing patterns of previous bookings and purchases, and the preferences displayed and services availed by them during those visits, and using them to offer loyalty rewards, special offers, upgrades, and providing prompts to staff and systems so they can appear to 'know' the customer (Sigala 2005). Brynjolfsson et al. (2011) report from a study involving 179 large publicly traded firms that those who adopt data-driven decision-making (DDD) 'have output and productivity that is 5–6% higher than what would be expected given their other investments and information technology usage'.

Big data are seen by many as the next stage in the ongoing process of seeking organisational efficiencies and structures that leverage competitive advantage, while reducing risks, costs and operational losses, and improving customer experience. What big data offer is the possibility of exhaustive, highly detailed, real-time intelligence on all aspects of an organisation. As the lobby group, TechAmerica Foundation (2012: 12) postulate, big data

> will lay the foundation for: replacing or supporting human decision-making with automated algorithms; reducing inefficiencies within an agency; creating transparency; improving performance by enabling experimentation to discover needs and expose variability; improving ROI [return on investment] for IT investments; improved decision-making and operational intelligence; providing predictive capabilities to improve mission outcomes; reducing security threats and crime; eliminating waste, fraud, and abuse; innovating new business models and stakeholder services.

In other words, big data will provide senior managers with a highly detailed and very timely knowledge of all aspects of their organisation from which they can formulate wise courses of action. Big data will enable organisations to be more nimble, opportune, flexible, innovative and smart in how they are organised and operate (Manyika et al. 2011).

An example of how a non-commercial organisation has successfully leveraged big data to restructure and manage its operations is the Democratic Party's election campaigns for Barack Obama. As noted in Chapter 4, the 2008 Obama campaign embraced big data, putting together an enormous set of data from multiple sources and generating significant amounts of real-time polling data, in order to manage in a reactive, evolving fashion its strategy, actions, and worker and volunteer tasks. Based on an analysis of the 2008 performance, for the 2012 election Obama's data analytics group grew in size fivefold and included leading technologists hired from industry (Scherer 2012). This group improved the relationality of data collected through different sources so that they could be more effectively linked together. They developed campaign apps and used social media such as Facebook to encourage peer pressure to register and to get out the vote, and dropped their own and third-party cookies onto the computers that visited their websites to track online habits (Crovitz 2012; Kaye 2012). They also improved their profiling and predictive modelling and how the information from their analytics was used to direct the campaign, as well as testing and honing ways to raise finance to fund the campaign (Scherer 2012). And they continuously added and processed new data and ran simulations to predict outcomes and the best responses. As one campaign official stated: 'We ran the election 66,000 times every night' to determine the odds of winning each swing state. 'And every morning we got the spit-out – here are your chances of winning these states. And that is how we allocated resources' (quoted in Scherer 2012). By continuously running their evolving datasets through sophisticated algorithms, Obama's team gained significant advantages over their rivals. Issenberg (2012: 246) thus argues that Obama's campaigns were 'the perfect political corporation: a well-funded, data-driven, empirically rigorous institution'. The promise of big data advocates is that the benefits that the Democratic Party gained from big data can be realised by all other organisations and businesses.

LEVERAGING VALUE AND PRODUCING CAPITAL

Beyond making companies more efficient and effective in their management, big data are being heavily promoted as a means for leveraging value from a company's activities and its relationships with suppliers and consumers. Indeed, as Gantz and Reinsel (2011) note, the prime driver of big data is not technological; it is financial and the promise of greater efficiencies and profits. The adoption of big data solutions is thus a strategy to realise untapped capital accumulation in a way that offers significant return on investment and provides competitive advantage (Manyika et al. 2011; Zikopoulos et al. 2012). There are several ways in which big data solutions can offer corporate intelligence that can grow turnover and profits. Using the retail sector as an example, Manyika et al. (2011) identify 16 solutions divided into 5 types – marketing, merchandising, operations, supply chain and new business models – that each leverage a potential gain in sales and efficiencies (see Table 7.1). These include generating data across the company and applying analytics in order to segment the market, tackle customer and employee churn, optimise various inputs (e.g., components, labour, utilities) and yield, and build various profiles and predictive models to answer a variety of questions:

- whether to contact the customer or not (target marketing);
- whether to provide the customer with a retention offer or not (customer retention);
- which type of ad or choice of words/images or product to present to a customer (content selection);
- which channel the customer should be contacted through (channel selection);
- whether a customer is offered a higher or lower price (dynamic pricing/discounting);
- whether a debtor is offered a deeper write-off (collections);
- whether a customer is offered a higher or lower credit limit or interest rate (credit risk) (Siegel 2013).

To focus on one of five solution types identifed by Manyika et al. (2011), marketing, a number of big data management tools and analytics, grouped into four themes (consolidation, segmentation, matching, optimisation), can be used to manage, process, analyse and interpret data into order to meet objectives (see Figure 7.1). The aim of behavioural marketing is to more effectively sell goods and services to individual customers and to build a long-term relationship with them in order to retain their custom by being more in tune to their characteristics, behaviours, preferences and desires (Schwartz and Solove 2011). By building individualised profiles and combining them with predictive analytics, companies seek to deliver a personalised experience through the micro-marketing of products and special offers. In so doing, they seek to 'anticipate a customer's intent to buy and to gently ease them into realising that intent', whilst at the same time building customer loyalty (Minelli et al. 2013). In this sense, Bill Stensrud contends that '[v]endors are using big data to try to acquire the consumer' (cited in Bollier 2010: 24).

　　Such a big data approach has already been implemented by a number of retailers such as Walmart and Tesco. These chains generate vast quantities of data daily within their ERP, SCM, and CRM systems, including checkout sales being tied to customers through loyalty and credit cards (in Walmart's case some 267 million transactions a day), using them to devise better pricing strategies, store layouts, staff rostering, inventory control, advertising campaigns, supplier costs, identify new store locations and products, and so on, and in so doing capture market share from rivals (Bollier 2010). Rather than conduct expensive, sampled consumer surveys where respondents state what they would do and what they value, the transaction and clickstream data explicitly reveal such information across all consumers. The projected benefits are high, with Manyika et al. (2011) suggesting that big data could increase retailers' operating margins by 60 per cent. While these solutions relating to retail and

Table 7.1   Forms of big data corporate intelligence

Marketing	*Cross-selling* (using customers' demographics, purchase history, preferences and other facts to increase the average purchase size)
	Location-based marketing (using real-time location, for example known by GPS embedded in smartphones, to target consumers in or close to stores)
	In-store behaviour analysis (tracking of smartphones, shopping cart transponders, video surveillance to help improve store layout, product mix and shelf positioning to increase sales)
	Customer micro-segmentation (using purchasing and browsing history to individually target customers with advertising and special offers)
	Sentiment analysis (tracking customer opinions on social media to identify sentiment towards a product and to alter marketing campaigns appropriately)
	Enhancing the multi-channel consumer experience (creating individually tailored Web experiences and catalogues based on customers' demographics, purchase history and preferences)
Merchandising	*Assortment optimisation* (allocating which products to stock in which stores based on local demographics, buyer perception and behaviour, and other local facts)
	Pricing optimisation (using demographics and purchasing behaviour to inform pricing decisions at different locations to maximise sales/revenue)
	Placement and design optimisation (using in-store behaviour and website interactions to guide store/website design and where to locate items to increase sales)
Operations	*Performance transparency* (fine-grained analysis, increasingly in real-time, of how well products, stores and employees are performing)
	Labour inputs optimisation (calculating the optimal levels of staffing and scheduling to avoid over- or under-capacity)
Supply chain	*Inventory management* (improved stock forecasting by monitoring sales histories, seasonal sales cycles, and local conditions and events to ensure suitable levels of desired stock)
	Distribution and logistics optimisation (real-time location of goods, calculating the most efficient routes in time and fuel, monitoring driver behaviour, scheduling maintenance)
	Informing supplier negotiations (using data concerning customer preferences and sales to inform the sourcing of products)
New business models	*Price comparison services* (third-party services providing customers with real-time price transparency on products across multiple retailers)
	Web-based markets (retailers that provide value-added services such as access to other sellers, product information, consumer-generated reviews, and price comparisons)

Source: Compiled from Manyika et al. 2011: 67–71.

Adapted from "Big data: The next frontier for innovation, competition, and productivity", May 2011, Mckinsey Global Institute, www. mckinsey.com/mgi.Mckinsey&Company.

marketing are potentially available across sectors, their salience varies, with different industries most benefiting from particular solutions (see Table 7.2).

As well as the pull of projected benefits, big data advocates also seek to push adoption by highlighting the consequences of failing to invest. For example, Manyika et al. (2011: 6) state that: 'Across sectors, we expect to see value accruing to leading users of big data at the expense of laggards.' In other words, those who do not adapt and adopt big data solutions will be left behind to flounder and wither as they lose market share. Regardless of whether using pull or push discourses, since 2012 big data for business have become pervasive within mainstream and business media, and given their touted benefits, their widespread roll-out as the next phase of technological innovation that delivers enhanced performance seems assured.

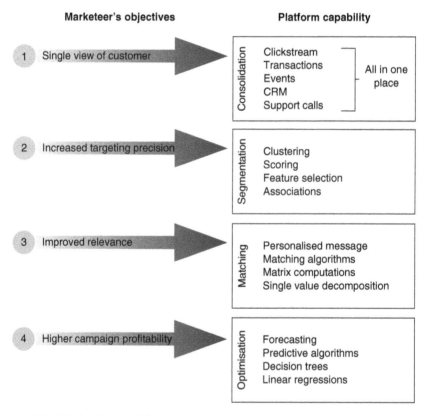

Figure 7.1 Marketing and big data

Source: Adapted from Claverie-Berge 2012.

Table 7.2   Big data benefits to ten selected industries

Automotive	*Insurance*
Advanced condition monitoring	Next best action
New car packaging and pricing	Catastrophe modelling
Warranty claims	Claims fraud
Banking	*Oil and gas*
Next best action	Advanced condition monitoring
System log analysis	Drilling surveillance and
Liquidity risk management	optimisation
	Production surveillance and
	optimisation
Energy and utilities	*Retail*
Smart meter analytics	Dynamic price optimisation
Distribution load forecasting and	Localised assortment
scheduling	Marketing optimisation
Condition-based maintenance	
Government	*Telecommunications*
Threat/crime prevention and prediction	Optimised service assurance
Fraud, waste and abuse analytics	Network intelligence
	New products and services creation
Health care	*Travel and transportation*
Measure and act on population health	Customer analytics and loyalty
Engage consumers in their health care	marketing
	Predictive maintenance

Source: IBM (n.d.) http://www-01.ibm.com/software/data/bigdata/industry.html

CREATING BETTER PLACES

Throughout history people have invented and adopted new technologies designed to create wealth and enhance everyday living. Many of these technologies have strongly impacted on the nature, structure, regulation and enactment of urban and rural life, in particular utilities, transportation, communication, and building infrastructure. These technologies often have paradoxical and adverse effects (e.g., factories that create wealth but also pollution), or become overloaded (e.g., overcrowding or traffic congestion), or produce dependencies that can become unsustainable (e.g., long-distance commuting). Information and communication technologies (ICTs) are the latest wave of new devices and infrastructure to be embedded into the fabric of environments, with a significant component of their discursive logic being that they provide solutions to the problems created by previous rounds of technology-led development – they will make them more efficient, sustainable, cleaner, safer, productive, and so on – as well as creating entirely new ways of acting in the world. As a consequence, over the past few decades, cities have embraced ICTs as a key component of their development strategies (Castells 1996; Graham and Marvin 1996; Kitchin 1998).

SMART
CITIES

The latest incarnation of such an ICT-led vision of urban development is the notion of smart cities, which conceives of places being increasingly composed of and monitored by pervasive and ubiquitous computing and whose economy and governance is driven by innovation, creativity and entrepreneurship, enacted by smart people. The smart city is densely instrumented and can be understood and regulated in real-time; it produces, shares, integrates, consumes and acts on big data (Kitchin 2014). Such big data provide a fine-grained, dynamic, cohesive understanding of cities and the inputs for systems that will create more liveable, secure, functional, competitive and sustainable places (Hancke et al. 2013; Townsend 2013). Such a smart city vision is being heavily promoted by a number of the world's largest software services and hardware companies (e.g., IBM, CISCO, Microsoft, Intel, Siemens, Oracle, SAP) and being enthusiastically adopted by municipal, national and supranational institutions who foresee smart city technologies producing socio-economic progress and renewing urban centres as hubs of innovation and work (Kourtit et al. 2012). Whilst some smart city projects are being built from the ground up (e.g., Songdo or Masdar City), most are piecemeal and consist of retrofitting existing infrastructure with digital technology and data solutions. The key function of big data in both cases is to provide real-time analytics to manage how aspects of the city function and are regulated.

Such real-time surveillance and data analytics have been employed for a number of years in some sectors. For example, many cities have implemented intelligent transport systems, where data concerning the movement of traffic around a system, generated by a network of cameras and transponders, are fed back to a central control hub and are used to monitor and regulate flow, adjusting traffic light sequences and speed limits and automatically administering penalties for traffic violations (Dodge and Kitchin 2007a). Similarly, the police might monitor a suite of cameras and live incident logs in order to efficiently and reactively direct appropriate resources to particular locations. Data relating to environmental conditions might be collated from a sensor network distributed throughout the city, for example measuring and tracking air pollution, water levels or seismic activity. Many local governments use management systems to log public engagement with their services. In nearly all cases, these are isolated systems dealing with a single issue and are controlled by a single agency.

More recently there has been an attempt to draw all of these kinds of surveillance and analytics into a single hub, supplemented by broader public and open data analytics. For example, the Centro De Operações Prefeitura Do Rio in Rio de Janeiro, Brazil, a partnership between the city government and IBM, has created a city-wide instrumented system that draws together data streams from 30 agencies, including traffic and public transport, municipal and utility services, emergency services, weather feeds, and information sent in by employees and the public via phone, Internet and radio, into a single data analytics centre (see Figure 7.2; Singer 2012c). Here, algorithms and a team of analysts process, visualise, analyse and monitor a vast amount of live service data, alongside data aggregated over time and huge volumes of administration data that are released on a more periodic basis, often mashing the datasets together to investigate particular aspects of city life and change over time, and to build predictive models with respect to everyday city development and management and disaster situations such as flooding. This is complemented by a virtual operations platform that enables city officials to log in from the field to access real-time information. For example, police at an accident scene can use the platform to see how many ambulances have been dispatched and when, and to upload additional information (Singer 2012c). The stated aim of the city's mayor, Eduardo Paes, was 'to knock down silos ... [between] departments and combine each one's data to help the whole enterprise' (Singer 2012c). Similar centres are being developed elsewhere, accompanied by a range of apps for citizens to access and utilise some streams of data.

For those developing and using integrated, real-time city data analytics, such centres and apps provide a powerful means for making sense of, managing and living in the city in the here-and-now, for envisioning and predicting future scenarios, and for undertaking evidence-based resource allocation and joined-up thinking across government (Flowers 2013; Kitchin 2014). Rather than basing

Figure 7.2   The Centro De Operações Prefeitura Do Rio in Rio de Janeiro, Brazil

Source: http://ipprio.rio.rj.gov.br/centro-de-operacoes-rio-usa-mapas-feitos-pelo-ipp/

decisions on anecdote or intuition or clientelist politics or periodic/partial evidence, it is possible to assess what is happening at any one time and to react and plan appropriately. Moreover, the use of large samples and the linking of diverse forms of data provide a deeper, more holistic and robust analysis. For advocates of such systems it thus becomes possible to develop, run, regulate and live in the city on the basis of strong, rational evidence rather weak, selective evidence and political ideology (Flowers 2013). Thus, it is argued, the use of such big data provides the basis for a more efficient, sustainable, competitive, productive, open and transparent city. Others warn that big data signals the possibilities of 'big brother', technocratic forms of governance, and the corporatisation of city management (see Chapter 10).

CONCLUSION

This chapter has charted the discursive drivers of big data with respect to four major tasks: governing people, managing organisations, leveraging value and producing capital, and creating better places (their potential with respect to science is discussed in the next chapter). The discussion has illustrated how big data are being framed politically and economically (see Chapter 1) and how a powerful set of rationalities is being developed to support the roll-out and adoption of big data technologies and solutions. The power of the discursive regimes being constructed is illustrated by considering the counter-arguments – it is difficult to contend that being less insightful and wise, productive, competitive, efficient, effective, sustainable, secure, safe, and so on, is a desirable situation. If big data provide all of these benefits, the regime contends that it makes little sense not to pursue the development of big data systems. Of course, the argument being presented is narrow and selective and deliberately avoids highlighting potential negative consequences with respect to civil liberties, dataveillance, social sorting, data security, control creep, anticipatory governance, technocratic and corporate governance, and technological lock-ins (see Chapter 10). It is the view of vested interests, particularly those seeking to sell big data technologies, and of governments pursuing a neoliberal vision of governance and regulation, not the view of citizens or communities who might still be advocates of big data and ubiquitous computing, but envisage them being used in emancipatory, empowering and participatory ways with the more negative effects being subject to regulation and oversight.

The analysis presented in the chapter has been quite cursory, providing a synoptic overview of some of the arguments being made. What is presently required, through specific case studies is a much more detailed mapping out and deconstruction of the unfolding discursive regimes being constructed. For example, with respect to the promotion of big data for smart cities there is a need to carefully chart and unpack how various supporting discourses are promoted with respect to specific places through trade magazines and websites, newspapers, corporate promotional materials, state records, political manifestos, and so on, and the intersections of various stakeholder interests and agendas. This needs to be accompanied not only by an analysis of how such discourses are being countered by alternative visions, the clashes and interplay between discursive arguments, genealogies of how they shift over time, and comparative analysis of the discursive landscape across locales, but also by an analysis of the effects of discourses on shaping how a domain works in practice and the consequences of implementing a big data solution.

With regards to the latter, Salmon (2014) details that once a data-driven solution is implemented it rarely delivers the benefits that its boosters expected and often produces a suite of new issues. He draws on Campbell's Law, formulated by sociologist Donald T. Campbell (1976), to explain this: 'The more any quantitative social indicator is used for social decision-making, the more subject it will be to corruption pressures and the more apt it will be to distort and corrupt the social processes it is intended to monitor.' Or in Salmon's terms:

> The more a field is run by a system, the more that system creates incentives for everyone (employees, customers, competitors) to change their behavior in perverse ways – providing more of whatever the system is designed to measure and produce, whether that actually creates any value or not.

In other words, people start to game the system in rational, self-interested but often unpredictable ways to subvert metrics, algorithms, and automated decision-making processes. For example, Porter (1995: 44) notes, '[w]hen business managers are judged by their accounts, they learn to optimise their accounts, perhaps through such artifices as putting off needed maintenance and other long term costs'. As a result, while organisations and government might be transformed in how they are managed and operate, becoming more data and metric-driven, these are likely to produce diverse and unanticipated effects and enact particular forms of governmentality, not all of which will be positive.

Studies of big data and their effects then need to open up to view the inherent politics and agendas of big data in different contexts and provide a basis for more normative conversations about the kind of big data worlds we might want to live in. These kinds of conversations are under-developed at present, partly due to the newness and rapidity of developments, but also because of the dominance of big data boosterist narratives and the machinations of vested interest stakeholders. Nonetheless, such conversations are needed given that big data are reshaping how citizens and places are governed, organisations managed, economies work, and science is practised.

8

THE REFRAMING OF SCIENCE, SOCIAL SCIENCE AND HUMANITIES RESEARCH

In an interview for *The Economist* in 2010, Sinan Aral, a business professor at New York University, stated that 'Revolutions in science have often been preceded by revolutions in measurement' (cited in Cukier 2010). This chapter explores the extent to which Aral's observation applies with respect to big data, data infrastructures and open data, and their effects with respect to how academic research and discovery is approached from a philosophical and methodological perspective. In particular, it examines how the availability of big data and data infrastructures, coupled with new analytic tools, challenges established epistemologies in different disciplines – how questions are asked and how they are answered – and is leading to the creation of new fields and disciplines. Thus, the chapter explores whether changes in how the raw material of information and knowledge is being produced, managed and analysed are radically altering the foundational tenets underpinning how the sciences, social sciences and humanities are understood and practised; in other words, is the data revolution leading to paradigm shifts across the principal domains of the academy?

As set out by Kuhn (1962), a paradigm constitutes an accepted way of interrogating the world and synthesising knowledge common to a substantial proportion of researchers in a discipline at any one moment in time. Researchers operating within the paradigm share a common philosophy, utilise a set of common methods, and ask and answer questions that build knowledge incrementally. Therefore, they tend to favour the same or very similar ontologies, epistemologies, theories, methods and ethical and ideological frames. Periodically, however, Kuhn argues, a new way of thinking emerges that challenges accepted theories or approaches. For example, Einstein's theory of relativity confronted and largely replaced Newtonian theory in physics. Similarly, Darwin's theory of evolution radically altered conceptual thought within the biological sciences, as well as challenging the religious doctrine of creationism. In both cases, some people clung on to the established ways of thinking, while others moved to the new position which quickly became hegemonic. In some academic domains there is little evidence of paradigms operating, notably in many social sciences, such as sociology and human geography where there is a diverse set of philosophical approaches employed (e.g., positivism, phenomenology, structuralism, poststructuralism, etc.), with these various theoretical camps providing competing views on how best to make sense of the world. In other domains, such as the sciences, there is more unity around a scientific method, underpinned by hypothesis testing to verify or falsify theories. That is not to say, however, that how the scientific method is conceived and deployed does not periodically shift, or that there are few competing theories with respect to explaining particular phenomena (theories about phenomena can differ while sharing the same wider approach to scientific endeavour).

Jim Gray, for example (as detailed in Hey et al. 2009), charts the evolution of science through four paradigms, the fourth of which he argues is in its infancy but is the result of the unfolding data revolution (see Table 8.1). Unlike Kuhn's proposition that paradigm shifts occur because the dominant mode of science cannot account for particular phenomena or answer key questions, thus demanding the formulation of new ideas, Gray's transitions are founded on advances in forms of data and the development of new analytical methods. This chapter explores the extent to which this fourth paradigm is coming into existence in science, and to what extent the data revolution is leading to alternative epistemologies in the humanities and social sciences. Given the relatively early point in the unfolding data revolution, it is perhaps no surprise that there are diverging opinions as to the effects of big data, open data, data infrastructures and new data analytics in producing new epistemologies, and there

Table 8.1 Four paradigms of science

Paradigm	Nature	Form	When
First	Experimental science	Empiricism; describing natural phenomena	Pre-Renaissance
Second	Theoretical science	Modelling and generalisation	Pre-computers
Third	Computational science	Simulation of complex phenomena	Pre-big data
Fourth	Exploratory science	Data-intensive; statistical exploration and data mining	Now

Source: Compiled from Hey et al. 2009.

will continue to be such. There is no doubt, however, that they do raise fundamental epistemological questions because extracting useful, valid information from the data deluge is not simply a technical issue that can be dealt with by technological solutions (Floridi 2012).

THE FOURTH PARADIGM IN SCIENCE?

While Jim Gray envisages the fourth paradigm of science to be data-intensive and an extension of the established scientific method, others suggest that big data usher in a new era of empiricism, wherein the volume of data, accompanied by techniques that can reveal their inherent truth, enable data to speak for themselves free of theory. The latter view has gained credence outside of the academy, especially within business circles, but its ideas have also taken root in the new field of data science and other sciences. Both approaches offer a challenge to the traditional scientific method and offer a possible alternative paradigm. In this section, the epistemological claims of both approaches are critically examined.

The re-emergence of empiricism

For some, the philosophy of the fourth paradigm is what Brooks (2013a) calls 'data-ism'; the attempt to capture everything as data and to extract some level of insight from them: 'everything that can be measured should be measured ... data is a transparent and reliable lens that allows us to filter out emotionalism and ideology; that data will help us do remarkable things – like foretell the future'. Such data-ist claims underpin much of the hype about big data within the business community, and they are generally expressed through an empiricist framing – that with enough volume, data can speak for themselves. Such empiricism is best embodied in the claims of Chris Anderson (2008), former editor-in-chief at *Wired* magazine, whose rallying call that big data signal 'the end of theory' struck a chord with many commentators. In a provocative piece, Anderson argues that 'the data deluge makes the scientific method obsolete'; that the patterns and relationships contained within big data inherently produce meaningful and insightful knowledge about social, political and economic processes and complex phenomena. He argues:

> There is now a better way. Petabytes allow us to say: 'Correlation is enough.' We can stop looking for models. *We can analyze the data without hypotheses about what it might show.* We can throw the numbers into the biggest computing clusters the world has ever seen and let statistical algorithms find patterns where science cannot ... Correlation supersedes causation,

and *science can advance even without coherent models, unified theories, or really any mechanistic explanation at all.* There's no reason to cling to our old ways. (my emphasis)

Similarly, Prensky (2009) argues: 'scientists no longer have to make educated guesses, construct hypotheses and models, and test them with data-based experiments and examples. Instead, they can mine the complete set of data for patterns that reveal effects, producing scientific conclusions *without* further experimentation' (my emphasis). Dyche (2012) thus argues that 'mining big data reveals relationships and patterns that we didn't even know to look for'. She continues, '[t]hese patterns are too specific and seemingly arbitrary to specify [through hypotheses]'. Likewise, Steadman (2013, my emphasis) argues:

> The big data approach to intelligence gathering allows an analyst to get the *full resolution* on worldwide affairs. Nothing is lost from looking too closely at one particular section of data; nothing is lost from trying to get too wide a perspective on a situation that the fine detail is lost. The algorithms find the patterns and the hypothesis follows from the data. *The analyst doesn't even have to bother proposing a hypothesis any more.* Her role switches from proactive to reactive, with the algorithms doing the contextual work ... *Algorithms will spot patterns and generates theories*, so there's a decreasing need to worry about inventing a hypothesis first and then testing it with a sample of data.

In other words, rather than testing whether certain hypothesised patterns or relationships exist within a dataset, algorithms are set to work on big data to discover meaningful associations between data without being guided by hypotheses. As Croll (2012: 56) puts it: 'In the old, data-is-scarce model, [we] had to decide what to collect first, and then collect it ... With the new, data-is-abundant model, we collect first and ask questions later.'

The examples used to illustrate such a position usually stem from marketing and retail. For example, Dyche (2012) details the case of a retail chain who analysed 12 years' worth of purchase transactions for possible unnoticed relationships between products that ended up in shoppers' baskets. Discovering correlations between certain items led to new product placements and alterations to shelf space management and a 16 per cent increase in revenue per shopping cart in the first month's trial. There was no hypothesis that Product A was often bought with Product H that was then tested. The data were simply queried to discover what relationships existed that might have previously been unnoticed. Similarly, Amazon's recommendation system produces suggestions for other items a shopper might be interested in without knowing anything about the culture and conventions of books and reading; it simply identifies patterns of purchasing across customers in order to determine whether, if Person A likes Book X, they are also likely to like Book Y given their own and others' consumption patterns.

Dyche's contention is that this open, rather than directed, approach to discovery is more likely to reveal unknown, underlying patterns with respect to customer behaviours, product affinities, and financial risks, that can then be exploited. While it might be desirable to explain why associations exist within the data and why they might be meaningful, such explanation is cast as largely unnecessary; what matters is knowing that it does. Siegel (2013: 90, my emphasis) thus argues with respect to predictive analytics: 'We usually don't know about causation, and we often don't necessarily care ... the objective is more to predict than it is to understand the world ... It just needs to work; *prediction trumps explanation*.' As Weinberger (2011: 33) contends with respect to Hunch – a website that makes recommendations based on the answers to questions that seemingly have little to do with the original question asked:

> The analysis is not in support of a theory and it produces no theory. Hunch has no idea why people who, say, prefer to wear sandals on a beach and who have not blown a dandelion in the past year might like those four movies [suggested to him]. It doesn't have a hypothesis and it doesn't have a guess. It just has statistical correlations.

Some data analytics software is sold on precisely this notion. For example, the data mining and visualisation software, Ayasdi, claims to be able to 'automatically discover insights – regardless of complexity – *without asking questions*. Ayasdi's customers can finally learn the answers to questions that they didn't know to ask in the first place. Simply stated, Ayasdi is "digital serendipity"' (Clark 2013; my emphasis). Further, it claims to have totally removed

> the human element that goes into data mining – and, as such, all the human bias that goes with it. Instead of waiting to be asked a question or be directed to specific existing data links, the system will – undirected – deliver patterns a human controller might not have thought to look for. (Clark 2013)

There is a powerful and attractive set of ideas at work in these arguments that runs counter to the deductive approach that is hegemonic within modern science. First, that big data can capture the whole of a domain and provide full resolution. Second, that there is no need for a priori theory, models or hypotheses. Third, that through the application of agnostic data analytics the data can speak for themselves free of human bias or framing, and that any patterns and relationships within big data are inherently meaningful and truthful. Fourth, that meaning transcends context or domain-specific knowledge.

KNOWING WITHOUT UNDERSTANDING

These work together to suggest that a new mode of science is being created, one in which the modus operandi is inductive in nature. As such, Gannon and Reid (2009) argue that the 'ready availability of diverse data is shifting scientific approaches from the traditional, hypothesis-driven scientific method to science based on exploration'. Likewise, Weinberger (2011: 127) suggests that the traditional aim of science – 'to construct theories that are both supported by and explain the facts' – is being transformed to 'producing complex models that account for complex relationships' where 'in some cases it is impossible to disentangle why certain effects work; instead there is observed a strong correspondence between simulation and the real world that provides confidence that other simulations will provide reliable results'. The example Weinberger uses is placing a column one metre in front of a door in a computer simulation of the exit flow of people in an evacuation. The column leads to a better flow, but there is no explanation from the model as to why it does. And in many ways, he suggests, we do not need to know why, just that it does and that such an implementation might save lives. This produces for Andrejevic (2013: 26) a state of 'knowing without understanding'.

The fallacies of empiricism

It is undeniable that big data are having, and will increasingly have, an effect on how science is practised and understood. However, the empiricist vision of how this new science will be constituted is based on fallacious thinking – all four ideas that underpin its formulation are problematic. They may well hold appeal, but critical and philosophical scrutiny reveals serious problems with each tenet. It is worth examining each in turn before detailing an alternative vision of data-driven science that blends aspects of abduction, induction and deduction.

First: big data can capture a whole of a domain and provide full resolution. Since big data strives for exhaustivity, its advocates argue that it is possible to see everything within a domain (e.g., all activity in Twitter, or all purchases within a supermarket chain), and that it is possible to make full sense of what is seen (Vis 2013). However, as discussed in Chapters 1, 2 and 9, big data may seek to be exhaustive, but it is both a representation and a sample. Indeed, all data provide oligoptic views of the world, not panoptic ones: views from certain vantage points, using particular tools, rather than an all-seeing, infallible god's eye view (Haraway 1991; Amin and Thrift 2002). Moreover, domains evolve and change; thus big data 'cannot reach everywhere, in part because they ... cannot know all spaces and times, and in part because many new spaces and times remain to be invented' (Amin and Thrift 2002: 128). As such, big data constitute 'a series of partial orders, localised totalities, with their ability to gaze in some directions and not others' (Latour cited in Amin and Thrift 2002: 92).

Vis (2013) thus concludes that '[i]t is important to remember that what you see is framed by what you are able to see or indeed want to see from within a specific ideological framework'.

Second: there is no need for a priori theory, models or hypotheses. The assumption here is that the data generation and analytics underpinning the use of big data seemingly come from nowhere; that they are somehow free from 'the regulating force of philosophy' (Berry 2011: 8). Contra, systems are designed to capture certain kinds of data, often for very specific purposes, and the analytics and algorithms underpinning big data are based on scientific reasoning and have been refined through scientific testing. A lot of thought goes into designing big data systems, drawing on an extensive scientific literature and the experience and knowledge of those working on the system. Time is spent choosing and testing different methods of identifying and extracting value from the data produced, evaluating the results and tweaking the analytics. Such work is guided by an agenda as to what outcomes are being sought (to increase turnover or profit, to understand a particular system, etc.), which draws on established theories as to what might be the salient ways of producing such effects. Whether such effects do in fact occur is then tested.

As Leonelli (2012) notes, an inductive strategy of identifying patterns within data is usually guided by scientific reasoning and does not occur in a scientific vacuum. Or, as Quintero (2012) puts it, 'explanations cannot simply be cranked out of statistical analyses, without the need for a precursor theory of some kind'. He continues, 'being data-driven is only useful if you have a strong theory by which to navigate; anything else can leave you heading blindly toward a cliff'. In fact, both deductive and inductive reasoning are always discursively framed and do not arise out of nowhere. Popper (1979, cited in Callebaut 2012: 74) thus suggests that all science adopts a searchlight approach to scientific discovery, with the focus of light guided by previous findings, theories and training; by speculation that is grounded in experience and knowledge. The same is true for Amazon, Hunch, Ayasdi, and Google. How Amazon constructed its recommendation system was based on scientific reasoning, underpinned by a guiding model and accompanied by empirical testing designed to improve the performance of the algorithms it uses. Likewise, Google undertakes extensive research and development, it works in partnership with scientists and it buys scientific knowledge, either funding research within universities or by buying the IP of other companies, to refine and extend the utility of how it organises, presents and extracts value from data. Thus, if statistical algorithms find patterns in data it is because pattern recognition science, along with domain-specific knowledge, has been employed.

Third: data can speak for themselves free of human bias or framing. Related to the notion that the production of knowledge from big data occurs unmoored from science is the idea that big data analytics enable data to speak for themselves

random correlations (patterns)
in data

unencumbered by contextualisation or the vagaries of human elucidation. Not only are data supposedly generated free from theory, but their interpretation and meaning can similarly take place in a scientific vacuum. Such a notion is a feature of empiricist thinking: that when presented and analysed in an appropriate manner, data in and of themselves constitute compelling evidence concerning a particular process or phenomenon, rather than its interpretation. In the case of big data, the volume of data adds to the weight of evidence. This 'deification of data' can lead, as Jenkins (2013) argues, to a 'data determinism in the arguments made for big data'. That is, a sense that data trumps theory; 'that data is real and theory is not real' (Hales 2013); that data tells the truth of the world, whereas theory is merely spin. There are three issues to consider here: the first is the assumption that the data are objective, neutral and free of bias; second, that patterns and relationships within big data are inherently meaningful and truthful; and third, that interpretation of such patterns and relationships lacks any kind of positionality or situatedness.

As argued in Chapter 1, data are not simply natural and essential elements that are abstracted from the world in neutral and objective ways and can be accepted at face value. Data do not pre-exist their generation and arise from nowhere. Rather data are created within a complex data assemblage that actively shapes its constitution. Data then can never just speak for themselves, but are always, inherently, speaking from a particular position (Crawford 2013). Further, Anderson's (2008) claim that '[c]orrelation supersedes causation', suggests that patterns found within a dataset are inherently meaningful. This is an assumption that all trained statisticians know is dangerous and false. Correlations between variables within a dataset can be random in nature and have no or little causal association (see Chapter 9). Interpreting every correlation as meaningful can therefore lead to serious ecological fallacies. This can be exacerbated in the case of big data because the empiricist position appears to promote the practice of data dredging – hunting for every correlation – thus increasing the likelihood of discovering random associations. However, while pattern recognition might identify potentially interesting relationships, the veracity of these needs to be further tested on other datasets to ensure their reliability and validity. In other words, the relationships should form the basis for hypotheses that are more widely tested, which in turn are used to build and refine a theory that explains them. Thus correlations do not supersede causation, but rather should form the basis for additional research to establish if such correlations are indicative of causation. Only then can we get a sense as to how meaningful are the causes of the correlation.

While the idea that data can speak for themselves free of bias or framing may seem like an attractive one, the reality is somewhat different. As Gould (1981: 166) notes, 'inanimate data can never speak for themselves, and we always bring to bear some conceptual framework, either intuitive and ill-formed, or tightly and formally structured, to the task of investigation, analysis, and interpretation'. Making sense of data is always framed; examined through a particular lens that casts how it is interpreted. Even if the process is automated in some way, the algorithms used to process the data are imbued with particular values and contextualised within a particular scientific approach. As Hales (2013) details: 'Any statistical test or machine learning algorithm expresses a view of what a pattern or regularity is ... One algorithm will find one kind of pattern and another will find something else.' If interpreted by a person, they inevitably draw on their accumulated knowledge, skills and intuition to distil insights, so that different analysts will draw varying conclusions from the same analytics. Interpretation then is always shaped by the eye of the beholder regardless of how neutral or value-free they claim to be. Moreover, interpretations are not fixed, altering as they are exposed to new knowledge through further research and discussion and debate. As such, data never simply speak for themselves. As Silver (2012: 9) contends, 'We speak for them.'

Fourth: meaning transcends context or domain-specific knowledge. A related aspect to the idea that data can speak for themselves is the notion that interpreting big data does not require contextual or domain-specific knowledge. Rather, what is important is to be able to make visible the meaning within the data which, because the data supposedly speak for themselves, anyone with a reasonable understanding of statistics should be able to interpret. There is little doubt that data and computer scientists and others have been moving into other disciplinary areas with the roll-out of computation and data infrastructures. In many cases, they are not just providing new tools, but are also actively involved in the interpretation of data. And yet these scientists have little deep understanding of the field they are commenting on and the empirically informed theories and knowledge which have been built up over a long period of time. In the social sciences and humanities, for example, new modes of analysis and data infrastructures are often being driven by computer scientists and physicists. The results often makes those steeped in a disciplinary perspective cringe.

By way of illustration, the emerging field of social physics, where physicists and others often make pronouncements about social and spatial processes based on big data analysis, especially relating to cities and the supposed laws that underpin their formation and functions (Bettencourt et al. 2007; Lehrer 2010; Lohr 2013), often wilfully ignore a couple of centuries of social science scholarship, including nearly a century of quantitative analysis and model building. The result is an analysis of cities that is largely reductionist, functionalist and ignores the effects of culture, politics, policy, governance and capital, and a rich tradition of work that has sought to understand how cities operate socially, culturally, politically, and economically (reproducing the same kinds of limitations generated by the quantitative/positivist social sciences in the mid-twentieth century)

(Kitchin 2014; Mattern 2013). It also cuts across rich and varied philosophical traditions and works to promote empiricist and positivist approaches as the best means to make sense of cities (a theoretical vision with which few in the post-positivist social sciences are likely to agree) (Kitchin 2013).

A similar set of concerns is shared by those in the sciences. Strasser (2012), for example, notes that within the biological sciences, bioinformaticians who have a very narrow and particular way of understanding biology are claiming ground once occupied by the clinician and the experimental and molecular biologist. He argues that 'shifting the analysis to digital data … opens up epistemic questions as to who is the most legitimate producer of knowledge – the museum collector (the clinician, or the molecular biologist) or the statistician analyzing the data' or producing the simulation or model (2012: 87). Some data scientists are thus undoubtedly ignoring the observations of Porway (2013):

> Without subject matter experts available to articulate problems in advance, you get [poor] results … Subject matter experts are doubly needed to assess the results of the work, especially when you're dealing with sensitive data about human behavior. As data scientists, we are well equipped to explain the 'what' of data, but rarely should we touch the question of 'why' on matters we are not experts in.

As Porway notes, what is really needed is for data scientists and domain experts to work with each other to ensure that the data analytics used make sense and that the results from such analytics are sensibly and contextually interpreted. Likewise, Lazer et al. (2009: 10–11) call for collaboration between 'computationally literate social scientists and socially literate computer scientists' (2009: 10–11), and with respect to business, Minelli et al. (2013) contend that data science teams should be coupled with business process experts to leverage appropriate insights (see also Table 9.1).

Data-driven science

Rather than being rooted in empiricism, data-driven science seeks to hold to the tenets of the scientific method, but is more open to using a hybrid combination of abductive, inductive and deductive approaches to advance the understanding of a phenomenon. It differs from the traditional, experimental deductive design in that it seeks to generate hypotheses and insights 'born from the data' rather than 'born from the theory' (Kelling et al. 2009: 613). In other words, it seeks to incorporate a mode of induction into the research design, though explanation through induction is not the intended end point (as with empiricist approaches). Instead, it forms a new mode of hypothesis generation before a deductive approach is employed. Nor does the process of induction arise from nowhere, but is situated and contextualised within a highly evolved theoretical domain. Thus, the epistemological strategy adopted within data-driven science is to use *guided* knowledge-discovery techniques to identify potential questions (hypotheses) worthy of further examination and testing.

The process is guided in the sense that existing theory is used to direct the process of knowledge discovery, rather than simply hoping to identify all relationships within a dataset and assuming they are meaningful in some way. Thus, how data are generated or repurposed is guided by certain assumptions, underpinned by theoretical and practical knowledge and experience, as to whether technologies and their configurations will capture or produce appropriate and useful research material. Data are not generated by every means possible, using every kind of available technology or every kind of sampling framework; rather, strategies of data generation and repurposing are carefully thought out, with strategic decisions made to harvest certain kinds of data and not others. Similarly, how these data are processed, managed and analysed is guided by assumptions as to which techniques might provide meaningful insights. The data are not subject to every ontological framing possible, nor every form of data mining technique, in the hope that they reveal some hidden truth. Rather, theoretically informed decisions are made as to how best to tackle a dataset so that it will reveal information which will be of potential interest and is worthy of further research. And instead of testing whether every relationship revealed has veracity, attention is focused on those – based on some criteria – that seemingly offer the most likely or a valid way forward. Indeed, many supposed relationships within datasets can quickly be dismissed as trivial or absurd by domain specialists, with others flagged as deserving more attention (H.J. Miller 2010).

Such decision-making with respect to methods of data generation and analysis is based on abductive reasoning. Abduction is a mode of logical inference and reasoning is put forward by C.S. Peirce (1839–1914) (H.J. Miller 2010). It seeks a conclusion that makes reasonable and logical sense, but is not definitive in its claim. For example, there is no attempt to deduce what is the best way to generate data, but rather to identify an approach that makes logical sense given what is already known about such data production. Abduction is very commonly used in science, especially in the formulation of hypotheses, though such use is not widely acknowledged. Any relationships revealed within the data do not then arise from nowhere and nor do they simply speak for themselves. The process of induction – of insights emerging from the data – is contextually framed. And those insights are not the end point of an investigation, arranged and reasoned into a theory. Rather, the insights provide the basis for the formulation of hypotheses and the deductive testing of their validity. In other words, data-driven science is a reconfigured version of the traditional scientific method, providing a new way in which to build theory. Nonetheless, the epistemological change is significant.

Data-driven science, it is argued, will become the new paradigm of scientific method in an age of big and scaled data because the epistemology favoured is suited to extracting additional, valuable insights that traditional 'knowledge-driven science' would fail to generate (Kelling et al. 2009; H.J. Miller 2010; Loukides 2010). Knowledge-driven science, using a straight deductive approach, has particular utility in understanding and explaining the world under the conditions of scarce data and weak computation. Continuing to use such an approach, however, when technological and methodological advances mean that it is possible to undertake much richer analysis of data – applying new data analytics and being able to connect together large, disparate data in ways that were hitherto impossible, and which produce new valuable data – and to identify and tackle questions in new and exciting ways, makes little sense. Data-driven science, it is argued, is much more suited to exploring, extracting value and making sense of massive, interconnected datasets; to fostering interdisciplinary research that conjoins domain expertise (as it is less limited by the starting theoretical frame); and will lead to more holistic and extensive models and theories of entire complex systems rather than elements of them (Kelling et al. 2009).

For example, it is argued that data-driven science will transform our understanding of environmental systems (Bryant et al. 2008; Lehning et al. 2009). It will enable high-resolution data generated from a variety of sources, often in real-time (such as conventional and mobile weather stations, satellite and aerial imagery, weather radar, stream observations and gauge stations, citizen observations, ground and aerial LIDAR, water quality sampling, gas measures, soil cores, and distributed sensors that measure selected phenomenon such as air temperature and moisture) to be integrated to provide very detailed models of environments in flux (as opposed to at freeze-points in time and space) and to identify specific relationships between phenomena and processes that generate new hypotheses and theories that can then be tested further to establish their veracity. It will also help to identify and further understand connection points between different environmental spheres such as the atmosphere (air), biosphere (ecosystems), hydrosphere (water systems), lithosphere (rocky shell of the Earth) and pedosphere (soils), and aid the integration of theories into a more holistic theoretical assemblage. This will provide a better comprehension of the diverse, interrelated processes at work and the interconnections with human systems, and can be used to guide models and simulations for predicting long-term trends and possible adaptive strategies.

COMPUTATIONAL SOCIAL SCIENCES AND DIGITAL HUMANITIES

While the epistemology of data-driven science seems set to transform the research approach taken in the natural, life, physical and engineering sciences, its trajectory in the humanities and social sciences is much less certain. These

Positivism

scientific methods draw on the idea of positivism.

areas of scholarship are highly diverse in their philosophical underpinnings, with only some scholars employing the epistemology common in the sciences. Those using the scientific method in order to explain and model social phenomena, in general terms, draw on the ideas of positivism (though they might not adopt such a label; Kitchin 2006). Such work tends to focus on factual, quantified information – empirically observable phenomena that can be robustly measured (such as counts, distance, cost and time), as opposed to more intangible aspects of human life such as beliefs or ideology – using statistical testing to establish causal relationships and to build theories and predictive models and simulations. Positivistic approaches are well established in economics, political science, human geography and sociology, but are very rare in the humanities. However, within those disciplines mentioned, there has been a strong move over the past half-century towards post-positivist approaches, especially in human geography and sociology.

For positivistic scholars in the social sciences, data infrastructures, open data and big data offer huge opportunities to develop more sophisticated, wider-scale, finer-grained models of human life. The data revolution offers the possibility of shifting: from data-scarce to data-rich studies of societies; from static snapshots to dynamic unfoldings; from coarse aggregations to high resolutions; from relatively simple models to more complex, sophisticated simulations (Kitchin 2013). The potential exists for a new era of computational social science that produces studies with much greater breadth, depth, scale, timeliness and is inherently longitudinal, in contrast to existing social sciences research (Lazer et al. 2009; Batty et al. 2012). Moreover, the volume, velocity, variety, exhaustivity, resolution, relationality, flexibility and extensionality of data, plus the growing power of computation and new data analytics, address some of the critiques of positivistic scholarship to date, especially those of reductionism and universalism, by providing more finely grained, sensitive and nuanced analysis that can take account of context and contingency, and can be used to refine and extend theoretical understandings of the social and spatial world. Further, given the extensiveness of data, it is possible to test the veracity of such theory across a variety of settings and situations. In such circumstances, knowledge about individuals, communities, societies and environments will become more insightful and useful with respect to formulating policy and addressing the various issues facing humankind. The challenge in such a scenario is no longer the data, but creating new statistical and modelling methods capable of dealing with millions or billions of observations (Batty et al. 2012).

For post-positivist scholars, the unfolding data revolution offers both opportunities and challenges. The opportunities are the digitisation and interlinking of analogue and unstructured data, much of it new (e.g., social media) and many of which have heretofore been difficult to access (e.g., millions of books, documents, newspapers, photographs, art works, material objects, etc., from across history that have been rendered into digital form over the past couple of decades by a range of organisations) (Cohen 2008); the provision of new tools of data curation, management and analysis; and a new means for fostering interdisciplinary collaboration and moving beyond the lone-scholar model, extending research linkages with non-academic institutions, and engaging with new and wider audiences (Sword 2008). These opportunities are being examined most widely through the emerging field of digital humanities, which brings together scholars from across the humanities (historians, linguists, creative artists, literary and media scholars, etc.) with librarians, and computer, data and information scientists.

Initially, the digital humanities consisted of the curation and analysis of data that were born digital, and the digitisation and archiving projects that sought to render analogue texts and material objects into digital forms that could be organised and searched and be subjected to basic forms of overarching, automated or guided analysis, such as summary visualisations of content or connections between documents, people or places (Schnapp and Presner 2009). Subsequently, its advocates have argued that the field has evolved to provide more sophisticated tools for handling, searching, linking, sharing and analysing data that seek to complement and augment existing humanities methods, and facilitate traditional forms of interpretation and theory building, rather than replacing traditional methods or providing an empiricist or positivistic approach to humanities scholarship (Berry 2011; Manovich 2011).

What the digital humanities offer is a way of curating and sharing data, of augmenting traditional analysis, of scaling up research across a much broader range and volume of sources, and the saving of time and effort. Rather than concentrating on a handful of Victorian novels or early-twentieth-century photographs or a couple of Renaissance artists and their work, it becomes possible to search and connect across a large number of related works; rather than focus on a handful of websites or chat rooms or photos or videos or online newspapers, it becomes possible to examine thousands of such media. Manovich (2011) thus contends that 'computer-assisted examination of massive cultural datasets typically reveals new patterns in ... data which even best manual "close reading" would miss – and of course, even an army of humanists will not be able to carefully "close read" massive datasets in the first place'. Moretti (2005) argues that digital humanities scholarship brings methodological rigour to disciplines that heretofore been unsystematic and random in their focus and approach. Counting, graphing and mapping literature, he argues, have the potential to offer new insights and bring a new lustre to tired fields.

At the same time as there are opportunities, there is a range of challenges. For its detractors, the use of new digital humanities methods promotes what Moretti (2005) has termed 'a distant reading' wherein computers can act as 'reading machines' (Ramsay 2010). Such an approach runs counter to the long established practice of providing 'a close reading' of sources. Culler (2010: 20), for example, argues that 'what contrasts with close reading is not distant reading but something like sloppy reading, or casual reading'. A close reading, he continues, involves paying 'attention to how meaning is produced or conveyed, to what sorts of literary and rhetorical strategies and techniques are deployed to achieve what the reader takes to be the effects of the work or passage' (p. 22), something that a distant reading is unable to do. His worry is that the digital humanities are not just facilitating and promoting 'distant reading', but are making it 'possible to do literary research without reading at all: find all the instances of the words *beg* and *beggar* in novels by two different authors and write up your conclusions' (p. 24).

Similarly, Trumpener (2009: 164) argues that the 'statistically driven model of literary history ... seems to necessitate an impersonal invisible hand'. Moreover, it identifies patterns but avoids assigning causality, which can only be addressed 'by tackling publishers' archives, reading individual manuscript drafts in rare book libraries, and trying to figure out, book for book, who determined each novel's title: author, publisher, or publicist' (p. 164). For her, such investigation involves 'real footwork' not the employment of algorithms. Analysing thousands of texts, she asserts, means 'any specific text becomes statistically almost irrelevant' (p. 164). She continues, 'any attempt to see the big picture needs to be informed by broad knowledge, an astute, historicised sense of how genres and literary institutions work, and incisive interpretive tools. And an appreciation of the aleatory' (pp. 170–71). She concludes, it is 'important that most of us forego counting to stay in the library ... [D]espair over the unavailability of universal knowledge shouldn't drive us to the opposite extreme of thinking we must begin processing literature by the ton to make any headway.'

Similarly, for Marche (2012) cultural artefacts, such as literature, cannot be treated as mere data. A piece of writing is not simply an order of letters and words, it is contextual and conveys meaning and has qualities that are ineffable. Algorithms are very poor at capturing and deciphering meaning or context and, Marche argues, treat 'all literature as if it were the same'. He continues,

> The algorithmic analysis of novels and of newspaper articles is necessarily at the limit of reductivism. The process of turning literature into data removes distinction itself. It removes taste. It removes all the refinement from criticism. It removes the history of the reception of works. *To the Lighthouse* is just another novel in its pile of novels.

Moreover, for others, rather than working with original sources, the digital humanities deal with digital objects, at once removed and qualitatively different from their originals (i.e., they are representations of representations), which inevitably will have an effect on their interpretation.

For many, then, the digital humanities are fostering weak, surface analysis, rather than deep, penetrating insight. They are thus critiqued for being overly reductionist and crude in their techniques, sacrificing complexity, specificity, context, depth and critique for scale, breadth, automation, descriptive patterns, and the impression that interpretation does not require deep contextual knowledge. Thus, Jenkins (2013) argues:

> the value of the arts, the quality of a play or a painting, is not measurable. You could put all sorts of data into a machine: dates, colours, images, box office receipts, and none of it could explain what the artwork is, what it means, and why it is powerful. That requires man [sic], not machine … Whilst I am sure there is a place for big data, it doesn't apply to many aspects of human life. It won't improve the human condition. Love, art, culture and politics are all essential to our lives but big data will tell us little about them. To put it concisely: don't believe all the data hype. It's not the answer to the big questions.

Moreover, the limited funding directed at the humanities is being refocused onto digital humanities projects at the expense of more traditional studies, starving some areas of scholarship of funds. Such redistributional effects are also at work within the digital humanities field itself, where funding is often directed at building data infrastructures and creating new tools, rather than funding projects that utilise digital collections to answer more fundamental questions. The consequence is to channel funding toward software engineering, the development of analytic tools, hardware, labs, and other resourcing aspects, rather than humanities scholarship per se.

The same kinds of argument can be levelled at computational social science. For example, in a discussion concerning the visualisation of Wikipedia authorship, Fernanda B. Viégas of IBM Visual Communications Lab argues that a visual mapping of the data can 'help researchers identify questions that might be explored statistically – for example, how often does vandalism occur and how quickly does the text get reverted?' (quoted in Bollier 2010: 11). Such questions, however, are relatively mundane. In this case it might well reveal that a topic is hotly contested and the extent to which Wikipedia editors intervene in the editing of data entries, but does little to answer much more interesting, revealing and useful questions, such as the reasons and nature of a dispute and the alternative narratives that are being produced, neither of which is best examined through statistics. Similarly, a map of the language of tweets in a city might reveal patterns of geographic concentration of different ethnic communities, but the important questions are who constitutes such concentrations, why they exist, what were

the processes of formation and reproduction, and what their social and economic consequences are. It is one thing to identify patterns; it is another to
explain them, which requires social theory and deep contextual knowledge. In
such cases, the danger is that research is being practised simply because the data
are available, which greatly limits the questions that can be asked because the
data were not generated with those questions in mind (Vis 2013). As González-
Bailón (2013) argues,

> mapping the spatial distribution of positive emotions, or the frequency
> with which certain words are mentioned in online communication, does
> not tell us much about the correspondence of those patterns with the
> social dynamics that underlie and generate them ... Measuring things
> just because they can be measured does not make them interesting or
> relevant.

In cases such as tweet maps, the pattern revealed should rarely be the end point
(which it seems to have been in some projects; Rogers 2013), but rather the
starting point, which almost certainly is going to require other forms of analysis
and most likely other datasets.

Just as with earlier critiques of quantitative and positivist social sciences,
computational social sciences are taken to task by post-positivists as being
mechanistic, atomising and parochial, reducing diverse individuals and complex,
multidimensional social structures to mere data points (Wyly, in press).
Moreover, the analysis is riddled with assumptions of social determinism, as
exemplified by Pentland (2012): 'the sort of person you are is largely determined by your social context, so if I can see some of your behaviors, I can infer
the rest, just by comparing you to the people in your crowd'. In contrast,
human societies, it is argued, are too complex, contingent and messy to be
reduced to formulae and laws, with quantitative models providing little insight
into explaining phenomena such as wars, genocide, domestic violence and rac-
ism (though quantitative data can illuminate aspects of them), and only circum-
scribed insight into other human systems such as the economy, inadequately
accounting for the role of politics, ideology, social structures, and culture
(Harvey 1972). People do not act in rational, predetermined ways, but rather
live lives full of contradictions, paradoxes, and unpredictable occurrences. How
societies are organised and operate varies across time and space and there is no
optimal or ideal form, or universal traits. Indeed, there is an incredible diversity
of individuals, cultures and modes of living across the planet. Reducing this
complexity to the abstract subjects that populate universal models does large
symbolic violence to how we create knowledge. Further, positivistic approaches
wilfully ignore the metaphysical aspects of human life (concerned with meanings, beliefs, experiences) and normative questions (ethical and moral dilemmas

on methodology

about how things should be as opposed to how they are) (Kitchin 2006). In other words, positivistic approaches only focus on certain kinds of questions, which they seek to answer in a reductionist way that seemingly ignores what it means to be human and to live in richly diverse societies and places. This is not to say that quantitative approaches are not useful – they quite patently are, especially with regards to explaining and modelling instrumental systems – but their limitations in understanding human life should be recognised and complemented with other approaches.

Brooks (2013b) thus contends that big data analytics: struggles with the social (people are not rationale and do not behave in predictable ways; human systems are incredibly complex, having contradictory and paradoxical relation); struggles with context (data are largely shorn of the social, political and economic and historical context); creates bigger haystacks (consisting of many more spurious correlations making it difficult to identify needles); has trouble addressing big problems (especially social and economic ones); favours memes over masterpieces (identifies trends but not necessarily significant features that may become a trend); and obscures values (of the data producers and those that analyse them and their objectives).

They do this because, as explained by Peter Gould (1981: 174), himself an advocate of statistical approaches to data analysis:

> our symbolic mathematical languages seem terribly constrained and limiting. Often they are damaging in that they not only limit, but actually crush out of existence that which might be open to our paying heed. If we project, as we so frequently do, the multidimensional nature that characterizes the complexity of contemporary life onto ... the spaces produced by that linear strainer called factor analysis, we may well crush information out of existence in the name of simplification. I am not sure exactly why we do this, except I have an almost certain feeling that the availability of large and fast computers, with 'on the shelf' programs, has something to do with it.

For Gould, understanding human behaviour and societies cannot and should not be reduced to rote, methodical and mechanistic analysis, and he called for sustained thinking about what kinds of techniques should be applied to what kinds of data, in what circumstances, to answer specific questions, rather than data being run through a statistical sausage factory that produces low-grade, ground-up meat rather than choice cuts.

Beyond the epistemological and methodological approach, part of the issue is that some big data analysis seems to be generated with no specific questions in mind, or the focus is driven by the application of a method or the content of the dataset rather than a particular question, or the dataset is being used to seek an answer to a question that it was never designed to answer in the first place. With respect to the latter, geotagged Twitter data have not been produced to provide answers with respect to the geographical concentration of language groups in a city and the processes driving such spatial autocorrelation. We should perhaps not be surprised then that it only provides a surface snapshot, albeit an interesting snapshot, rather than deep penetrating insights into the geographies of race, language, agglomeration and segregation in particular locales. It is for these reasons that small data studies will continue to be valuable.

In defence of the approach adopted by the digital humanities, Manovich (2011) contends that the aim is not to replace human experts with computers, but to use analytics to explore massive datasets (such as a billion tweets, or a million YouTube videos, or ten thousand novels) and then select particular representative objects for closer manual analysis. In other words, the digital humanities approach 'opens up the possibility for wide scale "surface" studies (across people) *as well as, rather than instead of,* "depth" studies (focused on a small number of individuals)' (Manovich 2011; my emphasis). Likewise, others argue that the approach spares 'the grunt work of poring through thousands of pages of news or watching hundreds of hours of programming', so that researchers 'can actually focus their energy on explaining' (Harris 2012). Thus Flaounas et al. (2013: 111) suggest:

> The automation of many tasks in news content analysis will not replace the human judgment needed for fine-grained, qualitative forms of analysis, but it allows researchers to focus their attention on a scale far beyond the sample sizes of traditional forms of content analysis. Rather than spending precious labour on the coding phase of raw data, analysts could focus on designing experiments and comparisons to test their hypotheses, leaving to computers the task of finding all articles of a given topic, measuring various features of their content such as their readability, use of certain forms of language, sources etc. (just a few of the tasks that can now be automated).

Likewise, Selisker (2012) argues that the digital humanities do not seek to 'replace literature with computer code, or to trade literary complexity for mindless formulae. Instead, these projects are merely thinking in creative ways about literary-historical problems that couldn't be easily addressed without computers'. For Ramsay (2003; 2010) computation can aid the process of interpretation. He contends that close reading involves the practices of selecting, isolating and noticing of patterns in texts, and that code is very efficient at such practices, and moreover does so in more objective and consistent ways than the subjective gaze of a scholar. Rather than replacing the identification of meaning, for him the employment of algorithms facilitates such a process.

The defence of computational social science is often quite different. Whereas nearly all digital humanists recognise the value of close readings, and stress how distant readings complement them by providing depth and contextualisation, positivistic forms of social science are oppositional to post-positivist approaches. The difference between the humanities and social sciences in this respect is because the statistics used in the digital humanities are largely descriptive – identifying patterns and plotting them as counts, graphs, and maps. In contrast, the computational social sciences employ the scientific method, complementing descriptive statistics with inferential statistics that seek to identify causality. In other words, they are underpinned by an epistemology wherein the aim is to produce sophisticated statistical models that explain, simulate and predict human life. This is much more difficult to reconcile with post-positivist approaches. The defence then rests on the utility and value of the method and models, not on providing complementary analysis of a more expansive set of data. There are alternatives to this position, such as that adopted within critical GIS (Geographic Information Science) and radical statistics, and those who utilise mixed-method approaches, that either employ models and inferential statistics while being mindful of their shortcomings, or more commonly only utilise descriptive statistics that are complemented with small data studies. Here, big and small data are used to provide different but complementary insights. Regardless of such complementarity, many post-positivists will continue to resist big data and statistical approaches in its various forms, and the debate will no doubt rumble on for the foreseeable future.

CONCLUSION

There is little doubt that the data revolution offers the possibility to reframe the epistemology of science, social science and humanities, and such a reframing is already actively taking place. Big data and the scaling of small data into data infrastructures enable the implementation of new approaches to data generation and analyses that make it possible to ask and answer questions in new ways. This has led some to make bold claims that the data revolution is a disruptive innovation that is ushering in a paradigm shift in how research is conducted. It is certainly the case that the shift from a data desert to a data deluge and new data analytics will transform research praxis. However, care needs to be taken in making assertions about the reframing of research and about the best path forward in such a reframing.

Science is ill served by arguments that the data revolution means that 'data can speak for themselves' or that it can unproblematically employ techniques such as data dredging, with correlation superseding causation (see Chapter 9).

Much more productive are approaches being developed within data-driven science that blend aspects of abduction, induction and deduction, where the scientific method is reframed rather than subverted. The philosophical under-pinnings of data-driven science are, however, in their infancy and there is a need for its epistemological tenets, principles and methodology to be thought through and elaborated.

The situation in the humanities and social sciences is somewhat more complex given the diversity of their philosophical underpinnings, with the data revolution being unlikely to lead to the establishment of a new paradigm. Rather, data infrastructures and big data will enhance the suite of data available for analysis and enable new approaches and techniques, but will not replace small data studies. As with the sciences, there is a need for wider critical reflection on the epistemological implications of the data revolution for the humanities and social sciences, a task that has barely begun to be tackled despite the speed of change in the data landscape.

9

TECHNICAL AND ORGANISATIONAL ISSUES

As discussed in the previous two chapters, data infrastructures, open data initiatives and the production of big data offer a range of new opportunities for measuring and understanding the world. They also pose a range of technical and organisational issues, and normative and ethical questions. In this chapter, the focus is on the former, concentrating on issues such as the scope of datasets, access to data, the quality of data, data integration and interoperability, the application of analytics and ecological fallacies, and skills and organisational capabilities and capacities. Some of these issues can be tackled through technical and management solutions, whereas others are more intractable and difficult to address. However, if issues concerning data quality and ecological fallacies cannot be adequately be addressed, then it does not matter what epistemology is employed (see Chapter 8), the analysis and interpretation will be suspect. Moreover, if access to data is tightly restricted, or if businesses, governments and civil society lack adequate skills to make sense of data, then the value and benefits of scaled, big and open data will be highly constrained. Consequently, the issues discussed in this chapter cannot be ignored or easily dismissed, and demand attention. In the next chapter, the focus turns to wider social and political issues concerning the generation, sharing, analysis and use of data, considering the ethical, security and legal dimensions of the data revolution.

DESERTS AND DELUGES

For all the talk of a data revolution it is often remarkably difficult to source a decent set of data with respect to many phenomena, especially data that are longitudinal and spatially resolute. Partly this is an issue of coverage and partly one of access. With respect to coverage, all sources of data are limited in sample, geographical extent, time, and indexical and attribute variables. Indeed, the world is vastly complex and it is impossible to capture a whole domain and all of its nuances, contradictions and paradoxes. Data generated from small data studies are explicitly samples, are generated on a non-continuous basis, and have a restricted number of variables given their tight focus and the cost to generate and analyse. Most are one-off studies or experiments that concentrate on particular cases (a specific group, institution, species, place, technology, etc.), and lack a longitudinal component. Those that study change over time are usually repeated at set intervals. Our understanding of a phenomenon is then usually based on a restricted set of data. Even when datasets are combined and scaled up within data infrastructures, the coverage is partial and selective. For example, Irish public administration datasets have a limited coverage, are full of gaps and silences about basic sectors such as housing and transport, and are often locked inside institutions (Kitchin et al. 2007).

Similarly, big data may seek to be exhaustive, but as with other datasets are both a representation and a sample, and they only partially solve the data desert issue. As noted in Chapter 2, what data are captured is shaped by the technology used, the context in which data are generated, and the data ontology employed. The data generated are usually what is relatively straightforward to capture, which is often a by-product of a system, and its immediate scope is limited by domain (e.g., supermarket chain, sensor network, social media site). In terms of science, big data are presently only being generated with respect to a select set of topics and are far from being rolled out across all scientific domains and foci. Moreover, resolution is not fixed but is scaled and focused to provide a variety of views, each of which compromises some element of what is captured (breadth, depth, detail, etc.). Even when combined with other datasets their scope is far from universal. Big data then do not, as yet, address the issue of data deserts with respect to many fields of study.

At the same time, while data deserts continue to exist, data infrastructures and big data have created a data deluge in some domains. As noted in Chapter 4, there has been a marked growth in the volume and velocity of data production (that is set to grow rapidly as new sources are created and rolled out), the complexity of datasets generated, and the ability to link data together. This deluge creates a number of challenges with respect to handling, processing, securing, storing and making sense of such data (Gantz and Reinsel 2011). Rather than small, discontinuous datasets, analysts are trying to cope with vast quantities of data being firehosed from a thick pipe. Much of these data become transient and are lost, never analysed or exploited. Others are dumped into data stores as largely 'unsupervised landfill' (Asay 2013), being held until such times as they can deliver up useful information. As a consequence, as the percentage of data increases exponentially, the percentage that is processed and analysed is shrinking (Zikopoulos et al. 2012). Wu (2012) thus notes that as data grow, less information is gained as a proportion of the data. In other words, the noise of data increases dramatically but the signal of information grows less, and moreover can be more difficult to isolate within the noise (see Silver 2012). This is inevitably a function of big data and data science being in their infancy, with the full potential of new techniques that can monitor, process and analyse vast quantities of data in real-time as yet largely unrealised. Even as big data analytics matures, it is likely to struggle to create methods that can extract detailed, rather than surface-level, analysis; to tackle 'why' as well as 'what' questions; to provide explanation rather than description (see Chapter 8). Moreover, it will need to diversify to cope with new forms of data created by innovative sources. Even so, keeping pace with the deluge and extracting a meaningful signal from the noise will be an ongoing struggle.

ACCESS

The other main blockage to sourcing decent datasets is how accessible they are and the licensing restrictions that define the parameters of use. Clearly, as discussed in Chapters 2 and 3, access is a key issue with respect to publicly funded research and data generated by public agencies. Data archives and infrastructures, and open data initiatives, are all centrally concerned with sharing and making data available for analysis. As the discussion in those chapters illustrates, despite the fact data are non-rivalrous, non-excludable and have marginal costs for replication (Floridi 2010), data are commonly restricted in distribution. In some cases, limited access to data is desirable given their sensitive and personal nature and ethical concerns related to their circulation and use (see Chapter 10). In others, data are limited in access to ensure that those who hold them can maximise their value and gain competitive advantage or leverage income through their sale or licensing (see Chapter 7). In others, an agency might seek to limit distribution for fear of what the data might reveal, which could have political or economic consequences, or in dread of exposing the poor quality of the data held.

While these barriers are slowly being eroded with respect to publicly generated and funded data in Western democratic countries, such moves are more patchy with respect to data generated by private interests. Indeed, it is somewhat of a paradox that despite the emerging big data deluge, access to such data is at present limited, with only a handful of entities drowning in such data (boyd and Crawford 2012; King 2011). Companies such as mobile phone operators, app developers, social media providers, financial institutions, retail chains, and surveillance and security firms are under no obligation to share freely the data they generate through their operations. Access to data is usually individually negotiated and involves signing a series of intellectual property right and non-disclosure agreements, as well as agreeing to terms and conditions that set out how and for what purposes the data can and cannot be used. Even then the data supplied are likely to be a limited sample (which might also lack contextual information as to how they were sampled), or be largely unprocessed (not cleaned or structured), or be aggregated, or stripped of useful variables, or manipulated in some way, that restricts modes of analysis. In some cases, a limited amount of the data might be made available to researchers or the public through Application Programming Interfaces (APIs). APIs consist of a set of commands that can be used to retrieve data stored in a databases on a publicly accessible server (Manovich 2011). For example, Twitter allows a few companies to access its firehose (stream of data) for a fee for commercial purposes (and have the latitude to dictate terms with respect to what can be done with such data), but researchers are restricted to a 'gardenhose' (c.10 per cent of public tweets), a 'spritzer' (c.1 per cent of public tweets), or to different subsets of content ('white-listed' accounts), with private and protected tweets excluded in all cases (boyd and Crawford 2012). In the case of websites (e.g., product listings and reviews, business directories) and social media (e.g., public profiles and feeds), companies such as 80legs (www.80legs.com/) and Mozenda (www.mozenda.com) provide webcrawling and scraping services to custom harvest data from such sites or access pre-built data feeds.

The worry is that the insights that privately owned and commercially sold big data can provide will be limited to the business sector, or maybe only opened to a privileged set of academic researchers whose findings cannot be replicated or validated (Lazer et al. 2009; King 2011). Neither scenario serves the public interest, but given the commercial value of the data in question leveraging access will be no simple task. The fact that socially and culturally rich big data are largely in the hands of private interests means that, at present, computational social science and digital humanities research is not necessarily easy to do in practice (Manovich 2011). As boyd and Crawford (2012: 673) note: 'Much of the enthusiasm surrounding big data stems from the perception that it offers easy access to massive amounts of data. But who gets access? For what purposes? In what contexts? And with what constraints?' These are all questions that require much further reflection and action.

DATA QUALITY, VERACITY AND LINEAGE

The quality and veracity of data are important because they underpin the extent to which one can trust the conclusions drawn from analysis. Data quality concerns how clean (error and gap free), untainted (bias free) and consistent (few discrepancies) the data are. Veracity refers to the authenticity of the data and the extent to which it accurately (precision) and faithfully (fidelity) represents what it is meant to. Establishing and documenting data quality and veracity is a key aspect of data lineage. Data lineage is

> information that describes the source of the observations, data collection and compilation methodologies, conversions, transformations, analyses, and derivations to which the data have been subjected. It also provides the assumptions and the criteria applied at any stage of its life, as well as any biases ... [L]ineage provides a dataset with its pedigree and allows the user to decide on its fitness for use. (Lauriault 2012)

It also details the provenance of the data. Weak data quality, veracity and lineage erode the degree of confidence and trust one can place in a dataset and analyses based upon it.

In traditional, data-scarce studies where sample sizes are typically small, data quality, veracity and lineage are of paramount importance. If one is going to infer conclusions about an entire population from a small, representative sample, that sample needs to be as clean and untainted as possible and have a high degree of precision and fidelity. Yet very few datasets are created fully formed and can be used without some form of data scrubbing, that is, checking for and correcting errors, adding missing data, and standardising and reformatting data so they can be combined with other data or are amenable to certain methods of analysis (see Chapter 6). Much work is thus expended on research design to limit sampling and methodological biases and to ensure that data are as rigorous and robust as possible before they are analysed or shared. Archives and infrastructures actively work to make sure that such data are kept reliable, accurate and authentic over time, maintaining data lineage through organisational stability, data and metadata management processes, and technological handshaking across generations (moving data across formats and platforms) (Lauriault 2012). Without such work the veracity of the data contained within them would soon diminish as trust dissipates.

In contrast, it has been argued by some that big data studies do not need the same standards of data quality and veracity because the exhaustive nature (n = all) of the dataset removes sampling biases and more than compensates for any errors or gaps or inconsistencies in the data or weakness in fidelity (Mayer-Schonberger and Cukier 2013). The argument for such a view is that 'with less error from sampling we can accept more measurement error' (p. 13) and 'tolerate inexactitude' (p. 16). The price of n = all is to embrace messiness, created in large part by the difficulty of cleansing high-velocity, often unstructured, data, and to accept data as being 'more probabilistic than precise' (p. 35). Viewed in this way, Mayer-Schonberger and Cukier (2013: 13) thus argue 'more trumps better'. Or to put it another way, '[i]f you have too much data, then "good enough" is good enough' (Helland 2011). Franks (2012: 211) thus argues that what is required is 'clean-enough data'; data that enables analysts to 'get the results that they can believe in'. Of course, this presumes that all uses of big data will tolerate inexactitude, when in fact many big data applications do require precision, or at least data with calculable error parameters. For example, OpenStreetMap aims to be as detailed and accurate as professional map prod-ucts, and needs to be for its users to trust it as a source of information. Similarly, Wikipedia seeks to be as accurate and authoritative as other encyclopaedias. Likewise, financial data or medical data need to be accurate and precise to instil confidence in traders, doctors and patients, and the list goes on. Such a view-point also presumes that data lineage and issues of data integrity and trust are not important to data users.

Regardless of the tolerance of some big data datasets to inexactitude, the warning 'garbage in, garbage out' still holds. Big datasets that generate dirty, gamed or biased data, or data with poor fidelity, are going to produce analysis and conclusions that have weakened validity and deliver fewer benefits to those that analyse and seek to exploit them. And by dint of their method of production big data can suffer from all of these ails. The data can be dirty through instrument error, even across technologies assumed to be highly accurate such as GPS which varies in precision by device, geographic context, user proficiency, and the num-ber of satellites available at any one time (Dodge and Kitchin 2013). Or the data might be gamed or faked through false accounts or hacking to influence trend-ing and direct clickstream trails (Vis 2013). For example, there are hundreds of thousands of fake Twitter accounts, constituting $c.4$ per cent of Twitter's user base (De Micheli and Stroppa 2013), with up to 46 per cent of some brands' Twitters followers being bots (Calzolari 2012), and more than two dozen services sell fake Twitter accounts (Baym 2013).

Data can be biased for a number of reasons. The demographics being sampled are rarely universal and are skewed by gender, race, income, location and other social and economic factors (not everybody uses Twitter or Facebook, or shops in a particular store, or is on a particular phone network, etc.) (Bollier 2010; Graham 2012; Crampton et al. 2012). The technology being used and their work-ing parameters affect the nature of the data. For example, which posts on social media are most read or shared can be strongly affected by ranking algorithms not simple interest (Baym 2013). Similarly, APIs structure what data are extracted, for example in Twitter only capturing specific hashtags associated with an event rather than all relevant tweets (Bruns 2013), with González-Bailón et al. (2012) finding that different methods of accessing Twitter data – search APIs versus streaming APIs – produced quite different sets of results. As a consequence, there is no guarantee that two teams of researchers attempting to gather the same data at the same time will end up with identical datasets (Bruns 2013). Further, the choice of metadata and variables that are being generated and which ones are being ignored paint a particular picture. Such biases 'skew, or even render invisible, ideas, trends, people, and patterns that aren't mirrored or represented in the dataset' (Graham 2012).

With respect to fidelity it is not always the case that the data truly represent that which they are being used to measure. For example, there are question marks over the extent to which social media posts really represent peoples' views and the faith that should be placed in them. Manovich (2011: 6) warns that '[p]eoples' posts, tweets, uploaded photographs, comments, and other types of online participation are not transparent windows into their selves; instead, they are often carefully curated and systematically managed' (though the same critique applies to interview and focus group data). Others have queried the veracity of crowdsourced and citizen science data, warning of the ignorance and unpredictability of crowds and the risks of uneven (in terms of coverage), variable (in terms of consistency and quality) and biased data generation inherent in egalitarian, largely leaderless projects that have a narrow demographic who are diverse in skills and motivation (Carr 2007). Indeed, social media are dominated by unrepresentative digital elites (Crutcher and Zook 2009) and large sections of society, such as the poor and elderly, do not engage in social media or they lack smart phones and therefore any data collected do not necessarily reflect their views or neighbourhoods (Crawford 2013). It is therefore imperative to determine and take such biases into account when analysing the data to gain a more holistic understanding of a phenomenon, especially if these are to be used in public policy and decisions that affect people's lives (e.g., health outcomes).

Moreover, there are concerns about the quality and consistency of content and metadata created across diversely skilled/motivated individuals, and how to provide documented degrees of reliability and generate a sense of trustworthiness (Dodge and Kitchin 2013). This has led some to posit that 'amateur', crowdsourced labour is best expended on data verification and correction, not creation (Carr 2007). The example Carr highlights is Wikipedia, which although popular and extensive, has grown in a haphazard way that matches the selective interests of participants, and has incomplete, sometimes poorly written, trivial and highly contested articles which undermine its authority and usability. Carr contends that 'if Wikipedia weren't free, it is unlikely its readers would be so forgiving of its failings' (2007: 4). OpenStreetMap can suffer from a lack of coverage in some areas where there are few volunteers. There are also concerns as to the sustainability of volunteered crowdsourced labour, with Carr (2007) arguing that the connections that bind a virtual crowd together are often superficial, lacking depth and obligatory commitment, are liable to dispersion, and are reliant on a small core group to keep the project going and provide the bulk of the labour. In contrast, others have noted with respect to OpenStreetMap, that the quality of data produced matches that of professional companies, and that the coverage is diverse (Haklay 2010; Mooney et al. 2011).

What this discussion highlights is that just because a dataset is huge in volume, it is not necessarily random, representative, clean, has fidelity, or is trustworthy. As boyd and Crawford (2012) note: 'Just because big data presents us with large quantities of data does not mean that methodological issues are no longer relevant. Understanding sample, for example, is more important now than ever' (p. 668). For Kelling et al. (2009: 615) this is an issue of provenance: 'information regarding the origins, identification, ownership, and structure' of datasets that enables their analysts to know how the data were generated and processed and to assess the quality and veracity of the data. And yet, the provenance of most big datasets is limited to those who generate the data, making it difficult to assess the validity of published studies based upon them. A key challenge for big data is to be able to detail lineage, including assessments of the levels of error and uncertainty in the dataset, and to create effective means to check, clean and standardise high-velocity, varied data.

DATA INTEGRATION AND INTEROPERABILITY

Part of the promise of the data revolution is the creation of datasets that have strong relationality which enables them to be combined to generate additional insights and value.

As is evidenced by the development of data infrastructures and data consolidators, many data are amenable to being conjoined. However, it is also clear that many data remain isolated in silos or can only be combined through significant additional processing. For data to be integrated into new datasets, or used in conjunction with any other, they require shared indexical fields and data standards, consistent metadata, and compatible organisation and format. While there has been much progress in data management, the rolling out of data standards, driven by organisations such as International Organisation for Standardisation (IOS), World Wide Web Consortium (W3C) and Open Geospatial Consortium (OGC), the aligning of data and metadata, and improved interoperability between different technological platforms that hold and process data, including the development of linked data, many datasets cannot be linked together. They constitute what Singh (2012) terms 'stranded data'.

Most small data studies still create stranded data because they use their own data ontologies and systems of data organisation that are fit for their purposes, but little consider wider issues of scaling and linking. This is often also the case within organisations, with separate departments using their own systems of management and classification. For example, in Ireland each of the 88 planning authorities uses its own land-use and zoning classification system. Moreover, they employ several different technological platforms for managing, storing and mapping the data. Combining these data into a single, national system is no easy task. Similarly, scaling up national datasets encounters similar problems. For example, linking together the Irish and Northern Irish censuses to create a single dataset for the whole island poses a number of technical challenges because only 30 per cent of the questions are the same, and another 35 per cent can be made to match through disaggregating classification schemes and reaggregating into common schemes; even then the data have different under-lying statistical geographies (they are aggregated into units that vary in size) (Kitchin et al. 2007).

These issues are multiplied across Europe, with each state and its institutions employing varying measures (units and classifications), temporalities (how often the data are generated), spatialities (the statistical geography), and tech-nologies (formats). Ruppert (2012: 118) thus concludes that even when there is extensive state data, it is most often 'struggling under the weight of myriad non-interoperable and often incomparable and conflicting datasets'. Initiatives such as the INSPIRE directive (Infrastructure for Spatial Information in the European Community) seek to produce common data across a shared European statistical geography, but producing alignment is a slow process because no state wants to unilaterally move to a new data system and in the process break their temporal record and lose their ability to conduct time series analysis, and each has different priorities with respect to what data it wants to generate and track.

The same challenges exist with respect to big data, which can be highly het-erogeneous, unstructured and variable in quality, as well as being flexible and extensible. Combining such data is no easy task and requires the development of a new set of tools and techniques, as well as the creation and adoption of new data standards. One solution, noted by Short et al. (2011), is ad hoc data integration, that enables users to control, on the fly, which data are to be inte-grated, though this requires the dataset to have certain qualities such as signifi-cant semantic infrastructure. Combining such data can also lead to cross-contamination with poor-quality, low-veracity data tainting more robust datasets and rendering them weak. As the data deluge grows, finding solutions to enable data integration and conjunction that retains integrity and robustness will be a pressing issue, though the inability to join data also has its positive aspects with respect to limiting dataveillance and improving data security (see Chapter 10).

POOR ANALYSIS AND ECOLOGICAL FALLACIES

All conclusions from studies are only as sound as the data used and the analysis conducted. Beyond data quality and veracity, within any research design it is important that an appropriate methodology and suitable techniques of analysis are employed. Failing to do so leads to severe ecological fallacies in the interpretation of the findings; that is, drawing conclusions that are fallacious and are not in fact supported by the data. There is a long history of debates concerning the relative strengths and weaknesses of different methodological approaches and techniques, and the circumstances in which they can be validly applied. In general, there are now well established guidelines and rules for how different kinds of data should be generated and analysed across disciplines. However, with respect to big data, data science is in its infancy and such norms are in the process of being formulated. New techniques are being invented, extended and evaluated.

Four methodological issues concerning big data analysis have attracted attention: assumptions and approximations within models can yield profoundly different answers (Silver 2012); the extent to which techniques induce apophenia (seeing patterns in random or meaningless data) or over-learning (overfitting) (boyd and Crawford 2012) or mistaking noise for information (Silver 2012; Siegel 2013); accusations that certain techniques constitute little more than data dredging (Webster 2011); and whether techniques can scale beyond test control data to trillions of real world, streaming records (Bryant et al. 2008).

Models seek to explain and express the relationships between variables and how a system works. Each model is founded on a theory, and is built using a set of assumptions and approximations as to how variables interact, with the validity of the model tested through empirical research. If the theory and its assumptions are wrong, then its predictions will be too. Even minor changes in a model's assumptions can lead to quite different results. In the case of the 2008 financial crisis, Silver (2012) argues that a highly significant factor in its production was the use of finance models that conflated risk (where the probability of a likely outcome could be calculated) with uncertainty (risk where the odds are very difficult to estimate). As a result, the models were based on uncertain assumptions but treated as if they were fully knowable risks. The consequence was to assume that novel securities that held massive systemic uncertainty were assets of low risk, an assumption that proved to be false. And in complex systems, such 'mistakes are not measured in degrees but in whole orders of magnitude. S&P and Moody's underestimated the default risk associated with CDOs (collateralized debt obligation) by a factor of two hundred' (Silver 2012: 45). Whatever the quality of the underlying data, if the model is faulty, any conclusions drawn from the model will be erroneous.

Granville (2013) and Taleb (2013) posit that the curse or tragedy of big data is multiple, falsely positive relationships between data; patterns in the dataset that are entirely coincidental, have no predictive power, are not replicable, and could be masking weaker patterns that are of significance. Datasets often contain data that appear to be associated even when the relationship is actually random. As the size of the dataset increases, the number of false positives multiplies, to the point where almost every relationship between data is statistically significant by the standards of traditional correlation tests (Pentland 2012; Rajaraman et al. 2012; Taleb 2013). Similarly, in data-mining techniques, such as decision trees, the model can be overfitted so that exceptional findings are extrapolated into generalisable findings thus producing ecological fallacies. Big data does not then mean better knowledge, but rather more confusion due to the difficulty of spotting a true signal in a mass of signals; 'sometimes less is more' (Verhulst, cited in Bollier 2010: 14).

A significant aspect of the problem of false positives is not solely the size of the dataset, but how the dataset is processed and analysed. Part of the strategy of much big data analytics is to examine a dataset prior to formulating hypotheses (see Chapter 6). One way to do this is to calculate correlations between all variables to identify potential relationships between data that are worthy of further examination. This process constitutes data dredging (sometimes called data fishing), a practice that is severely frowned upon by many statisticians (Webster 2011; Piatetsky-Shapiro 2012). The problem of such an approach is twofold. First, it identifies potentially thousands of false positives without determining which ones are random and which are significant. Second, it can lead to the cherry-picking and presentation of findings that confirm an analyst's beliefs, with the evidence from the analysis used to make the claim seem reasonable and considered (Webster 2011; Taleb 2013). The thorny question, as Granville (2013) notes, is how to discriminate between a real and an accidental signal in vast amounts of data? How not to succumb to apophenia or overlearning?

There are a couple of potential solutions. Rajaraman et al. (2012: 5) suggest using the Bonferroni principle, which seeks to identify events that are so rare that they are unlikely to occur in random data, in order to sort real associations from random. Lusk (2013) argues for the use of enhanced standard levels, citing the five-sigma threshold now used in physics to counter spurious correlations and claim discovery (1 in 3.5 million chance that the result was due to statistical fluctuations). Another solution is to cross-validate with other datasets, or to randomly divide the existing dataset into samples and to see if the relationship holds across samples (Jensen 2000). With respect to overlearning, H.J. Miller (2010) discusses the strategy of using background knowledge, which consists of utilising known facts about the dataset derived from assumptions about the system, observable facts, expert knowledge, or theory, or interestingness measures, that assess the simplicity, certainty, utility and novelty of the generated patterns, to separate the meaningful patterns from the noise. It is clear, however, that more work is needed to develop techniques for evaluating significance and meaningfulness in an era of big data.

Given that new data analytics are in their early stages of development, and have predominantly been applied to control, test data, there are also concerns as to the robustness of such techniques to cope with messy, uncontrolled data. As Bryant et al. (2008: 4) note, '[m]any algorithms do not scale beyond datasets of a few million elements or cannot tolerate the statistical noise and gaps found in real-world data'. If there are flaws or biases built into the algorithms these will skew the findings and their interpretation (boyd and Crawford 2012). Aligned to this concern is an anxiety that there is an over-reliance and too much faith being placed in algorithms to undertake analysis, screening out the benefits that human experience, knowledge and intuition would bring to understanding a phenomenon (Lohr 2012). Thus, work remains to be done in establishing and evaluating the integrity of new analytics and the confidence of the conclusions that can be drawn from them.

One other critique of big data analysis is its focus on the here and now; given its newness, in general, big data lack historical depth. New sensor networks or crowdsourced data might provide rich and continuous data, but have short longitudinal timelines. As a consequence, much of the analysis is timely but lacks temporal depth. That is fine if one is interested in the present, such as using social media to track an unfolding event (e.g., a major political moment such as the Arab Spring), or one is analysing a physical process that is unchanging over time (e.g., a physics experiment), but is more problematic when being used to understand processes which unfold over thousands of years or more (e.g., environmental and geological systems). Such a critique, of course, also holds for many small data studies, which are also snapshots taken at particular places and times.

SKILLS AND HUMAN RESOURCING

While some data analysis is ceded to algorithms, especially the grunt work of processing and calculating, direction and interpretation is still largely the preserve of a human analyst. Drawing on their skills, experience, and knowledge, researchers and analysts make decisions concerning where to focus attention, how to frame and undertake analysis, and make sense of the findings and act upon them. People then remain key actors in building, maintaining and running data-driven projects. For example, constructing a data infrastructure requires software and hardware engineers, digital curators, policy and requirements specialists, and domain experts and analysts. These workers ensure a decent system design that generates useful, valid and reliable data, provides the means to store and share data, and a suite of appropriate management and analytic tools, that can extract value and knowledge. And they know what questions to ask and what to do with the answers. Human talent then is a premium commodity. But as a number of reports have highlighted there is an emerging shortage of staff with data skills, especially data analysts and managers who can turn data and information into knowledge and wisdom (Gantz and Reinsel 2011; Manyika et al. 2011; Shah et al. 2012; Rooney 2012).

Manyika et al. (2011: 3) contends that '[t]he United States alone faces a shortage of 140,000 to 190,000 people with deep analytical skills as well as 1.5 million managers and analysts to analyse big data and make decisions based on their findings'. They go on to note that such talent is 'difficult to produce, taking years of training' or retraining (p. 10). Shah et al. (2012) evaluated 5,000 employees at 12 global companies as to their ability to handle data analytics in a productive way. They grouped employees into three groups: 'unquestioning empiricists' who trust analysis over judgement (43 per cent), 'visceral decision makers' who ignore analysis and go with their gut instincts (19 per cent), and 'informed skeptics' (38 per cent) who balance judgement and analysis, seeking to interpret and contextualise data in making decisions. Worryingly, those who 'let the data speak for themselves' and those who routinely ignore data and analytics, outnumber those best able to make sense of big data. Moreover, they observe that companies suffer from four problems that hinder them in leveraging the potential of big data: analytic skills are concentrated in too few employees and do not trickle down to others; IT functions typically concentrate on the 'T' and much less on the 'I', which is where the value is gained; data storage is haphazard and it is difficult for any one employee to locate material if they were not responsible for its collection; managers understand the value of talent, capital and brand, but not of information and do not put enough effort into understanding data or organising it efficiently and effectively. Such skill shortages also exist in the academy, where domain experts trained in a time of data scarcity are largely unprepared for the era of data infrastructures and big data beyond a handful of scholars and centres.

The worry for many commentators is that the potential benefits of data-driven business and science will not be fully realised due to a shortage of human talent, in particular 'data scientists, who combine the skills of software programmer, statistician and storyteller/artist to extract the nuggets of gold hidden under mountains of data' (Cukier 2010), and managers who understand how to convert such nuggets into wise decisions. With respect to the latter, as Shah et al. (2012: 23) note, '[i]nvestments in analytics can be useless, even harmful, unless employees can incorporate that data into complex decision making'. Universities are now starting to create new data science programmes and research centres, and to adapt existing courses to include training in new skills sets, in an effort to ameliorate some skills gaps. Some of these programmes are being organised in conjunction with corporations. For example, IBM has begun to work with several universities to develop courses and curricula, and others such as Teradata are offering university-certified

Table 9.1 Expertise needed to build data infrastructures and conduct big data research

Domain expertise	• a deep theoretical and factual knowledge of relevant field(s) • familiarity with types of data to be examined, their provenance, and their significance to the relevant field(s) • the ability to identify knowledge gaps • familiarity with disciplinary literature and conventions • the ability to teach others from different backgrounds to appreciate all of the above
Data expertise	• an understanding of how data have been collected and curated and of relationships between material objects and digital representations of those objects (if applicable) • familiarity with data models and/or conventions of description • an understanding of how relevant data are accessed and stored • the ability to facilitate data-sharing and manual error-correction, both during and after the project • the ability to predict future or alternative uses for data • an understanding of new forms of publication that can incorporate data
Analytical expertise	• understand the strengths and weaknesses of individual research tools • select and customise appropriate tools to support research goals • predict problems that might arise with using the selected tool to perform project asks • predict and detect error rates in data and data analysis algorithms and choose statistical methods that account for these errors when appropriate • teach others to interpret results of analysis
Project management expertise	• an ability to frame project parameters • an ability to set appropriate goals and deadlines and to coordinate parallel work streams if necessary • an ability to select the most appropriate communication and documentation strategies for the project • a mastery of collaborative research tools • a strong desire to work toward outcomes that benefit all team members

Source: Adapted from Williford and Henry (2012: 16–20).

courses (Bertolucci 2013), though these run the risk of channelling students to particular corporate visions and software.

Data science is not the only expertise that needs to be produced. As Williford and Henry (2012) contend, building data infrastructures and conducting big data research requires the marriage of four kinds of expertise for successful delivery (see Table 9.1). These, Ruppert (2013) argues, can only be produced through an interdisciplinary and cross-sectoral approach, combining skills and viewpoints that cut across disciplines, and collaboration between the academy, industry and government. Until such time that a new generation of suitable talent matures, and cross-disciplinary/sector approaches develop, projects will be vulnerable to under-performing and failure.

CONCLUSION

This chapter has examined the technical shortcomings of scaled small data and big data. It has argued that big data has a number of issues that presently constrain its utility and development, not least the rather narrow scope of datasets, limited access to data, poor data quality, veracity and fidelity, ill-defined lineage, poor interoperability, suspect analytics and ecological fallacies, and a weakly developed skills base and organisational receptiveness. This has led Dembosky et al. (2012) to contend that '[e]arly movers may be overpromising and under-delivering', with those adopting big data solutions becoming 'jaded by technology that is so new and unrefined, it is more cumbersome and frustrating than helpful'. Over time many of these issues will be addressed to an extent through technical and management solutions, but there will continue to be concerns that require ongoing remedial work and diligence. The same is true for data infra-structures and open data projects. In fact, as noted here and in Chapter 3, many of the issues affecting big data afflict open data projects. For example, some open data sites are little more than data dumps of selective variables, being poorly organised with weakly structured and dirty data, and lacking full record sets, documentation, and policies for preservation, backup, auditing, reuse, privacy and ethics policies.

We need to be careful to recognise that the data revolution is in its infancy and has the qualities of an infant in terms of its maturity and development. At present, the rush seems to be to roll out systems with the aim of demonstrating potential and securing early market share without sufficient due diligence being paid to their trustworthiness, robustness and utility, or to management and human resource issues regarding organisational readiness and appropriate skill sets. Indeed, the mantra of some projects is to 'go ugly early' and to deal with issues arising on an unfolding basis. Consequently, tightly focused research designed to determine the nature and extent of the technical and organisational shortcomings of big data, open data and data infrastructures, and to find workable solutions that are widely applicable and easily implementable, is lagging behind other development work. Such research is vital, however, to produce systems that offer valid findings and conclusions, and which add sufficient value to the organisations adopting and using them. This research needs to be conducted across sectors and types of data to establish the issues and solutions pertaining to different data and systems. Moreover, there needs to be investment in re-skilling existing workers and training a new generation of data scientists. Without such research, big data, open data and data infrastructures will potentially suffer reputational damage that will slow their roll-out and adoption. Another set of issues that will also perform the same role are those relating to ethics and the social and political implications of new data systems, which is the focus of the next chapter.

10

ETHICAL, POLITICAL, SOCIAL AND LEGAL CONCERNS

As discussed in Chapter 7, data are generated and employed for many ends, including governing societies, managing organisations, leveraging profit, and regulating places. In all these cases, data are key inputs into systems that para-doxically are implemented in the name of making societies more secure, safe, competitive, productive, efficient, transparent and accountable, yet do so through processes that monitor, discipline, repress, persuade, coerce, and exploit people. There is a fine balance then between using data in emancipa-tory and empowering ways, and using data for one's own ends and to the detriment of others, or in ways contrary to the wishes of those the data rep-resent. It is not a case, however, that data are used simply in either good or bad ways; it is more complex than that. Often seemingly opposing outcomes are bound together so that people can be both liberated and coerced simultaneously – they gain personal benefit at the same time as they become enmeshed in a system that seeks to gain from their participation. In Althusser's (1971) terms, such an arrange-ment works through interpellation, ensnaring people in its logic through persua-sion and incentives. For example, supermarket loyalty cards provide customers with savings at the same time as they work to produce store loyalty and provide a rich seam of data that are used to try and sell more goods to those customers, thus increasing profits. Similarly, the price of being more secure from terrorist attacks is invasive surveillance of all members of society; citizens gain safety at the price of privacy.

The generation of data and the work these data do are inherently infused with ethical, social and political concerns. Such concerns have long been recognised and debated within scientific and public fora, leading to the creation of a raft of professional ethical guidelines and legislation that delimits how data are pro-duced, managed, shared and employed. No form of data generation and analysis is free from such concerns. Even scientific projects which are seemingly benign and neutral can raise ethical questions and have social and political consequences. For example, the measurement and modelling of environmental systems might seem like it is confined to understanding natural phenomena, but can also be used to shape policy that affects the people living within such systems. Such ethical debates are ongoing and evolve in tandem with the broader discursive realm concerning societal attitudes and opinions, and the development of new technologies. With respect to the latter, the scaling of small data into data infrastructures, the creation of an enormous data marketplace, the opening up of institutional data, and the flows of big data, pose fundamental ethical, social and political questions as they radically alter the data landscape. The volume and variety of data being generated about all aspects of daily life and the world we live in is growing exponentially and these data are ever more timely, resolute, exhaustive, and relational. What was private or unknown is increasingly being revealed to a diverse set of interests, and decision-making within government and business is becoming more data-driven, evidence-informed and technocratic.

This chapter examines a selection of the ethical, social, political and legal concerns that the data revolution raises, including dataveillance and data footprints and shadows, privacy, data security, profiling, social sorting and redlining, control creep, anticipatory governance, technocratic and corporate governance and technological lock-ins, and ownership and intellectual property. How each of these issues is thought about is contested, with views varying within and between science, companies, government and civil society, who have differing agendas, vested interests, and political sensibilities. Thus, there are no easy answers to resolving the issues discussed, and resolutions always consist of compromises. It is certain, therefore, that as the data revolution unfolds, the debates around these concerns are likely to intensify, especially as attempts are made to produce new legislation to address technological developments which enable new ways of generating, consolidating and analysing data, thus producing new issues and rendering old laws obsolete.

DATA SHADOWS AND DATAVEILLANCE

As discussed in previous chapters, an enormous amount of data are presently generated with respect to citizens in all nation states. The production and remit of such data is growing and widening, with state, corporate and civil society organisations actively seeking to capture data about their citizens, customers and members and their activities. Indeed, it is becoming increasingly more difficult to take part in daily life without leaving some trace of participation due to the mediating role of digital technologies, software and the use of indexical identifiers (Kitchin and Dodge 2011). Even if a buyer does not use a credit card to purchase goods in a store, their presence is recorded by surveillance cameras; even if a person uses an anonymous username on social media, their IP and MAC addresses are recorded. We thus routinely leave a trail of data in our wake, though we often have little control over its form, extent, or how it is used.

Koops (2011), for example, reports that the Dutch Data Protection Authority estimates that the average Dutch citizen is included in 250–500 databases, with more socially active people included in up to 1,000 databases. These databases not only include individuals' digital footprints (data they themselves leave behind) but also individuals' data shadows (information about them generated by others), and increasingly provide data trails of location and interactions and transactions across space and time (Clarke 1994a; Lyon 2007; Dodge and Kitchin 2005; Koops 2011). Moreover, whereas footprints and shadows are ephemeral, their digital counterparts are largely persistent and can be stored in databases indefinitely (Koops 2011), producing a world that potentially remembers all data points and never forgets (Dodge and Kitchin 2007b). These footprints and shadows are fragmented and dispersed, divided across dozens of organisations and servers, and are subject to integration and division (Raley 2013). At best, they constitute oligopticons – limited views from partial vantage points from fixed positions with defined view sheds (Amin and Thrift 2002) – rather than slotting together to create a panopticon; an all-seeing, god's-eye view. However, given the relationality of data and the value of data amplification, the trend is towards combining oligoptical views to create a more powerful visioning.

Collectively, data footprints and shadows provide a highly detailed record of an individual's daily life: their patterns of consumption, work, travel, communication, play, interactions with organisations, and their thoughts and interests. And it is not only individuals who are subject to such an intensive gaze, but also objects, institutions, transactions and territories (Dodge and Kitchin 2005). Never before has so much data about people and their social and economic worlds been so readily generated, and through data markets, infrastructures, and open data initiatives been so widely available. Indeed, gaining access to sensitive data is not the preserve of government, companies and organisations, with peer-to-peer surveillance becoming relatively straightforward to undertake without the subject's knowledge or permission (Andrejevic 2007). Of course, this was always possible through snooping and gossiping, but is now easier through the Internet (either through searching for or purchasing data) or by browsing the logs of digital devices (e.g., on a mobile phone, Internet browser, car satnav, etc.) or by installing relatively cheap surveillance devices such as miniature cameras. As discussed in Chapter 2, data brokers allow the histories of individuals to be examined with respect to issues such as marital status, solvency, property ownership, employment history, tax status, criminal records, sexual or domestic abuse allegations, educational background, and so on.

The data deluge is thus open to dataveillance and exploitation. Dataveillance is a mode of surveillance enacted through sorting and sifting datasets in order to identify, monitor, track, regulate, predict and prescribe (Clarke 1988; Raley 2013); it works to transform the complex myriad of actions and thoughts that data represents into a legible landscape and 'visible forms of order' (Curry et al. 2004: 359) and is a key component of modern forms of governance and governmentality. With respect to exploitation, as discussed in Chapter 7, data are being used to profile and target individuals with the aim of leveraging profit. Data are thus often being repurposed and used in ways that were never intended when generated. Dataveillance and data shadows thus raise a number of ancillary concerns especially with respect to issues such as privacy, profiling and social sorting, and enacting different modes of governance.

PRIVACY

Privacy is a condition that many people expect and value. It is considered a basic human right and is enshrined in national and supranational laws in various ways. In the United States it is mostly covered under the rubric of privacy laws, whereas in the European Union it falls within the realm of data protection (Minelli et al. 2013). It is a term that is multidimensional in its meaning and is often used in context-dependent ways, but generally refers to acceptable practices with regards to accessing and disclosing personal and sensitive information (Elwood and Leszczynski 2011). One way to unpack its multidimensionality is to examine the various ways in which it can be breached and their associated harms (Solove 2006; see Table 10.1). What is clear from this taxonomy is that breaching privacy can have a number of effects on the emotional and physical well-being of individuals, as well as opening them up to the pernicious activities of others and to asymmetric power imbalances.

There is little doubt that the concept of privacy is changing. As noted above, people are subject to much greater levels of scrutiny and modes of surveillance than ever before. Tasks that were considered largely private are now being monitored and recorded. For example, what programmes one watched on television used to be known only to those present in the room, whereas now cable companies can monitor what is being viewed on each television because one-way broadcasts have been replaced by a two-way connection. What one bought was only known by the customer and the person serving them, whereas now it is routinely collected through digital checkout tills. Where one travelled was largely unknown to everyone but the traveller and their companions, but now

Table 10.1 A taxonomy of privacy

Domain	Privacy breach	Description
Information collection	Surveillance	Watching, listening to, or recording of an individual's activities
	Interrogation	Various forms of questioning or probing for information
Information-processing	Aggregation	The combination of various pieces of data about a person
	Identification	Linking information to particular individuals
	Insecurity	Carelessness in protecting stored information from leaks and improper access
	Secondary use	Information collected for one purpose used for a different purpose without the data subject's consent
	Exclusion	Failure to allow the data subject to know about the data that others have about them and participate in its handling and use, including being barred from being able to access and correct errors in that data
Information dissemination	Breach of confidentiality	Breaking a promise to keep a person's information confidential
	Disclosure	Revelation of information about a person that impacts the way others judge their character
	Exposure	Revealing another's nudity, grief or bodily functions
	Increased accessibility	Amplifying the accessibility of information
	Blackmail	Threat to disclose personal information
	Appropriation	The use of the data subject's identity to serve the aims and interests of another
	Distortion	Dissemination of false or misleading information about individuals
Invasion	Intrusion	Invasive acts that disturb one's tranquillity or solitude
	Decisional interference	Incursion into the data subject's decisions regarding their private affairs

Source: Compiled from Solove (2006).

GPS embedded into cars or mobile phones, or signal triangulation with phone masts, or the use of RFID cards on public transport systems or at toll booths, reveals the location and paths traversed. And such data are being repackaged, circulated and sold.

Moreover, we live in much more open and transparent societies than we used to. Information that was previously considered private is being more freely shared, such as résumés (via LinkedIn), family photographs and videos (via Flickr, Instagram and YouTube), personal and family stories (via Facebook and blogs), and personal thoughts (via Twitter, chat rooms and online reviews). What might have been shared with a handful of people (family, close friends, employers) in limited forums (the home, a local bar, an HR office) is now being globally broadcast for anyone to tune in to and view (Minelli et al. 2013). That said, not everyone is so free and easy with personal data and, even when they are, they do not necessarily anticipate that the data might be culled, processed, packaged and sold on. They also do not anticipate that software apps that have no social media element and which they consider to be private might be generating and transmitting data back to their developers, or that some companies might be trying to reverse engineer privacy protection strategies such as anonymisation to create unified profiles. And yet this is happening regularly. For example, in a test of 101 smart phone apps, the *Wall Street Journal* found that 56 transmitted the phone's unique device identifier to other companies without users' awareness or consent, 47 sent the phone's location, 5 sent the users personal details, and 45 did not have any associated privacy policies that users could view (Efrati et al. 2011). TRUSTe found that only 19 per cent of 340 top apps link to a privacy policy and neither Apple nor Google stores require that apps have such policies (Coterill 2011). Yet as Gralla et al. (2011) detail, apps can trace and communicate 'your Web habits, look into your contact list, make phone calls without your knowledge, track your location, examine your files and more'.

The privacy landscape is thus in flux, challenging both social and legal expectations. For some, the notion of privacy is largely dead (Rambam 2008; Rubenking 2013). It is seen as difficult to maintain in practice, it curtails user experience, it is an economic hindrance, the majority of people do not seem 'to mind being mined', and if you have nothing to hide what is the problem with data being open? (Raley 2013: 126; Solove 2007). For others, privacy is a right that has to be protected as it is foundational to 'informed and reflective citizenship' and to freedom of expression (Cavoukian 2009). As such, it is viewed as an 'indispensable structural feature of liberal democratic political systems' (Cohen 2012: 2). If denied the various forms of privacy outlined in Table 10.1, people are opened up to different kinds of personal harm and more pernicious forms of governance. All commentators appear to be of the view that privacy legislation is no longer fit for purpose and needs to be updated to suit the times we live in.

At present, privacy legislation is largely constructed around personal rights and consent regarding the generation, use, and disclosure of personal data (Solove 2013). It consists of seven global privacy principles (Minelli et al. 2013: 156; see Table 10.2), also known as Fair Information Practice Principles (Solove 2013). Within these principles, individuals are thus, in theory, given control over their personal data and provide consent to others with regards to it. Moreover,

Table 10.2 Fair information practice principles

Principle	Description
Notice	Individuals are informed that data are being generated and the purpose to which the data will be put
Choice	Individuals have the choice to opt in or opt out as to whether and how their data will be used or disclosed
Consent	Data are only generated and disclosed with the consent of individuals
Security	Data are protected from loss, misuse, unauthorised access, disclosure, alteration and destruction
Integrity	Data are reliable, accurate, complete and current
Access	Individuals can access, check and verify data about themselves
Accountability	The data holder is accountable for ensuring the above principles and has mechanisms in place to assure compliance

Source: Minelli et al. (2013: 156).

data holders are meant to adhere to data protection laws that limit the disclosure of personally identifiable information (PII), sensitive information, and other data that can be used to infer an identity (see Table 10.3), and advocate data minimisation wherein only the data required for a specific purpose is generated (Tene and Polonetsky 2012). In general, the solution to PII stipulations is to use anonymisation techniques such as deidentification (removing PII), pseudonyms or aggregation, alongside encryption, secure storage and access limitations (Coterill 2011).

Table 10.3 Types of protected information

Personally identifiable information (PII): any information that directly or indirectly identifies a person	Sensitive information: any information whose unauthorised disclosure could be embarrassing or detrimental to the individual	Other information that can be used to infer the identity of a person
Name	Race/ethnicity	Preferences
Postal address/zip code	Political opinions	Cookie ID
Email address	Religious/philosophical beliefs	Static IP address
Telephone/cell number	Trade union membership	
Social security number	Health/medical information	
Driver's licence number	Marital status/sexual life	
Financial account number	Age	
Credit/debit card number	Gender	
	Criminal record	

Source: Adapted from Minelli et al. (2013: 159).

There are several cognitive and structural problems with existing privacy legislation.

States routinely circumvent privacy laws for the purposes of security and intelligence-gathering, as has been recently revealed by the secret data-gathering and analysis programmes of the US, UK and other governments (see Chapter 7). Many companies do not feel compelled to present individuals with a privacy policy because they claim to generate anonymised data, thus falling outside of fair information practices. Or they present a policy at initial inception of engagement (e.g., when installing software or signing up for a service) that is full of complex and ambiguous language and which often reserves the right to be modified at a later date without further consultation (Rubinstein 2013).

With respect to data generated without an individual's knowledge it is difficult to discover and legally challenge such practices. In the case of self-managing privacy, as Solove (2013) details, it is simply too onerous and difficult for individuals to police their privacy across dozens of entities, to weigh up the costs and benefits of agreeing to terms and conditions without knowing how the data might be used now and in the future, and to assess the cumulative and holistic effects of their data being merged with other datasets. Consequently, he notes:

> (1) people do not read privacy policies; (2) if people read them, they do not understand them; (3) if people read and understand them, they often lack enough background knowledge to make an informed choice; and (4) if people read them, understand them, and can make an informed choice, their choice might be skewed by various decision-making difficulties. (Solove 2013: 1888)

Consent is thus 'too often an empty exercise' (Rubinstein 2013: 2), with individuals unwittingly signing away rights without realising the extent or consequences of their actions. Thus, 'privacy policies often serve more as liability disclaimers for businesses than as assurances of privacy for consumers' (Tene and Polonetsky 2012). Moreover, it is clear that in an age of big data the strategy of deidentification provides only a weak form of privacy because it is possible to reverse engineer the process by combing and combining datasets (Narayanan and Shmatikov 2010). For example, Niv Singer of Traxc (quoted in Minelli et al. 2013: 31) explains such a deidentification process:

> It can sometimes be a real challenge to unify social profiles for a single user who may be using different names or handles on each of their social networks, so we've built an algorithm that combs through key factors including content of posts, and location, among others, to provide a very robust identity unification.

As a result of these concerns, the European Union has been reconsidering its data protection policies (see European Commission 2012; Hon et al. 2011; Koops 2011; Rubinstein 2013). The EU proposals include consent to be explicit and not assumed, greater and easier access for individuals to data concerning them, the right to data portability (i.e., the ability to transfer personal data from one service provider to another), a right to be forgotten, wherein individuals can seek to have their data deleted if there are no legitimate grounds for retaining them, and that these rules apply to companies outside of the EU if they are active in the EU market and offer their services to EU citizens (European Commission 2012). Similarly, the Federal Trade Commission in the US has proposed three alterations to more effectively protect privacy: privacy by design wherein privacy is inherently built into every stage of product development; simplified choice for businesses and consumers that gives them the ability to make decisions about their data, including implementing a do not track mechanism and obtaining express consent for sensitive data, or before using data in a materially different manner than the purpose for which it was generated; and greater transparency about data, collection and usage, including reasonable access to data by those the data represent and the ability to correct or suppress data (Federal Trade Commission 2012).

Table 10.4 The 7 foundational principles of *Privacy by Design*

Principle	Description
Proactive not reactive; preventative not remedial	IT systems should seek to anticipate privacy concerns rather than seeking to resolve privacy infractions once they have incurred
Privacy as the default setting	Privacy is automatically protected and does not require action on behalf of an individual
Privacy embedded into design	Privacy protections are core features of the design and architecture of IT systems and is not a bolt-on feature
Full functionality – positive-sum, not zero-sum	All legitimate interests and objectives are accommodated, rather than there being trade-offs between privacy and other considerations such as security
End-to-end security – full life cycle protection	Privacy is embedded into the system from ingestion to disposal
Visibility and transparency – keep it open	Component parts and operations are visible and transparent to users and providers alike and are subject to independent verification
Respect for user privacy – keep it user-centric	A system should be built around, protect the interests of, and empower individuals

Source: Cavoukian (2009).

Privacy by design pursues a different strategy from regulatory and legislative compliance and proposes that privacy must be the default mode of operation; a system explicitly and actively seeks to assure privacy (Cavoukian 2009). The approach is underpinned by the seven principles listed in Table 10.4.

Several privacy scholars and industry lobby groups have also suggested alternative approaches to how privacy is handled. Privacy scholars have considered: legislative reform designed to protect citizen rights, including issues such as the 'right to a clean slate' and expiration dates for data (Koops 2011); who should hold the responsibility for ensuring privacy (developers, agencies, users) and the technical and administrative means of implementing these (Coterill 2011); and what constitutes private information and framing privacy around risk and extent of harm rather than content definition (Hon et al. 2011). They have also proposed: individuals entering into partnerships with developers wherein they can more proactively select what data they are willing to release, to whom, and under what circumstances; companies providing users access to their own data in a usable format for their own benefit; and that companies 'share the wealth' in the monetisation of personal data (Tene and Polonetsky 2012; Rubinstein 2013). An example of such a co-beneficial sharing of the wealth of data are smart grids where data generated by smart meters concerning household electricity consumption are used by the power company to produce supply efficiencies, with households supplied with apps that enable them to monitor their own use and adapt behaviour to save money. Industry, by and large, wants either the present provisions to continue or to be relaxed, with privacy administered through market-led regulation that does not stifle the economic leveraging of data. Here, it is envisaged that companies will self-regulate for fear of reputational damage and customers voting with their feet if they overly infringe on privacy issues (Minelli et al. 2013; Mayer-Schonberger and Cukier 2013).

DATA SECURITY

Given the value of data, especially personal data that can facilitate identity theft, or commercial data that can be pirated or used to gain competitive advantage, data security has become an important aspect of data protection. Individuals can have multiple personal and work accounts with a variety of agencies and vendors, with as many ID codes, usernames and passwords. They can have their own data, and data about them, stored in dozens of places (e.g., computers, digital devices, smartphones, external hard drives, data sticks, and servers). These accounts and digital devices are vulnerable to hacking (breaking into accounts or accessing machines), malware (code that is secretly installed on a computer that can access sensitive data or record keystrokes and communicate them to a third party), and phishing (scam e-mails or social engineering through phone calls that try to get an individual to volunteer account information), resulting in the theft and misappropriation of data.

Gantz and Reinsel (2011) detail five levels of data security, each of which has slightly different drivers, though they all demand proactive security procedures: (1) privacy: to maintain the privacy of information and limit circulation; (2) compliance-led: to protect data that might be discoverable in litigation or subject to retention rules; (3) custodial: to protect data which could lead to or aid in identity theft; (4) confidential: to ensure confidential information, such as trade secrets, are protected; (5) lockdown: to protect highly restricted information such as financial transactions, personnel files, medical records or military intelligence, that could have consequences beyond personal theft. Managing these levels of data security is an important task for individuals, companies and institutions. In general, this is achieved by controlling access through security software and system/network design (e.g., installing firewalls and malware, virus, trojan and spam detection software), and encryption that requires a password to unlock. Given that, once accessed, data can be easily copied and distributed, digital rights management seeks to limit such practices and also make them easier to track.

And yet, despite these threats, digital devices, services and data, and potential weak points in their configuration, are growing faster than the ability to secure them (Gantz and Reinsel 2011). While many PCs and laptops are relatively secure (as long as their protective software is regularly updated), tablets, mobile phones, faxes, external hard drives, peripheral devices (such as printers, scanners and networked photocopiers), and the diverse set of digital devices that compose the Internet of things often have few protections (Rezendes and Stephenson 2013; Rose 2013). This has led Mims (2013) to contend that once everything in an environment contains digital code and is connected to a network then they can be hacked, with objects potentially being controlled remotely, or forced to exceed their design parameters or operate in ways that are unpleasant or dangerous, or misdirect users leading to error and damage, or spy on occupants and users. Moreover, the methods used by hackers and phishers are becoming increasingly sophisticated and invasive, and the security industry is always in a race to keep up with them (Goldberg 2012).

As the data revolution unfolds, and more and more devices produce, share and utilise data, it seems that security issues are going to multiply, not lessen (Gantz et al. 2007). In turn, this is going to exacerbate crimes such as identity theft, undermine trust in data systems, and raise a series of legal questions concerning responsibility and liabilities in protecting systems when data are mishandled, misappropriated and stolen (Weber 2010).

PROFILING, SOCIAL SORTING AND REDLINING

Beyond the widening of the surveillance gaze, the infringements of privacy, and the vulnerabilities of data security are concerns about what the data deluge is being employed to achieve. As noted in Chapter 7, not only has the nature of data changed, but there has been a qualitative shift in how data can be analysed, to what ends data and analytics can be employed, and who has the power to utilise and extract value from data. Data have long been used to profile, segment and manage populations, but these processes have become much more sophisticated, fine-grained, widespread and routine. While state agencies produce citizen profiles for the purposes of security and fraud detection, most of the growth in profiling has been by commercial enterprises seeking to understand and target its existing and potential customer base (see Chapter 2).

In the past, companies practised mass marketing, broadcasting a rather generic message to a very large audience through mass advertising using television, radio, print, and mail shots in order to reach their target group (Schwartz and Solove 2011). Over time this was complemented by targeted marketing using relatively crude profiling. Here, a small number of specialist companies created generic population classifications wherein households were categorised into aggregate profile classes, usually denominated by a selection of demographic variables and location, for example using census data, or lifestyle variables, for example using subscription data (e.g., to certain periodicals) (Goss 1995). Rather than attempt to profile their own customers, companies would purchase profiles and contact details in order to segment and target particular population classes with a more narrowly framed message while also creating efficiencies in the marketing budget by reducing wasteful advertising. More recently, profiling companies have started to produce individual, rather than aggregate, profiles by combining data from various sources such as credit and store card transactions, clickstreams, social media posts, and other kinds of personal data (Siegel 2013). Moreover, companies themselves are utilising the vast amounts of data they generate about customers (e.g., through sales, CRM, clickstreams), combining them with other sources of data, to produce their own profiles and engage in behavioural marketing.

On the surface predictive profiling looks to be a win–win situation for customers and vendors – customers receive personalised treatment and vendors gain sales and reduce churn. However, predictive profiling can be used to socially sort and redline populations, selecting out certain categories to receive a preferential status and marginalising and excluding others (Graham 2005; Leyshon and Thrift 1999). For example, a company might profile customers with respect to their credit risk and how likely they are to be able to meet payments, or their projected lifetime value if they remain loyal and how likely they are to move their custom (Minelli et al. 2013). Using such profiles they can prioritise attention and resources, usually focusing on high-value customers. Consumers are thus being routinely measured and ranked, and receive differential services, some of which are discriminatory such as the redlining of populations deemed unprofitable, or not profitable enough, or high risk, which in turn can affect life chances (Curry

1997; Danna and Gandy 2002; Wyly in press). These profiles are products and can be sold to other companies interested in assessing potential customer value and risk; thus their negative consequences can haunt an individual across domains and over time.

Such discriminatory practices can also include dynamic and personalised pricing. It is already common for a supermarket chain to have the same goods differentially priced across stores dependent on the characteristics of the people who shop in them, or the prices of products to vary by volume (e.g., 1 for $1, or 3 for $2), or prices to vary across groups (e.g, students or senior citizens receiving discounts) (Varian 1996). The desire of many companies is the rolling out of such practices on an individualised basis, tailored to personal profiles, so that different people pay varying amounts for the same product (as with airline fares, but based on a personalised model). Prices will also vary dynamically and contextually, depending on circumstance. Such individualised and dynamic practices have already started to be applied, including in the supermarket sector. For example, Clifford (2012) provides examples where shoppers in the same store pay different amounts for the same product based on their customer profile. In some cases, stores will even alter prices as consumers shop depending on their in-store location and shopping history (e-coupons are generated on the spot when shoppers scan items using a phone app). The aim of personalised and dynamic pricing is to 'usurp the entire value surplus available in the transaction by pricing goods or services as close as possible to the individual's reservation price' (Tene and Polonetsky 2012: 17). In other words, it is designed to leverage optimal spending in the store's favour.

Given their power to shape and sort consumer experience and life chances, individual profiles and the data and data practices underpinning them demand further attention. At present, both the data used and the analytics applied are opaque to consumers and citizens. If one ends up on a no-fly list or is negatively treated or excluded from a product by a company, for example being credit blacklisted, it is difficult to determine the grounds for discrimination and to challenge them. Critics contend that we have entered an age where

> the data body [shadow] not only claims to have ontological privilege, but actually has it. What your data body says about you is more real than what you say about yourself. The data body is the body by which you are judged in society, and the body which dictates your status in the world. What we are witnessing at this point in time is the triumph of representation over being. (Critical Art Ensemble 1995)

Yet we know that big data and the data body are messy – they are full of gaps, inconsistencies and errors (see Chapter 9) – and we also know that software and algorithms work in selected and biased ways (Kitchin and Dodge 2011). Thus, systems based on big data, which are not transparent and lack proper scrutiny and recourse, pose all kinds of potential problems when they privilege the data body. Indeed, predictive profiling is ripe for regulatory and legal oversight and for measures that unsettle its ontological privileging of data and protect people from pernicious and discriminatory practices.

SECONDARY USES, CONTROL CREEP AND ANTICIPATORY GOVERNANCE

One of the foundations of privacy and data protection policy in the European Union and North America is the concept of data minimisation. This stipulates that agencies and vendors should only generate data necessary to perform a particular task, that the data are only retained for as long as they are required to perform that task (or as long as legal considerations dictate), and that the data generated should only be used for this task (Tene and Polonetsky 2012). In other words, the collectors of data should not capture everything that they can, nor should they store them indefinitely or put them to secondary uses. Such aspirations are clearly antithetical to the rationale of big data and the functioning of data markets which seek to hoard data in case they have possible future value (Tene and Polonetsky 2012; Andrejevic 2013). The solution for vendors has been to repackage data by deidentifying them or creating derived data, with only the original dataset being subjected to data minimisation. The repackaged data can then be sold on and used in a plethora of ways. Such repurposing of data is common, with vendors arguing that there is no need to inform the person the data refers to, or gain their consent, as the data are anonymised, derived or aggregated (Solove 2007). The speculative harvesting of vast quantities of data, much of it captured without individuals' knowledge or understanding, and then being put to secondary uses, clearly raises ethical questions concerning not only privacy and data protection, but also governance. One of the clearest examples related to governance is control creep.

Control creep is where the data generated for one form of governance is appropriated for another (Innes 2001). This has mostly clearly occurred with respect to security, particularly in the post 9/11 era, with airline industry data and government administrative data being repurposed for profiling and assessing the security risk of passengers (Lyon 2003b). Similarly, road traffic and congestion charge cameras in London have been repurposed for security tasks, rather than simply monitoring traffic offences (Dodge and Kitchin 2007a). A commercial example of control creep is in-car navigation systems in rental vehicles being repurposed from helping drivers find their way to monitoring and fining those that drive out of state or off-road (Elliott 2004). Control creep systematically undermines the rationale for data minimisation and its roll-out poses clear threats to civil liberties, with all citizens – both innocent and guilty – subject to its gaze and disciplinary action.

Another example of a secondary use of data that impinges on civil liberties is anticipatory governance. Here, predictive analytics are used to assess likely future behaviours or events and to direct appropriate action. Such anticipatory governance has been a feature of air travel for a number of years, with passengers profiled for risk and levels of security checks prior to starting their journey (Dodge and Kitchin 2004). Similarly, a number of US police forces are using predictive analytics to anticipate the location of future crimes and to direct police officers to increase patrols in those areas (Siegel 2013). Likewise, some companies such as Hewlett Packard are using predictive analytics to assess who might potentially leave the company and to proactively intervene to minimise employee churn (Siegel 2013). In such cases, a person's data shadow does more than follow them; it precedes them (Stalder 2002).

Such anticipatory modes of governance raise ethical issues because they target attention at particular groups and places, and seek to police behaviours that may never occur, and in the process reshape how people act through self-disciplining (Harcourt 2006). Moreover, such predictive analytics often work to intensify prejudice and discrimination and act to create self-fulfilling prophecies (Harcourt 2006; Siegel 2013). Raley (2013: 128) thus argues that

> [d]ata is in this respect performative: the composition of flecks and bits of data into a profile of a terror suspect, the re-grounding of abstract data in the targeting of an actual life, will have the effect of producing that life, that body, as a terror suspect

and thus making it the focus of the gaze and practices of state policing and subject to the consequence of being a suspect, though not a proven, terrorist. In other words, the person is treated differently in anticipation of being something they may or may not be or do. While it might have honourable intentions, anticipation thus has consequences beyond preventing predicted events (Harcourt 2006). As with other forms of profiling, anticipatory governance is largely directed by black box algorithms working on data of unknown provenance, and is generally closed to recourse. It has been the focus of very little critical attention or debate as to its effects, yet is being actively developed for use by governments and companies.

MODES OF GOVERNANCE AND TECHNOLOGICAL LOCK-INS

Beyond control creep and anticipatory profiling, the data revolution has a number of potential impacts with regards to the organisation and operation of governance. Given the widening net of data collection, and its fine-grained resolution and timeliness, the worry for many commentators is that the emerging era of big data precedes that of Big Brother. That is, an age where state and corporations know and anticipate so much about individuals through dataveillance and predictive profiling that they possess the power to enforce rigid and pernicious forms of disciplinary control.

As noted throughout the chapter, there is no doubt that we live in an age of massively increased surveillance, where oligopticons are becoming ever more connected, and are underpinned by a growing 'culture of control' that desires security, orderliness and risk minimisation (Lyon 2007). Here, a different kind of governance is enacted, one where the regulation of certain aspects of everyday life is devolved to technological systems that are imbued with secondary agency (Kitchin and Dodge 2011). For example, the capture, processing and administering of traffic violations are increasingly becoming automated, enacted through software that processes data concerning number plates, speed and right of access, and cross-references them with ownership databases to automatically impose fines or penalty points (Dodge and Kitchin 2007a). Unlike traditional forms of surveillance that seek to encourage self-discipline, automated systems actively reshape behaviour (Agre 1994; Kitchin and Dodge 2011). In such systems, the mechanisms of data generation and disciplining are an integral aspect of the system, rather than being external to it. For example, rather than a checkout-till worker self-disciplining their work rate because they may or may not be monitored via a CCTV camera, the act of scanning the goods and processing payments is the means by which work rate is constantly overseen. In such systems, surveillance and its associated data shadow become continuous, pervasive, distributed, persistent, reactive to the subject's behaviour, but outside of the subject's control (Cohen 2012).

Not all automated data generation is used to enact automated management, but this is increasingly the trend, especially for highly regulated systems. Moreover, new modes of control are not, as yet, being enacted in the heavy-handed way that George Orwell's Big Brother vision anticipates; they are ordinary, routine and seductive, interpellating citizens to willingly and actively participate in its practices (Kitchin and Dodge 2011; Cohen 2012). As a consequence, for Solove (2007), big data are not so much about ushering in Orwell's vision, but rather that of Kafka: it raises issues of due process and accountability (bureaucratic indifference, errors, abuses, frustration, lack of transparency and recourse) more than domineering power and totalitarianism. In contrast, for Boellstorff (2013), the master metaphor for big data and surveillance is not the panopticon, but rather the confession, wherein rather than being subjected purely to an invasive gaze, people willingly confess their data (via social media, by joining loyalty card programmes, etc.). Regardless of the conceptualisation of operation, these new systems clearly have consequences with respect to power and control and differentially shape life experiences and chances, and the role of data and dataveillance in such systems requires further critical attention.

One of the ways in which governance is being transformed through data-driven technologies is by making it more technocratic in nature. For example, the drive towards managing and regulating cities via information and analytic systems promotes a technocratic mode of urban governance which presumes that all aspects of a city can be measured and monitored and treated as technical problems which can be addressed through technical solutions (Kitchin 2014); it displays what Mattern (2013) terms 'instrumental rationality' and Morozov (2013) calls 'solutionism', wherein complex social situations can be disassembled into neatly defined problems that can be solved or optimised through computation. Here, there is a reification of big data; they can provide the answer to all problems (Mattern 2013). By capturing phenomena as real-time data it seemingly becomes possible to model, understand, manage and fix a situation as it unfolds. As Hill (2013) puts it: '[smart city thinking] betrays a technocratic view that the city is something we might understand in detail, if only we had enough data – like an engine or a nuclear power station – and thus master it through the brute of force of science and engineering'. Indeed, Mattern (2013) suggests that big data urbanism suffers from 'datafication, the presumption that all meaningful flows and activity can be sensed and measured'. Within such thinking there is 'an often-explicit assumption that the universe is formed with knowable and definable parameters [that] assure us that if we were only able to measure them all, we would be able to predict and respond with perfection accordingly' (Haque 2012). Technological solutions on their own are not, however, going to solve the deep-rooted structural problems in cities because they do not address their root causes. Rather they only enable the more efficient management of the manifestations of those problems. Thus, while smart city technologies such as real-time analytics are promoted as the panacea for tackling urban governance issues, they largely paper over the cracks rather than fixing them, unless coupled with a range of other policies (Kitchin 2014). The same can be said with respect to technocratic approaches applied to other domains; data-driven modes of governance do ensure the implementation of evidence-informed strategies, but these have to be contextualised, flexible and properly targeted, not simply be management by numbers and algorithms.

Alongside the critique that governance is becoming too omniscient and technocratic is a concern that it is being captured and overtly shaped by corporate interests for their own gain. Continuing with the smart city agenda and municipal governance example, as noted in Chapter 7, a number of the world's largest software services and hardware companies are actively seeking to subcontract aspects of urban management and to make their wares a core, indispensable part of how various aspects of city life are monitored and regulated (Kitchin 2014; Townsend 2013). The concern around such a corporatisation of urban governance is three-fold (Kitchin 2014). First, that it actively promotes a neoliberal political economy and the marketisation of public services wherein city functions are administered for private profit (Hollands 2008). Second, that it creates a technological lock-in that makes cities beholden to particular technological platforms and vendors over a long period of time, creating monopoly positions (Hill 2013). The danger here is the creation of a corporate path dependency that cannot easily be undone or diverted (Bates 2012). Third, that it leads to 'one size fits all smart city in a box' solutions that take little account of the uniqueness of places, peoples and cultures and straitjackets city administrations into a narrowly visioned technocratic mode of governance (Townsend 2013). Indeed, IBM is now selling a product called 'IBM Intelligent Operations Center', which combines a number of the systems that were designed for Rio de Janeiro into a single product that can be applied to any city (Singer 2012c, see Chapter 7). This is not to say that corporate lock-ins are inevitable, but it is clear that it is the desire of a number of very large corporate players. Likewise, other forms of governance are being increasingly targeted by corporations seeking to find markets for technocratic solutions. Again, the consequences of such forms of governance demand further scrutiny.

CONCLUSION

This chapter has examined some of the ethical, social, political and legal implications of the changes taking place with respect to data generation, data integration and data use. It is clear that while such practices have benefits for governments, companies and citizens, they also have differential and negative consequences. Given how rapidly the data landscape is changing, keeping track of developments, determining their potential implications, and thinking through appropriate social and legal responses is a challenge. Indeed, there are many fundamental normative questions that need reflexive consideration concerning who can generate, access, share, analyse datasets, 'for what purposes, in what contexts, and with what constraints' (boyd and Crawford 2012: 673). The need for answers to such questions is rather pressing, however, given the extent and effects of dataveillance, infringements of privacy, lax data security, the pernicious effects of social sorting and redlining, and the changing nature and modes of governance. Even if the response was quick and fulsome, the answers produced would be diverse, with different stakeholders seeking alternative strategies to deal with various concerns, as is evidenced by the suggested approaches to the erosion and breaches of privacy. Consequently, one can expect much debate in the coming years with respect to managing the various elements of the data revolution. In particular, as discussed in Chapter 2, the work of data brokers is likely to come under increasing scrutiny from governments and citizens.

From an academic perspective it is vital that scholars take an active role in researching and thinking through the ethical, social, political and legal questions arising from the data revolution, and track and contribute to the various ongoing debates. Such work needs to consist of, on the one hand, detailed empirical case studies that document the discursive and material effects of how data are employed and, on the other, synoptic and normative treatises that set out the implications of various data assemblages and possible alternative paths forward. To date, most contributions, such as this chapter and the work it discusses, have consisted of the latter, with relatively few empirical studies of specific sociotechnical systems and their consequences. Such studies are important because they reveal the concrete ways in which data assemblages are grounded and function in practice and how they are embraced, reworked, resisted, subverted and transgressed by communities, and provide an evidence base from which to envisage how such systems might be reframed or repurposed.

11

MAKING SENSE OF THE DATA REVOLUTION

This book has argued that there needs to be a more critical and philosophical engagement with data and that a data revolution is presently taking place. With respect to the former, it has been contended that data are fundamental elements of knowledge production and yet, to date, little attention has been paid to their ontological framing and the assemblage surrounding their production and use. Rather, the focus has been more methodological with respect to their generation, or has concentrated on their derivative forms of information and knowledge. In relation to the latter, it has been argued that the scaling of small data into data infrastructures, the opening-up of data that were previously limited in access, and the phenomenon of big data are disruptive rather than sustaining innovations; they change the nature of data with respect to their volume, velocity, exhaustivity, relationality and indexicality, flexibility and extensionality, variety, openness and interoperability, and give rise to new data assemblages and ways of making sense of, and doing work in, the world. The disruptive effects of the data revolution have many implications for government, companies and civil society by creating new knowledges and practices that can be used to reframe how people are governed, organisations managed, value leveraged and capital produced, places improved, and science reimagined and practised. They also raise many challenges and questions, enabling more pervasive modes of dataveillance, privacy to be undermined, people and places to be profiled and socially sorted, and new forms of governance to be enacted. This final chapter sets out an indicative road map to making sense of data and the data revolution given the present gaps in conceptual thought and knowledge. It suggests that such sense-making needs to occur in two ways: first, through philosophical reflection and synoptic, conceptual and critical analysis; second, through detailed empirical research concerning the genesis, constitution, functioning and evolution of data assemblages.

UNDERSTANDING DATA AND THE DATA REVOLUTION

Given the utility and value of data, there is a critical need to engage with them from a philosophical and conceptual point of view. Philosophy, Wittgenstein (1921) argued, is the logical clarification of thought. Each school of thought is a system of ideas and a lens for making sense of the world. In general terms, each school and its variants is shaped by four components – ontology, epistemology, ideology, methodology – that define its parameters. Ontology is a set of tenets about the nature of existence; it concerns what exists and can be observed and known. With respect to data, it concerns what data are. What is the essential nature of data? Epistemology concerns how knowledge is derived or arrived at; assumptions about how we can know the world. How do we come to know data? But also, how are data mobilised in the praxis of knowing? Ideology concerns the underlying politics and purpose for producing knowledge, the extent to which an approach seeks to be neutral, objective and value-free or actively seeks to intervene and change the world. Are data pre-factual, pre-analytical and rhetorical or are they social, political and actively framed? Methodology is the set of procedures used to operationalise a question or theory within the ontological and epistemological assumptions of the overall philosophy of investigation. It frames the choice of techniques by which data are generated and analysed. Data, methodology and techniques are intimately linked, but what is the nature of their relationship?

Chapter 1 set out to provide some initial answers to these questions and to provide a conceptual framing for understanding data from a philosophical perspective that decouples them from merely being the 'raw' material of information and knowledge. It was argued that data are both social and material, and that they do not merely represent the world but actively produce it. Data, it was contended, do not exist independently of the ideas, techniques, technologies, people and contexts that produce, process, manage, analyse and store them. Indeed, they are organised and stored in databases and data infrastructures that form the core of complex sociotechnical assemblages. As detailed in Chapter 1, these apparatus include systems of thought, forms of knowledge, finance, political economy, governmentalities and legalities, materialities and infrastructures, practices, organisations and institutions, subjectivities and communities, places and the marketplace, each of which has numerous elements (see Table 1.3) that work together in multifarious, contingent and relational ways to discursively and materially produce a data assemblage (see Figure 1.3). Throughout the book numerous assemblages have been discussed such as research infrastructures, national archives, cyber-infrastructures, open data projects, data brokers, governmental data systems, and business systems. Each of these assemblages, while sharing commonalities, evolves and operates in different ways, is composed of a set of apparatus and elements that are variously scaled (e.g., from local organisations and materialities to dispersed teams, national and supranational laws, to global markets) but are nonetheless bound in a unique constellation.

Such a conceptual framing enables us to, on the one hand, think through the production of data, how they are variously framed technically, politically and economically, ethically, spatially and temporally, their uses, and the work they do in the world, and, on the other, guide empirical research concerning data assemblages (see the next section). It is, however, just one of a suite of potential ways to make sense of data and no doubt over time scholars will produce a set of diverse conceptual lenses through which to understand data, and the diversity of views will create productive counterpoints for new ideas, as well as conceptual vantage points to direct empirical research. These might include theorising data through a more structural lens that focuses on their role in the operation of late capitalism, or draws on Deleuzian poststructural notions concerning rhizomic modes governance, or on feminist or postcolonial critiques of the gendered and politicised production and employment of data. Regardless of the lens, what is required is deep, careful and critical reflection and putting theory to work through empirical case studies.

Not only do we need to explore the conceptualisations of data but, as discussed in Chapter 8, we need to examine how the data revolution presents some challenges to existing philosophies of science. Big data and new data analytics, in particular, offer the possibility of a new scientific paradigm, a new epistemological approach to development of scientific theory that is data-intensive and exploratory in nature. Initial attempts to think through what such a paradigm shift might mean has often been confused and misleading, promoting a form of empiricism that many scientists will find alienating and a step backwards, not forwards. This needs to be replaced with a much more robust vision of what data-driven science might consist of: its philosophical and methodological tenets. Such thinking has barely started, yet is desperately needed in order to catch up with the pace of technical change and the roll-out of ad hoc and pragmatic approaches, and to replace proliferating forms of weak empiricism. A paradigm shift is less likely in the humanities and social sciences, but nonetheless big data, open data and data infrastructures offer new approaches to social, cultural, political, economic and historical questions. Chapter 8 mapped out some of the relative merits and critiques of the digital humanities and computational social science being developed, but a full and frank debate is required that teases out the consequences of an epistemological shift in thought and praxis. Such a debate needs to also assess the role and merits of small data studies, as well as hybrid approaches that mix small and big data methods.

Such thinking needs to be complemented with more normatively orientated reflection on the generation and uses of data, and the construction and functioning of data assemblages. As discussed in Chapter 10, the data revolution poses a number of thorny questions with respect to the extent to which everyday lives are being captured in data assemblages and how people's data body precedes and conditions their lives in all kinds of unanticipated ways. For example, should people be able to access all data held about them and have the right to correct and challenge data, data analysis and profiling? To what extent should people be able to exercise the right to be forgotten? In what ways should data brokers be subject to independent oversight and regulation, especially when their data and algorithms affect life chances? How secure should different kinds of data be and what should be the punishments for security breaches? What are the legitimate bounds for governments in collecting and amalgamating data about their citizens? To what extent should corporations be involved in government work and governance systems? These questions concern what kind of society is desirable in an age of data abundance, and the answers to them have consequences with respect to how data assemblages might be reconceived and reconfigured, including new forms of governance and regulation. Legal scholars have begun to think through issues such as the consequences for privacy of big data and to propose alternative ways of dealing with their more pernicious effects, but it is clear that such issues are far from resolved and they will be the focus of an evolving debate and legislative struggles, and there is a need for others to contribute to a robust, open and ongoing conversation.

Alongside developing a better and deeper conceptual and normative understanding of data, there is a need to provide synoptic and critical overviews of data infrastructures, open data, big data and their consequences. Rather than presenting a thesis based on extensive empirical research, this book has supplied such an overarching analysis, drawing on academic, industry and media writings. This approach has utility because it pulls together ideas and observations from diverse sources to provide a wider view of the unfolding landscape, enabling the larger dynamics at play to be charted and to think through their potential effects. As yet, however, thoughtful, challenging, synoptic overviews of the data revolution are thin on the ground. Instead, there is a handful of mainly business, management and technical books that breathlessly engage in data boosterism and lack critical edge. In contrast, what is required are accounts that are interdisciplinary and sophisticated in their thinking. While it is useful to examine the data revolution through a disciplinary lens, such a lens is inherently limiting given the broad agenda and implications at stake. Similarly, the notion that the data revolution produces data that can be interpreted free of context or domain-specific knowledge needs to be quashed. Instead, it is necessary to draw from the insights and ideas across disciplines, with scholars who possess different expertises working together in order to provide a more fulsome and rounded picture (Ruppert 2012).

Further, the analysis produced needs to be careful not to slip into simple polemics that either set out passionately the case for big data, open data and data infrastructures, or supply an entrenched critique decrying their more negative consequences. A situation is rarely as black and white, good or bad, as such polemics present. Rather, we need to recognise that the developments taking place are contingent, relational and contextual, and unfold in messy and sometimes contradictory and paradoxical ways. As noted in Chapter 9, data assemblages often work to both liberate and coerce simultaneously and data consumers are sometimes also data producers; systems seek to interpellate users in diverse ways. As such, assemblages are often quite entangled and need to be carefully unpacked to reveal their various shades of grey. And where there are effects that work in harmful and discriminatory ways we need to determine appropriate social and legal responses that protect individual and collective rights but do not throw the baby out with the bath water.

RESEARCHING DATA ASSEMBLAGES

Detailed empirical research on the formation, functioning and sustenance of data assemblages is required to accompany and underpin wider conceptual, synoptic and critical analysis. At present, we have little in-depth understanding of both the overall construction of data assemblages and their apparatus and individual elements. Consequently, there is a pressing need for case studies that trace out the sociotechnical arrangements of whole assemblages, such as the assemblage of a data broker or a research data infrastructure or an open data movement in a city, or document in detail specific aspects of an assemblage, such as the sociology and political economy of hackathons and data dives, or the communities of practice within a sector of big data. Ideally, such studies would also be comparative in nature, contrasting iterations of an assemblage, such as across locales or contexts, or across various types of assemblage. Such comparative research enables generalities and specificities to be identified, and the various contingent and relational ways in which assemblages unfold to be charted.

There are many ways in which such research could be operationalised, including the use of data analytics as discussed in Chapter 6 to identify the constitution of an assemblage and the connections and relationships between elements. Such an approach would have much utility by using the power of data mining and machine learning to identify patterns within and across large data assemblages and to establish the relative strength of associations. This would provide a broad, comparative explanation of assemblages and their operation. However, with respect to understanding the contextual, contingent and relational processes at play within an assemblage – the complex intersections of agency and structure – perhaps, somewhat ironically, a suite of small data methods is likely to produce more fine-grained, perceptive and illuminating insights. These methods include, but are not limited to, genealogies, deconstruction, ethnographies, and observant partici-pation (a suite of methods that I have previously advocated using to make sense of software (Kitchin and Dodge 2011) and mapping (Dodge et al. 2009; Kitchin et al. 2012a). Each method seeks to carefully identify and unpack social phenom-ena and, as the eleven elements make clear, data assemblages are thoroughly social in nature. And by using them in combination the unfolding discursive and material production of data assemblages can be dissected, providing what Wang (2013) has termed 'thick data'; contextual stories and insights about data and their production.

Genealogy is most often used to trace out the contingent unfolding of a sys-tem of thought or set of actions over time and space, rather than producing a sanitised, teleological historiography (Crowley 2009). It illustrates how the future is built upon the past, but is not necessarily determined by it in simple cause–effect ways. As such, genealogy is employed to untangle and make sense histori-cally of the multiple, complex and sometimes contradictory or paradoxical iterations of an assemblage, or one of its elements – the evolving and situated unfolding of ideas, decisions, constraints, actions and actors that shape their development, along with dead-ends and apparent failures (Foucault 1977). In so doing, it identifies points of confluence when people or ideas come together and give rise to new assemblages and the complex and messy ways in which these then develop. In the case of the data revolution a genealogical method would be employed to trace out the formation and evolution of open data, data infrastruc-tures and big data more generally, and specific instantiations of them.

For example, one might produce a detailed genealogy of the development of the open data movement in broad terms, tracing the emergence of actors, organisations, funding models, ideas and events over time and across space, and the interlinkages, alliances and disagreements between them, and their effects in reshaping the data landscape by redefining the politics surrounding government-produced and held data and opening up such data for wider use. Or one might undertake a genealogy of a single entity such as the Open Knowledge Foundation, a non-for-profit organisation founded in 2004 in the UK, that has quickly grown to become an influential international movement campaigning for open data and open government. Here, one would seek to trace out the genesis of the organisation, the evolution of its mission and values, the development of its infrastructures, governance, funding, activities, programmes and publications, the spread of its influence, its interactions with other bodies, and so on, in order to understand the contingent and relational way such an entity unfolds and operates and its present position and author-ity within the wider open data movement.

Performing a genealogical analysis is often accompanied by utilising decon-struction. This method of analysis teases apart and reveals meaning within texts broadly conceived (writing, pictures, maps, speech and combinations of these in the form of brochures and websites). Texts are understood to be mediators of both explicit and implicit messages, and through a forensic examination of a text its deeper meanings can be revealed and understood. In essence, deconstruction looks beyond surface signs and face values to challenge the taken-for-granted readings of a text in order to open up the hidden, or tangle up the overly simple, meanings within that text (Burman and MacLure 2005; Harley 1989). It is a critical reading that uses techniques like displacing assumed meaning or power, identifying points of paradox or contradiction, untangling intertextuality and embedding within wider materialities and contexts, and reflecting on the positionality of the speaker and their intended audience (Burman and MacLure 2005). As detailed in Chapters 2, 3 and 7, open data, data infrastructures and big data are all accompanied by discursive regimes that seek to persuade people, companies and institutions to their logic – to support, adopt and invest in their rationale and product. These discursive regimes are not universal, but are complex and messy, the amalgam of collaborating and competing interests. By using deconstruction the discursive regime of an assemblage or specific elements of it, such as the various factions in the open data movement or specific companies promoting big data solutions to urban issues, can be teased apart and its composition and message unpacked, revealing the meanings, ideology and power inherent within their design and presentation.

Ethnographic studies provide immersive and holistic analyses of communities of practice by documenting in detail their organisation, operation, culture, internal dynamics and external engagements (Herbert 2000). Typically, an ethnographic approach employs a mix of participant observation undertaken over an extended period of time and in-depth interviews with a wide range of internal and external stakeholders, complemented by other techniques such as a hermeneutic reading of related documents and artefacts (such as websites, e-mail exchanges, work spaces, etc.). In essence, ethnography seeks a nuanced understanding of the lifeworld of a community – its social relations, its rhythms, its cultural meanings, its patterns of power and decision-making, ways of being, and so on – in order to comprehend how it is constituted and continuously unfolds (Crang and Cook 2007). The researcher goes beyond providing surface descriptions to document the complex ways in which communities work by being embedded in the relations and practices being studied. Ethnographies of data assemblages would then provide detailed, holistic accounts of how they are constituted and operate in practice. For example, an ethnography of the Open Knowledge Foundation would consist of a researcher being embedded within that organisation, taking part in planning meetings, activities and events, observing workers interacting, and interviewing key stakeholders, to gain first-hand insight into the operations of a key player in the open data movement, and how the various components of a data assemblage (i.e., systems of thought; political economy; governmentalities; materialities and infrastructures, etc.) are grounded and managed within and through it. Similarly, one might conduct an ethnography within a particular data infrastructure or data broker, or within a big data company, or within specific kinds of events such as hackathons, or industry exhibitions and conferences, or big data teams within election campaigns, and so on.

Such ethnographies can be complemented with observant participation, a kind of self-ethnography wherein a researcher undertakes sustained examination of their own and other peoples' engagement with a phenomenon or practice (Crang and Cook 2007; Morton 2005). With respect to the data revolution this might be participant observation of being part of a team building a data infrastructure, or being a member of the open data movement, or working as a data scientist employing big data to tackle a particular issue, and so on. Employing such a method is an inherently a self-reflexive exercise, one that is subjective and personal, in which the researcher strives to rigorously examine their own and others' practices in a field in which they are a key player. The principal benefit of such an approach is that the researcher is fully aware of the diverse and complex landscape (socially, politically, economically) within which they are operating and is an active participant, experiencing the various processes at play. The main critique of such an approach is that it can be highly inflected and situated personally, lacking in wider representation, and is perhaps best utilised in combination with other methods that provide a wider context.

These methods are a subset of a range of possible ways of making sense of data assemblages and their elements, and there is no doubt that many other approaches will be employed to conduct empirical research on the nature of the unfolding data revolution, each providing different insights. Indeed, a mixed methods approach that combines the in-depth and contextual insights of qualitatively orientated small data studies with broader studies that employ data analytics might be a profitable route to follow. In such a study, data analytics might be used to provide a broad-based overview of a data assemblage, or the links or overlaps between assemblages, which is then followed by more focused research using the methods detailed to provide more in-depth insights into the relationships and processes at work within and between elements. Or the combination might be purely quantitative in formulation, as detailed in the discussion of data science in Chapter 8, wherein exploratory analysis of an assemblage is followed more traditional hypothesis-testing to identify the most salient factors at play. The approach can also work in reverse, with focused, in-depth research being used to guide the deployment of data analytics across a much larger sample. In both cases, the first and second stages work in concert with each other to enhance insight and knowledge. In the former case, the broad picture is used to help frame, contextualise and deepen understanding. In the latter case, in-depth understanding provides the basis for trying to establish wider explanation.

FINAL THOUGHTS

The data revolution is in its infancy, but is unfolding quickly. In just a handful of years open data, data infrastructures and big data have had a substantial impact on the data landscape, accompanied by vocal boosterist discourses declaring their positive disruptive effects. The speed of the developments taking place has meant that measured, in-depth and extended critical analysis has been struggling to catch up. No doubt over the next few years there will be a veritable flood of such studies seeking to document the nature and implications of the emerging data assemblages. Such studies, as argued in this chapter, are sorely needed. On the one hand, such works will set out ways of making sense of the data revolution, both through conceptual reflection and empirical studies, and on the other they will provide the platform for more normative thinking concerning how the data landscape should evolve and be regulated and managed. At present, the latter is often quite reactionary, weakly conceived, or dominated by vested interests. This book has sought to provide an initial and balanced conceptual, critical and synoptic analysis which might help inform the studies that follow. For too long data and the constitution and operation of the assemblages surrounding them have been taken for granted, with attention focused on the information and knowledge distilled from them. It is time to rectify this neglect.

REFERENCES

Adler, M.J. (1986) *A Guidebook to Learning: For a Lifelong Pursuit of Wisdom*. Macmillan, London.

Agre, P. (1994) 'Surveillance and capture: two models of privacy', *Information Society*, 10(2): 101–27.

Alder, K. (2002) *The Measure of All Things – The Seven-Year-Odyssey that Transformed the World*. Abacus, London.

Alonso, W. and Starr, P. (1987) *The Politics of Numbers*. Russell Sage Foundation, New York.

Althusser, L. (1971) *Lenin and Philosophy and Other Essays*, translated by B. Brewster. New Left Books, London.

Amin, A. and Thrift, N. (2002) *Cities: Reimagining the Urban*. Polity, London.

Amin, A. and Thrift, N. (2013) *Arts of the Political: New Openings for the Left*. Duke University Press, Durham, NC.

Amoore, L. (2006) 'Biometric borders: governing mobilities in the war on terror', *Political Geography*, 25: 336–51.

Anderson, B. (2009) 'Affective atmospheres', *Emotion, Space and Society*, 2: 77–81.

Anderson, C. (2008) 'The end of theory: the data deluge makes the scientific method obsolete', *Wired*, 23 June, http://www.wired.com/science/discoveries/magazine/16-07/pb_theory (last accessed 12 October 2012).

Andrejevic, M. (2007) *iSpy: Surveillance and Power in the Interactive Era*. University of Kansas, Lawrence, KS.

Andrejevic, M. (2013) *Infoglut: How Too Much Information is Changing the Way We Think and Know*. Routledge, New York.

Anthony, S. (2013) 'DARPA shows off 1.8-gigapixel surveillance drone, can spot a terrorist from 20,000 feet', *ExtremeTech*, 28 January 2013, http://www.extremetech.com/extreme/146909-darpa-shows-off-1-8-gigapixel-surveillance-drone-can-spot-a-terrorist-from-20000-feet (last accessed 1 February 2013).

Arthur, C. and Cross, M. (2006)' Give us back our crown jewels', *Guardian*, 9 March. http://www.theguardian.com/technology/2006/mar/09/education.epublic (last accessed 21 October 2013).

Asay, M. (2013) 'Big data and the landfills of the digital enterprise', *Readwrite*, 11 February. http://readwrite.com/2013/02/11/big-data-and-the-landfills-of-our-digital-lives (last accessed 19 February 2013).

Bamford, J. (2009) *The Shadow Factory: The Ultra-secret NSA from 9/11 to the Eavesdropping on America*. Anchor Books, New York.

Barnes, T.J. and Hannah, M. (2001) 'The place of numbers: histories, geographies, and theories of quantification', *Environment and Planning D: Society and Space*, 19: 379–83.

Barnett, C. (2013) 'Theory as political technology', *Antipode* (online first), http://radica-lantipode.files.wordpress.com/2013/07/book-review_barnett-on-amin-and-thrift.pdf (last accessed 2 August 2013).

Bates, J. (2012) '"This is what modern deregulation looks like": co-optation and contestation in the shaping of the UK's Open Government Data Initiative', *The Journal of Community Informatics*, 8(2), http://www.ci-journal.net/index.php/ciej/article/view/845/916 (last accessed 6 February 2013).

Bates, J. (2013) 'Opening up public data', *SPERI Comment*, 21 May. http://speri.dept.shef.ac.uk/2013/05/21/opening-public-data/ (last accessed 18 September 2013).

Batty, M. (2007) *Cities and Complexity: Understanding Cities with Cellular Automata, Agent Based Models, and Fractals*. MIT Press, Cambridge, MA.

Batty, M., Axhausen, K.W., Giannotti, F., Pozdnoukhov, A., Bazzani, A., Wachowicz, M., Ouzounis, G. and Portugali, Y. (2012) 'Smart cities of the future', *European Physical Journal Special Topics*, 214: 481–518.

Baym, N.K. (2013) 'Data not seen: the uses and shortcomings of social media metrics', *First Monday*, 18(10), http://firstmonday.org/ojs/index.php/fm/article/view/4873/3752 (last accessed 3 January 2014).

Beagrie, N., Lavoie, B. and Woollard, M. (2010) *Keeping Research Data Safe 2*, JISC, London and Bristol. http://www.beagrie.com/jisc.php.

Becker, H. (1952) 'Science, culture, and society', *Philosophy of Science*, 19(4): 273–87.

Beer, D. and Burrows, R. (2007) 'Sociology and, of and in Web 2.0: some initial considera-tions', *Sociological Research Online*, 12(5), http://www.socresonline.org.uk/12/5/17.html.

Beer, D. and Burrows, R. (2013) 'Popular culture, digital archives and the new social life of data', *Theory, Culture and Society*, 30(4): 47–71.

Benkler, Y. (2006) *The Wealth of Networks: How Social Production Transforms Markets and Freedom*. Yale University Press, New Haven, CT.

Berners-Lee, T. (2009) *Linked Data*, http://www.w3.org/DesignIssues/LinkedData.html (last accessed 30 January 2013).

Berry, D. (2011) 'The computational turn: thinking about the digital humanities', *Culture Machine*, 12, http://www.culturemachine.net/index.php/cm/article/view/440/470 (last accessed 3 December 2012).

Bertolucci, J. (2013) 'IBM, universities team up to build data scientists', *InformationWeek*, 15 January. http://www.informationweek.com/big-data/big-data-analytics/ibm-universities-team-up-to-build-data-scientists/ (last accessed 16 January 2014).

Bettencourt, L.M.A., Lobo, J., Helbing, D., Kuhnert, C. and West, G.B. (2007) 'Growth, innovation, scaling, and the pace of life in cities', *Proceedings of the National Academy of Sciences*, 104(17): 7301–06.

Bielsa, A. (2013) 'The Smart City Project in Santander', *Sensors*, 1 March, http://www.sensorsmag.com/wireless-applications/smart-city-project-santander-11152 (last accessed 27 May 2013).

Boellstorff, T. (2013) 'Making big data, in theory', *First Monday*, 18(10), http://firstmonday.org/ojs/index.php/fm/article/view/4869/3750 (last accessed 3 January 2014).

Bollier, D. (2010) *The Promise and Peril of Big Data*. The Aspen Institute. http://www.aspeninstitute.org/sites/default/files/content/docs/pubs/The_Promise_and_Peril_of_Big_Data.pdf (last accessed 1 October 2012).

Bonney, R., Ballard, H., Jordan, R., McCallie, E., Phillips, T., Shirk, J. and Wilderman, C.C. (2009) *Public Participation in Scientific Research: Defining the Field and Assessing Its Potential for Informal Science Education.* http://www.informalscience.org/documents/PPSR report 20FINAL.pdf. A CAISE Inquiry Group Report, Center for Advancement of Informal Science Education (CAISE). Washington, DC (last accessed 17 January 2014).

Borgman, C.L. (2007) *Scholarship in the Digital Age.* MIT Press, Cambridge, MA.

Borgman, C.L. (2012) 'The conundrum of sharing research data', *Journal of the American Society for Information Science and Technology,* 63(6): 1059–78.

Bowker, G. (2005) *Memory Practices in the Sciences.* MIT Press, Cambridge, MA.

Bowker, G. and Star, L. (1999) *Sorting Things Out: Classification and Its Consequences.* MIT Press, Cambridge, MA.

boyd, D. and Crawford, K. (2011) 'Six provocations for big data', SSRN, http://ssrn.com/abstract=1926431 (last accessed 22 February 2013)

boyd, D. and Crawford, K. (2012) 'Critical questions for big data', *Information, Communication and Society,* 15(5): 662–79.

Brooks, D. (2013a) 'The philosophy of data', *New York Times,* 4 February, http://www.nytimes.com/2013/02/05/opinion/brooks-the-philosophy-of-data.html (last accessed 5 February 2013).

Brooks, D. (2013b) 'What data can't do', *New York Times,* 18 February, http://www.nytimes.com/2013/02/19/opinion/brooks-what-data-cant-do.html (last accessed 18 February 2013).

Bruns, A. (2013) 'Faster than the speed of print: reconciling "big data" social media analysis and academic scholarship', *First Monday,* 18(10), http://firstmonday.org/ojs/index.php/fm/article/view/4879/3756 (last accessed 3 January 2014).

Bryant, R., Katz, R.H. and Lazowska, E.D. (2008) *Big-Data Computing: Creating Revolutionary Breakthroughs in Commerce, Science and Society.* December, Computing Community Consortium, http://www.cra.org/ccc/docs/init/Big_Data.pdf (last accessed 12 October 2012).

Brynjolfsson, E., Hitt, L.M. and Kim, H.H. (2011) *Strength in Numbers: How Does Data-Driven Decision-making Affect Firm Performance?* SSRN, http://ssrn.com/abstract=1819486 (last accessed 22 February 2013).

Burman, C. and MacLure, M. (2005) 'Deconstruction as a method of research', in B. Somekh and C. Lewin (eds), *Research Methods in the Social Sciences.* Sage, London, pp. 282–92.

Callebaut, W. (2012) 'Scientific perspectivism: a philosopher of science's response to the challenge of big data biology', *Studies in History and Philosophy of Biological and Biomedical Sciences,* 43: 69–80.

Calzolari, M.C. (2012) 'Analysis of Twitter followers of leading international companies', 8 June, http://www.camisanicalzolari.com/MCC-Twitter-ENG.pdf (last accessed 3 January 2014).

Campbell, D.T. (1976) *Assessing the Impact of Planned Social Change.* The Public Affairs Center, Dartmouth College, New Hampshire.

Carr, N.G. (2007) 'The ignorance of crowds', *Strategy + Business Magazine,* 47: 1–5.

Carroll, R. (2013) 'Welcome to Utah, the NSA's desert home for eavesdropping on America', *Guardian,* 14 June. http://www.guardian.co.uk/world/2013/jun/14/nsa-utah-data-facility (last accessed 8 July 2013).

Case, D.O. (2002) *Looking for Information: A Survey of Research on Information Seeking, Needs, and Behavior*. Academic Press, Amsterdam.

Castells, M. (1988) *The Informational City: Information Technology, Economic Restructuring and the Urban-regional Process*. Blackwell, Oxford.

Castells, M. (1996) *Rise of the Network Society*. Blackwell, Oxford.

Cavoukian, A. (2009) *Privacy by Design: A Primer*. http://www.privacybydesign.ca/content/uploads/2013/10/pbd-primer.pdf (last accessed 15 October 2013).

CCSDS (2012) *Reference Model for an Open Archival Information System (OAIS)*. Consultative Committee for Space Data Systems, Washington, DC. http://public.ccsds.org/publications/archive/650x0m2.pdf (last accessed 21 October 2013).

Chignard, S. (2013) 'A brief history of open data', *Paris Tech Review*, 29 March, http://www.paristechreview.com/2013/03/29/brief-history-open-data/ (last accessed 18 September 2013).

Chopra, S. and Meindl, P. (2012) *Supply Chain Management: Strategy, Planning and Operation*, 5th edition. Pearson, Harlow.

Christensen, C.M. (1997) *The Innovator's Dilemma*. Harvard Business Review Press, Cambridge, MA.

CIPPIC (2006) *On the Data Trail: How Detailed Information About You Gets into the Hands of Organizations With Whom You Have No Relationship. A Report on the Canadian Data Brokerage Industry*. http://www.cippic.ca/uploads/May1-06/DatabrokerReport.pdf, The Canadian Internet Policy and Public Interest Clinic, Ottawa (last accessed 17 January 2014).

Clark, L. (2013) 'No questions asked: big data firm maps solutions without human input', *Wired*, 16 January, http://www.wired.co.uk/news/archive/2013-01/16/ayasdi-big-data-launch (last accessed 28 January 2013).

Clarke, R. (1988) 'Information technology and dataveillance', *Communications of the ACM*, 31(5): 498–512.

Clarke, R. (1994a) 'The digital persona and its application to data surveillance', *The Information Society*, 10(2): 77–92.

Clarke, R. (1994b) 'Human identification in information systems: management challenges and public policy issues', *Information Technology and People*, 7(4): 6–37.

Claverie-Berge, I. (2012) 'Solutions big data IBM', IBM corporation. http://www-05.ibm.com/fr/events/netezzaDM_2012/Solutions_Big_Data.pdf (last accessed 9 July 2013).

Clements, A. (2013) Democratic State Surveillance, Transparency and Trust. Cyberdialogue conference, University of Toronto, 17–18 March. http://www.cyberdialogue.ca/2013/03/democratic-state-surveillance-transparency-and-trust-by-andrew-clement/ (last accessed 8 July 2013).

Clifford, S. (2012) 'Shopper alert: price may drop for you alone', *New York Times*, 9 August, http://www.nytimes.com/2012/08/10/business/supermarkets-try-customizing-prices-for-shoppers.html (last accessed 8 August 2013).

Codd, E.F. (1970) 'A relational model of data for large shared data banks', *Communications of the ACM*, 13(6): 377–87.

Cohen, D. (2008) 'Contribution to: The Promise of Digital History' (round table discussion), *Journal of American History*, 95(2): 452–91.

Cohen, J. (2012) 'What is privacy for?' Social Sciences Research Network, http://papers.ssrn.com/sol3/papers.cfm?abstract_id=2175406 (last accessed 16 July 2013).

Constine, J. (2012) 'How big is Facebook's data? 2.5 billion pieces of content and 500+ terabytes ingested every day', *TechCrunch,* 22 August, http://techcrunch. com/2012/08/22/how-big-is-facebooks-data-2-5-billion-pieces-of-content-and-500-terabytes-ingested-every-day/ (last accessed 28 January 2013).

Coterill, C. (2011) 'Location privacy: who protects?', *URISA,* 23(2): 49–59.

CRA (2003) *Grand Research Challenges in Information Systems,* The Computing Research Association. http://archive.cra.org/reports/gc.systems.pdf (last accessed 16 January 2014).

Crampton, J., Graham, M., Poorthuis, A., Shelton, T., Stephens, M., Wilson, M.W. and Zook, M. (2012) *Beyond the Geotag? Deconstructing 'Big Data' and Leveraging the Potential of the Geoweb,* http://www.uky.edu/~tmute2/geography_methods/readingPDFs/2012-Beyond-the-Geotag-2012.10.01.pdf (last accessed 21 February 2013).

Crang, M. and Cook, I. (2007) *Doing Ethnographies.* Sage, London.

Crawford, K. (2013) 'The hidden biases of big data', *Harvard Business Review Blog,* 1 April, http://blogs.hbr.org/2013/04/the-hidden-biases-in-big-data/ (last accessed 18 September 2013).

Critical Art Ensemble (1995) 'The mythology of terrorism on the Net', http://www. critical-art.net/books/digital/tact2.pdf (last accessed 31 May 2013).

Croll, A. (2012) 'Big data is our generation's civil rights issue, and we don't know it', in *Big Data Now: Current Perspectives from O'Reilly Media.* O'Reilly Media, Sebastopol, CA, pp. 55–9.

Crovitz, L.G. (2012) 'Obama's "Big Data" Victory', *Wall Street Journal,* 18 November, http://online.wsj.com/article/SB10001424127887323353204578126671124151266. html (last accessed 19 November 2012).

Crowley, U. (2009) 'Genealogy method', in R. Kitchin and N. Thrift (eds), *International Encyclopedia of Human Geography,* vol. 4. Elsevier, Oxford, pp. 341–4.

Crutcher, M. and Zook, M. (2009) 'Placemarks and waterlines: racialized cyberscapes in post-Katrina Google Earth', *Geoforum,* 40(4): 523–34.

Cukier, K. (2010) 'Data, data everywhere', *The Economist,* 25 February, http://www. economist.com/node/15557443 (last accessed 12 November 2012).

Culler, J. (2010) 'The closeness of close reading', *ADE Bulletin,* 149: 20–25.

Curry, M.R. (1997) 'The digital individual and the private realm', *Annals of the Association of American Geographers,* 87: 681–99.

Curry, M.R., Philips, D.J. and Regan, P.M. (2004) 'Emergency response systems and the creeping legibility of people and places', *The Information Society,* 20: 357–69.

Cyberinfrastructure Council (2007) 'Cyberinfrastructure vision for 21st century discovery', http://www.nsf.gov/pubs/2007/nsf0728/index.jsp?org=EEC, National Science Foundation, Washington, DC (last accessed 17 January 2014).

Danna, A. and Gandy, O.H. (2002) 'All that glitters is not gold: digging beneath the surface of data mining', *Journal of Business Ethics,* 40: 373–86.

Darnton, R. (2000) 'An early information society: news and the media in eighteenth-century Paris', *American Historical Review,* 105: 1–30.

Dasish (2012) *Roadmap for Preservation and Curation in the Social Sciences and Humanities,* http://dasish.eu/publications/projectreports/D4.1_-_Roadmap_for_Preservation_ and_Curation_in_the_SSH.pdf/ (last accessed 15 October 2013).

Data Seal of Approval (2010) *Quality Guidelines for Digital Research Data*, http://www.datasealofapproval.org/media/filer_public/2013/09/27/dsa-booklet_1_june2010.pdf (last accessed 8 October 2013).

DataRemixed (2013) *Worldwide Open Data Sites*, 8 August, http://dataremixed.com/2013/08/worldwide-open-data-sites (last accessed 4 November 2013).

Davenport, T.H., Barth, P. and Bean, R. (2012) 'How "Big Data" Is Different', *MIT Sloan Management Review,* 30 July, http://sloanreview.mit.edu/the-magazine/2012-fall/54104/how-big-data-is-different/ (last accessed 28 January 2013).

de Goes, J. (2013) '"Big data" is dead. What's next?', *VB/Big Data,* 23 February, http://venturebeat.com/2013/02/22/big-data-is-dead-whats-next/ (last accessed 26 February 2013).

De Micheli, C. and Stroppa, A. (2013) 'Twitter and the underground market', 11th Nexa Lunch Seminar, 22 May, http://nexa.polito.it/nexacenterfiles/lunch-11-de_micheli-stroppa.pdf (last accessed 3 January 2013).

de Vries, M., Kapff, L., Negreiro Achiaga, M., Wauters, P., Osimo, D., Foley, P., Szkuta, K., O'Connor, J. and Whitehouse, D. (2011) *Pricing of Public Sector Information Study (POPSIS)*, http://epsiplatform.eu/sites/default/files/models.pdf (last accessed 11 August 2013).

Deloite (2012) *Open Data: Driving Ingenuity, Innovation and Growth.* Deloitte, London. http://www.deloitte.com/assets/Dcom-UnitedKingdom/Local%20Assets/Documents/Market%20insights/Deloitte%20Analytics/uk-insights-deloitte-analytics-open-data-june-2012.pdf (last accessed 14 August 2013).

Dembosky, A., Waters, R. and Steel, E. (2012) 'Questions raised over power of big data', *Financial Times, Tech Hub,* 11 December, http://www.ft.com/intl/cms/s/0/92f76 77a-40dd-11e2-aafa-00144feabdc0.html (last accessed 11 December 2012).

Dery, K., Hall, R. and Wailes, N. (2006) 'ERPs as technologies-in-practice: social construction, materiality and the role of organisational factors', *New Technology, Work and Employment,* 21(3): 229–41.

Desrosières, A. (1998) *The Politics of Large Numbers: A History of Statistical Reasoning,* translated by C. Naish. Harvard University Press, Cambridge, MA.

Dicken, P. (2003) *Global Shift.* Sage, London.

Diebold, F. (2012) 'A personal perspective on the origin(s) and development of "big data": the phenomenon, the term, and the discipline', http://www.ssc.upenn.edu/~fdiebold/papers/paper112/Diebold_Big_Data.pdf (last accessed 5 February 2013).

Dietrich, D. (2012) 'Linked data', *ePSIplatform Topic Report,* no: 2012 11, http://epsiplatform.eu/content/topic-report-linked-data (last accessed 14 August 2013).

Dodge, M. and Kitchin, R. (2004) 'Flying through code/space: the real virtuality of air travel', *Environment and Planning A,* 36: 195–211.

Dodge, M. and Kitchin, R. (2005) 'Codes of life: identification codes and the machine-readable world', *Environment and Planning D: Society and Space,* 23(6): 851–81.

Dodge, M. and Kitchin, R. (2007a) 'The automatic management of drivers and driving spaces', *Geoforum,* 38(2): 264–75.

Dodge, M. and Kitchin, R. (2007b) '"Outlines of a world coming in existence": pervasive computing and the ethics of forgetting', *Environment and Planning B,* 34(3): 431–45.

Dodge, M. and Kitchin, R. (2013) 'Mapping experience and knowledge: crowdsourced cartography', *Environment and Planning A,* 45(1): 19–36.

Dodge, M., Perkins, C. and Kitchin, R. (2009) 'Mapping modes, methods and moments: a manifesto for map studies', in M. Dodge, R. Kitchin and C. Perkins (eds), *Rethinking Maps.* Routledge, London, pp. 220–43.

Donovan, K. (2012) 'Seeing like a slum: towards open, deliberative development', *Georgetown Journal of International Affairs,* 13(1): 97–104.

Dourish, P. (2001) *Where the Action Is.* MIT Press, Cambridge, MA.

Dourish, P. and Bell, G. (2007) 'The infrastructure of experience and the experience of infrastructure: meaning and structure in everyday encounters with space', *Environment and Planning B,* 34: 414–30.

Driscoll, K. (2012) 'From punched cards to "big data": a social history of database populism', *communication +1,* 1(4), http://scholarworks.umass.edu/cpo/vol1/iss1/4 (last accessed 22 February 2013).

Dumbill, E. (2012) 'What is big data?' in *Big Data Now: Current Perspectives from O'Reilly Media.* O'Reilly Media, Sebastopol, CA. pp. 3–10.

Dwoskin, E. (2013) 'Data broker discloses what it knows', *Wall Street Journal,* 4 September, http://blogs.wsj.com/digits/2013/09/04/data-broker-discloses-what-it-knows/ (last accessed 11 October 2013).

Dyche, J. (2012) 'Big data "eurekas!" don't just happen', *Harvard Business Review Blog,* 20 November, http://blogs.hbr.org/cs/2012/11/eureka_doesnt_just_happen.html (last accessed 23 November 2012).

Eaves, D. (2013) 'The value of open data – don't measure growth, measure destruction', 25 April, http://eaves.ca/2013/04/25/the-value-of-open-data-dont-measure-growth-measure-destruction/ (last accessed 18 September 2013).

Economist, The (2010) 'All too much: Monstrous amounts of data', 25 February, http://www.economist.com/node/15557421 (last accessed 12 November 2012).

Economist, The (2013) 'Open data: a new goldmine', 18 May, http://www.economist.com/news/business/21578084-making-official-data-public-could-spur-lots-innovation-new-goldmine (last accessed 16 September 2013).

Edwards, J. (2013) 'Facebook is about to launch a huge play in "big data" analytics', *Business Insider,* 10 May, http://www.businessinsider.com/facebook-is-about-to-launch-a-huge-play-in-big-data-analytics-2013-5 (last accessed 18 September 2013).

Efrati, A., Thurm, S. and Searchy, D. (2011) 'Mobile-app makers face U.S. privacy investigation', *Wall Street Journal,* 5 April, http://online.wsj.com/article/SB10001424052748703806304576242923804770968.html (last accessed 17 July 2013).

Elliott, C. (2004) 'Some rental cars are keeping tabs on the drivers', *New York Times,* 13 January, http://www.nytimes.com/2004/01/13/business/13gps.html (last accessed 8 August 2013).

Ellis, J. (2013) 'Hiding in public: how the National Archives wants to open up its data to Americans', *Nieman Journalism Lab,* 25 February, http://www.niemanlab.org/2013/02/hiding-in-public-how-the-national-archives-wants-to-open-up-its-data-to-americans/ (last accessed 26 February 2013).

Elwood, S. and Leszczynski, A. (2011) 'Privacy reconsidered: new representations, data practices, and the geoweb', *Geoforum,* 42: 6–15.

European Commission (2012) *Commission Proposes a Comprehensive Reform of the Data Protection Rules*, 25 January, http://ec.europa.eu/justice/newsroom/data-protection/news/120125_en.htm (last accessed 6 August 2013).

Farber, D. (2013) 'Counting the Internet of things in real time', *CNet*, 30 July, http://news.cnet.com/8301-11386_3-57596162-76/counting-the-internet-of-things-in-real-time/ (last accessed 18 September 2013).

Farber, M., Cameron, M., Ellis, C. and Sullivan, J. (2011) *Massive Data Analytics and the Cloud: A Revolution in Intelligence Analysis*. Booz Allen Hamilton. http://www.boozallen.com/media/file/MassiveData.pdf (last accessed 16 July 2013).

Federal Trade Commission (2012) *Protecting Consumer Privacy in an Era of Rapid Change*, http://www.ftc.gov/os/2012/03/120326privacyreport.pdf (last accessed 14 October 2013).

Ferro, E. and Osella, M. (2013) *Eight Business Model Archetypes for PSI Re-Use. Open Data on the Web*, Workshop, 23–24 April 2013, Google Campus, Shoreditch, London. http://www.w3.org/2013/04/odw/odw13_submission_27.pdf (last accessed 13 August 2013).

Fitzgerald, A.M. (2010) *State of Play: PSI Reuse in Australia. European Public Sector Information Platform*, Topic Report No. 13, http://epsiplatform.eu/sites/default/files/ePSIplatform%20Topic%20Report%20No.%2013%20Australia%20final.pdf (last accessed 14 August 2013).

Flaounas, I., Ali, O., Lansdall-Welfare, T., De Bie, T., Mosdell, N., Lewis, J. and Cristianini, N. (2013) 'Research methods in the age of digital journalism', *Digitial Journalism*, 1(1): 102–16.

Floridi, L. (2005) 'Is information meaningful data?', *Philosophy and Phenomenological Research*, 70(2): 351–70.

Floridi, L. (2008) 'Data', in W.A. Darity (ed.), *International Encyclopedia of the Social Sciences*, 2nd edition. Detroit: Macmillan. Preprint online: http://www.philosophyofinformation.net/publications/pdf/data.pdf.

Floridi, L. (2010) *Information: A Very Short Guide*. Oxford University Press, Oxford.

Floridi, L. (2012) 'Big data and their epistemological challenge', *Philosophy and Technology*, 25(4): 435–7.

Flowers, M. (2013) 'Beyond open data: the data-driven city', in B. Goldstein and L. Dyson (eds), *Beyond Transparency: Open Data and the Future of Civic Innovation*. Code for America Press, San Francisco, CA. pp. 196–209.

Foucault, M. (1977) *Discipline and Punish*. Allen Lane, London.

Foucault, M. (1978) *The History of Sexuality*, Volume One. Random House, New York.

Foucault, M. (1981) *Power/Knowledge: Selected Interviews and Other Writings 1972–1977*. Harvester, London.

Franks, B. (2012) *Taming the Big Data Tidal Wave: Finding Opportunities in Huge Data Streams with Advanced Analytics*. Wiley, Hoboken, NJ.

Fry, J., Lockyer, S., Oppenheim, C., Houghton, J.W. and Rasmussen, B. (2008) *Identifying Benefits Arising from the Curation and Open Sharing of Research Data Produced by UK Higher Education and Research Institutes*, JISC, London and Bristol. http://repository.jisc.ac.uk/279/ (last accessed 21 October 2013).

Gannon, D. and Reid, D. (2009) 'Parallelism and the cloud', in T. Hey, S. Tansley and K. Tolle (eds), *The Fourth Paradigm: Data-Intensive Scientific Discovery*. Microsoft Research, Redmond, WA, pp. 131–5.

Gantz, J. and Reinsel, D. (2011) *Extracting Value from Chaos*. IDC, Framingham, MA http://idcdocserv.com/1142 (last accessed 1 October 2012).

Gantz, J., Reinsel, D., Chute, C., Schlichting, W., McArthur, J., Minton, S., Xheneti, I., Toncheva, A. and Manfrediz, A. (2007) *The Expanding Digital Universe: A Forecast of Worldwide Information Growth Through 2010*. IDC, Framingham, MA, http://www.emc.com/collateral/analyst-reports/expanding-digital-idc-white-paper.pdf (last accessed 26 October 2012).

Garvey, E.G. (2013) '"*facts* and FACTS": abolitionists' database innovations', in L. Gitelman (ed), *'Raw Data' is an Oxymoron*. MIT Press, Cambridge, MA, pp. 89–102.

Gershenfeld, N., Krikorian, R. and Cohen, D. (2004) 'The internet of things', *Scientific American*, October, 291(4): 76–81.

Gilder, G. (2000) *Telecosm: How Infinite Bandwidth will Revolutionize Our World*. Free Press, New York.

Gilheany, S. (2000) 'Projecting the cost of magnetic disk storage over the next 10 years', http://www.teqnium.in/images/MagneticStorageOvertheNext10years.pdf (last accessed 16 January 2014).

Gitelman, L. and Jackson, V. (2013) 'Introduction', in L. Gitelman (ed.), *'Raw Data' is an Oxymoron*. MIT Press, Cambridge, MA, pp. 1–14.

Gleeson, J., Kitchin, R., Bartley, B. and Treacy, C. (2009) 'New ways of mapping social inclusion in Dublin City', http://www.nuim.ie/nirsa/mappinginclusion.pdf, Dublin City Partnership/Dublin City Development Board (last accessed 13 August 2013).

Goddard, L. and Byrne, G. (2010) 'Linked data tools: semantic Web for the masses', *First Monday*, 15(11), http://firstmonday.org/ojs/index.php/fm/article/view/3120/2633 (last accessed 14 August 2013).

Goldberg, J. (2012) 'Big data ushers in era of security intelligence', *Wired: Innovation Insights*, 30 November, http://www.wired.com/insights/2012/11/big-data-ushers-in-era-of-security-intelligence/ (last accessed 3 December 2012).

Golledge, R. and Stimson, R. (1997) *Spatial Behaviour*. Guilford, New York.

González-Bailón, S. (2013) '"Big data" and the capillaries of human geography', *Dialogues in Human Geography*, 3(3): 292–6.

González-Bailón, S., Wang, N., Rivero, A., Borge-Holtoefer, J. and Moreno, Y. (2012) *Assessing the Bias in Communication Networks Sampled from Twitter*. Working Paper, http://arxiv.org/abs/1212.1684 (last accessed 17 January 2014).

Goodchild, M.F. (2007) 'Citizens as sensors: the world of volunteered geography', *GeoJournal*, 69: 211–21.

Goodchild, M.F. (2009) 'Uncertainty', in R. Kitchin and N. Thrift (eds), *International Encyclopedia of Human Geography*, vol 12. Elsevier, Oxford, pp. 1–5.

Gordon, G. (2013) 'Towards an overarching narrative on open government', *Open Government Partnership UK*, 12 February, http://www.opengovernment.org.uk/towards-an-overarching-narrative-on-open-government/ (last accessed 19 February 2013).

Gorman, S. (2013) 'The danger of a big data episteme and the need to evolve geographic information systems', *Dialogues in Human Geography*, 3(3): 285–91.

Goss, J, (1995) '"We know who you are and we know where you live": the instrumental rationality of geodemographics systems', *Economic Geography*, 71: 171–98.

Gould, P. (1981) 'Letting the data speak for themselves', *Annals of the Association of American Geographers,* 71(2): 166–76.

Graham, M. (2012) 'Big data and the end of theory?' *Guardian,* 9 March, http://www.guardian.co.uk/news/datablog/2012/mar/09/big-data-theory (last accessed 12 November 2012).

Graham, M., Stephens, M. and Hale, S. (2013) 'Mapping the geoweb: a geography of Twitter', *Environment and Planning A,* 45: 100–02.

Graham, S. (2005) 'Software-sorted geographies', *Progress in Human Geography,* 29(5): 562–80.

Graham. S. and Marvin, S. (1996) *Telecommunications and the City.* Routledge, London.

Graham, S. and Marvin, S. (2001) *Splintering Urbanism.* Routledge, London.

Gralla, P., Sacco, A. and Faas, R. (2011) 'Smartphone apps: is your privacy protected?', *ComputerWorld,* http://www.computerworld.com/s/article/9218163/Smartphone_apps_Is_your_privacy_protected (last accessed 17 July 2013).

Grant, D., Harley, B. and Wright, C. (2006) 'Editorial introduction: the work and organisational implications of Enterprise Resource Planning systems', *New Technology, Work and Employment,* 21(3): 196–8.

Granville, V. (2013) 'The curse of big data', *analyticbridge,* 5 January, http://www.analytic-bridge.com/profiles/blogs/the-curse-of-big-data (last accessed 28 January 2013).

Greenfield, A. (2006) *Everyware: The Dawning Age of Ubiquitous Computing.* New Riders, Boston.

Greenwald, G. and MacAskill, E. (2013) 'NSA Prism program taps in to user data of Apple, Google and others', *Guardian,* 7 June, http://www.guardian.co.uk/world/2013/jun/06/us-tech-giants-nsa-data (last accessed 8 July 2013).

Grimes, S. (2011) 'Unstructured data and the 80 percent rule', *Clarabridge,* http://clarabridge.com/default.aspx?tabid=137&ModuleID=635&ArticleID=551 (last accessed 4 March 2013).

Grochowski, E. and Halem, R.D. (2003) 'Technological impact of magnetic hard disk drives on storage systems', *IBM Systems Journal,* 42: 338–46.

Gurstein, M. (2011) 'Open data: empowering the empowered or effective data use for everyone', *First Monday,* 16(2), http://www.uic.edu/htbin/cgiwrap/bin/ojs/index.php/fm/article/view/3316/2764 (last accessed 6 February 2013).

Gurstein, M. (2013) 'Should "Open Government Data" be a product or a service (and why does it matter?)', *Gurstein's Community Informatics,* 3 February, http://gurstein.wordpress.com/2013/02/03/is-open-government-data-a-product-or-a-service-and-why-does-it-matter/ (last accessed 6 February 2013).

Haklay, M. (2010) 'How good is volunteered geographical information? A comparative study of OpenStreetMap and Ordnance Survey datasets', *Environment and Planning B,* 37: 682–703.

Hales, D. (2013) 'Lies, damned lies and big data', *Aid on the Edge of Chaos,* 1 February 2013, http://aidontheedge.info/2013/02/01/lies-damned-lies-and-big-data/ (last accessed 5 February 2013).

Han, J., Kamber, M. and Pei, J. (2011) *Data Mining: Concepts and Techniques,* 3rd edition. Morgan Kaufmann, Waltham, MA.

Hancke, G.P., de Carvalho e Silva, B. and Hancke Jr., G.P. (2012) 'The role of advanced sensing in smart cities', *Sensors,* 13: 393–425.

Hannah, M. (1997) 'Space and the structuring of disciplinary power: an interpretative review', *Geografiska Annaler Series B, Human Geography,* 79: 171–80.

Hannah, M. (2011) *Dark Territory in the Information Age.* Ashgate, Farnham.

Haque, U. (2012) 'What is a city that it would be "smart"?', *Volume #34: City in a Box* http://volumeproject.org/blog/2012/12/21/volume-34-city-in-a-box/.

Haraway, D. (1991) *Simians, Cyborgs and Women: The Reinvention of Nature.* Routledge, New York.

Harcourt, B.E. (2006) *Against Prediction: Profiling, Policing and Punishing in an Actuarial Age.* Chicago University Press, Chicago.

Harley, J.B. (1989) 'Deconstructing the map', *Cartographica,* 26: 1–20.

Harris, D. (2012) 'Researchers mine 2.5m news articles to prove what we already know', *Gigaom,* 26 November 2012, http://gigaom.com/2012/11/26/researchers-mine-2-5m-news-articles-to-prove-what-we-already-know/ (last accessed 28 January 2013).

Hart, J.A., Reed, R.R. and Bar, F. (1992) 'The building of the Internet: implications for the future of broadband networks', *Telecommunications Policy,* 16: 666–89.

Harvey, D. (1972) *Social Justice and the City.* Blackwell, Oxford.

Hastie, T., Tibshirani, R. and Friedman, J. (2009) *The Elements of Statistical Learning: Data Mining, Inference, and Prediction,* 2nd edition. Springer, New York.

Hausenblas, M. (2012) '5 ★ open data', http://5stardata.info/ (last accessed 30 January 2013).

Helbig, N., Cresswell, A.M., Burke, G.B. and Luna-Reyes, L. (2012) The Dynamics of Opening Government Data: A White Paper. Centre for Technology in Government, State University of New York, Albany. http://www.ctg.albany.edu/publications/reports/opendata/opendata.pdf (last accessed 6 February 2013).

Helland, P. (2011) 'If you have too much data, then "good enough" is good enough', *ACM Queue,* https://queue.acm.org/detail.cfm?id=1988603 (last accessed 4 July 2013).

Herbert, S. (2000) 'For ethnography', *Progress in Human Geography,* 24(4): 550–68.

Hewitt, R. (2010) *Map of a Nation: A Biography of the Ordnance Survey.* Granta Books, London.

Hey, T., Tansley, S. and Tolle, K. (2009) 'Jim Gray on eScience: A transformed scientific method', in T. Hey, S. Tansley and K. Tolle (eds), *The Fourth Paradigm: Data-Intensive Scientific Discovery.* Microsoft Research, Redmond, WA, pp. xvii–xxxi.

Hilbert, M. and López, P. (2011) 'The world's technological capacity to store, communicate, and compute information', *Science,* 10(331): 703–05.

Hill, D. (2013) 'On the smart city: or, a "manifesto" for smart citizens instead', *City of Sound,* 1 February, http://www.cityofsound.com/blog/2013/02/on-the-smart-city-a-call-for-smart-citizens-instead.html (last accessed 5 February 2013).

Hollands, R.G. (2008) 'Will the real smart city please stand up?', *City,* 12(3): 303–20.

Hon, W.K., Millard, C. and Walden, I. (2011) *The Problem of 'Personal Data' in Cloud Computing – What Information is Regulated?,* Queen Mary University of London, School of Law Legal Studies Research Paper No. 75/2011, http://papers.ssrn.com/sol3/papers.cfm?abstract_id=1783577 (last accessed 16 July 2013).

Houghton, J. (2011) *Costs and Benefits of Data Provision.* Report to the Australian National Data Service. Centre for Strategic Economic Studies, Victoria University. http://ands.org.au/resource/houghton-cost-benefit-study.pdf (last accessed 14 August 2013).

Howe, J. (2008) *Crowdsourcing*. Random House, New York.

Huijboom, N. and Van der Broek, T. (2011) 'Open data: an international comparison of strategies', *European Journal of ePractice*, 12 (March/April), http://www.epractice.eu/files/European%20Journal%20epractice%20Volume%2012_1.pdf (last accessed 15 August 2013).

IBM (2012) *What is Big Data?*, http://www-01.ibm.com/software/data/bigdata/ (last accessed 12 November 2012).

IBM (n.d.) *Big Data at the Speed of Business*, http://www-01.ibm.com/software/data/bigdata/industry.html (last accessed 9 July 2013).

Innes, M. (2001) 'Control creep', *Sociological Research Online*, 6(3), http://www.socresonline.org.uk/6/3/innes.html (last accessed 14th January 2014).

Issenberg, S. (2012) *The Victory Lab: The Secret Science of Winning Campaigns*. New York, Crown.

InterPARES 2 (2013) *Dictionary Definitions*. InterPARES 2 Terminology Database: http://www.interpares.org/ip2/ip2_terminology_db.cfm (last accessed 21 October 2013).

Jacobs, A. (2009) 'The pathologies of big data', *ACM Queue*, 1 July, http://queue.acm.org/detail.cfm?id=1563874 (last accessed 12 November 2012).

Janssen, K. (2012) 'Open Government Data: right to information 2.0 or its rollback version?', *ICRI Working Paper*, 8/2012, http://papers.ssrn.com/sol3/papers.cfm?abstract_id=2152566 (last accessed 14 August 2013).

Jenkins, T. (2013) 'Don't count on big data for answers', *Scotsman*, 12 February, http://www.scotsman.com/the-scotsman/opinion/comment/tiffany-jenkins-don-t-count-on-big-data-for-answers-1-2785890 (last accessed 11 March 2013).

Jensen, H.E. (1950) 'Editorial note', in H. Becker (1952), *Through Values to Social Interpretation*. Duke University Press, Durham, NC, pp. vii–xi.

Jensen, D. (2000) *Data Snooping, Dredging and Fishing: The Dark Side of Data Mining*, http://www.martinsewell.com/datamining/Jens00.pdf (last accessed 20 February 2013).

Johnson, S. (2003) 'Offloading your memories', *The New York Times*, 14 December, http://www.nytimes.com/2003/12/14/magazine/14OFFLOADING.html (last accessed 16 January 2014).

Johnson, J.A. (2013) *From Open Data to Information Justice*. Paper Presented at the Annual Conference of the Midwest Political Science Association, 13 April, Chicago, Illinois. http://papers.ssrn.com/abstract=2241092 (last accessed 16 August 2013).

Kaye, K. (2012) 'Obama's approach to big data: do as I say, not as I do', *AdAge*, 16 November, http://adage.com/article/digital/obama-s-approach-big-data-i-i/238346/ (last accessed 19 November 2012).

Keim, D., Kohlhammer, J., Ellis, G. and Mansmann, F. (2010) *Mastering the Information Age – Solving Problems with Visual Analytics*. Eurographics Association. http://www.vismaster.eu/book/ (last accessed 16 August 2013).

Kelling, S., Hochachka, W., Fink, D., Riedewald, M., Caruana, R., Ballard, G. and Hooker, G. (2009) 'Data-intensive science: a new paradigm for biodiversity studies', *BioScience*, 59(7): 613–20.

King, G. (2011) 'Ensuring the data-rich future of the social sciences', *Science*, 331(February): 719–21.

Kinsley, S. (2011) 'Anticipating ubiquitous computing: logics to forecast technological futures', *Geoforum,* 42(2): 31–240.

Kinsley, S. (2012) 'Futures in the making: practices to anticipate "ubiquitous computing"', *Environment and Planning A,* 44(7): 1554–69.

Kitchin, R. (1996) 'Methodological convergence in cognitive mapping research: investigating configurational knowledge', *Journal of Environmental Psychology,* 16(3): 163–85.

Kitchin, R. (1998) *Cyberspace: The World in the Wires.* John Wiley and Sons, Chichester.

Kitchin, R. (2006) 'Positivistic geography and spatial science', in S. Aitken and G. Valentine (eds), *Approaches in Human Geography.* Sage, London. pp. 20–9.

Kitchin, R. (2013) 'Big data and human geography: opportunities, challenges and risks', *Dialogues in Human Geography,* 3(3): 262–7.

Kitchin, R. (2014) 'The real-time city? Big data and smart urbanism', *GeoJournal,* 79 (1): 1–14.

Kitchin, R. and Dodge, M. (2006) 'Software and the mundane management of air travel', *First Monday,* 11(9), http://firstmonday.org/issues/special11_9/kitchin/ (last accessed 6 March 2014).

Kitchin, R. and Dodge, M. (2011) *Code/Space: Software and Everyday Life.* MIT Press, Cambridge, MA.

Kitchin, R. and Fotheringham, A.S. (1997) 'Aggregation issues in cognitive mapping research', *Professional Geographer,* 49(3): 269–80.

Kitchin, R. and Tate, N. (1999) *Conducting Research in Human Geography: Theory, Methodology and Practice.* Prentice Hall, Harlow.

Kitchin, R., Bartley, B., Gleeson, J., Cowman, M., Fotheringham, S. and Lloyd, C. (2007) 'Joined-up thinking across the Irish border: making the data more compatible', *Journal of Cross Border Studies,* 2: 22–33.

Kitchin, R., Gleeson, J. and Dodge, M. (2012a) 'Unfolding mapping practices: a new epistemology for cartography', *Transactions of the Institute of British Geographers,* 38(3): 480–96.

Kitchin, R., O'Callaghan, C., Boyle, M., Gleeson J. and Keaveney, K. (2012b) 'Placing neoliberalism: the rise and fall of Ireland's Celtic Tiger', *Environment and Planning A,* 44: 1302–26.

Koops, B.J. (2011) 'Forgetting footprints, shunning shadows: a critical analysis of the "right to be forgotten" in big data practice', *SCRIPTed,* 8(3): 229–56.

Kourtit, K., Nijkamp, P. and Arribas-Bel, D. (2012) 'Smart cities perspective – a comparative European study by means of self-organizing maps', *Innovation,* 25(2): 229–46.

Kuhn, T. (1962) *The Structure of Scientific Revolutions.* University of Chicago Press, Chicago.

Lake, C. (2013) '24 beautifully-designed web dashboards that data geeks will love', 3 June, *Econsultancy,* http://econsultancy.com/ie/blog/62844-24-beautifully-designed-web-dashboards-that-data-geeks-will-love (last accessed 12 November 2013).

Laney, D. (2001) '3D data management: controlling data volume, velocity and variety', *Meta Group,* http://blogs.gartner.com/doug-laney/files/2012/01/ad949-3D-Data-Management-Controlling-Data-Volume-Velocity-and-Variety.pdf (last accessed 16 January 2013).

Latour, B. (1989) *Science in Action*. Harvard University Press, Cambridge, MA.

Lauriault, T.P. (2012) *Data, Infrastructures and Geographical Imaginations: Mapping Data Access Discourses in Canada*. Ph.D. Thesis, Carleton University, Ottawa.

Lauriault, T.P., Craig, B.L., Taylor, D.R.F. and Pulsifier, P.L. (2007) 'Today's data are part of tomorrow's research: archival issues in the sciences', *Archivaria*, 64: 123–79.

Lauriault, T.P., Hackett, Y. and Kennedy, E. (2013) *Geospatial Data Preservation Primer*. Ottawa, Hickling, Arthurs and Low.

Lazer, D., Pentland, A., Adamic, L., Aral, S., Barabási, A.-L., Brewer, D., Christakis, N., Contractor, N., Fowler, J., Gutmann, M., Jebara, T., King, G., Macy, M., Roy, D. and Van Alstyne, M. (2009) 'Computational social science', *Science*, 323: 721–33.

Lehning, M., Dawes, N., Bavay, M. Parlange, M., Nath, S. and Zhao. F. (2009) 'Instrumenting the Earth: next-generation sensor networks and environmental science', in T. Hey, S. Tansley and K. Tolle (eds), *The Fourth Paradigm: Data-Intensive Scientific Discovery*. Microsoft Research; Redmond, WA. pp. 45–51.

Lehrer, J. (2010) 'A physicist solves the city', *New York Times*, 17 December, http://www.nytimes.com/2010/12/19/magazine/19Urban_West-t.html (last accessed 23 December 2013).

Leonelli, S. (2012) 'Introduction: making sense of data-driven research in the biological and biomedical sciences', *Studies in History and Philosophy of Biological and Biomedical Sciences*, 43: 1–3.

Leyshon, A. and Thrift, N. (1999) 'Lists come alive: electronic systems of knowledge and the rise of credit-scoring in retail banking', *Economy and Society*, 28: 434–66.

Linehan, T.P. (1991) History and development of Irish population censuses', *Journal of the Statistical and Social Inquiry Society of Ireland*, XXVI(IV): 91–125.

Lohr, S. (2012) 'Sure, big data is great. But so is intuition', *New York Times*, 29 December. http://www.nytimes.com/2012/12/30/technology/big-data-is-great-but-dont-forget-intuition.html (last accessed 3 January 2013).

Lohr, S. (2013) 'SimCity, for real: measuring an untidy metropolis', *New York Times*, 23 February, http://www.nytimes.com/2013/02/24/technology/nyucenter-develops-a-science-of-cities.html (accessed 1 April 2013).

Longo, J. (2011) '#OpenData: digital-era governance: thoroughbred or new public management Trojan horse?', *PP+G Review*, 2(2), http://ppgr.files.wordpress.com/2011/05/longo-ostry.pdf (last accessed 16 September 2013).

Loukides, M. (2010) 'What is data science?', *O'Reilly Radar*, 2 June, http://radar.oreilly.com/2010/06/what-is-data-science.html (last accessed 28 January 2013).

Lucas, P., Ballay, J. and McManus, M. (2012) *Trillions: Thriving in the Emerging Information Ecology*. John Wiley, Hoboken, NJ.

Lusk, G. (2013) 'Big. Bad. Big data', *The Bubble Chamber*, 13 February, http://thebubblechamber.org/2013/02/big-bad-big-data/ (last accessed 19 February 2013).

Lyon, D. (2002) 'Everyday surveillance: personal data and social classifications', *Information, Communication and Society*, 5: 242–57.

Lyon, D. (2003a) 'Surveillance as social sorting: computer codes and mobile bodies', in Lyon, D. (ed.), *Surveillance as Social Sorting: Privacy, Risk and Digital Discrimination*. Routledge, London, pp. 13–30.

Lyon, D. (2003b) 'Airports as data filters: converging surveillance systems after September 11th', *Information, Communication and Ethics in Society*, 1: 13–20.

Lyon, D. (2007) *Surveillance Studies: An Overview*. Polity, Cambridge.

Mann, S., Nolan, J. and Wellman, B. (2003) 'Sousveillance: inventing and using wearable computing devices for data collection in surveillance environments', *Surveillance and Society,* 1(3): 331–55.

Manovich, L. (2011) 'Trending: the promises and the challenges of big social data', http://www.manovich.net/DOCS/Manovich_trending_paper.pdf (last accessed 9 November 2012).

Manyika, J., Chiu, M., Brown, B., Bughin, J., Dobbs, R., Roxburgh, C. and Hung Byers, A. (2011) *Big Data: The Next Frontier for Innovation, Competition, and Productivity*. McKinsey Global Institute.

Marche, S. (2012) 'Literature is not data: against digital humanities', *Los Angeles Review of Books,* 28 October, http://lareviewofbooks.org/article.php?id=1040&fulltext=1 (last accessed 4 April 2013).

Marchetti, N. (2012) 'In Portugal, a smart city from the ground up', *Sustainable Cities Collective,* 7 June, http://sustainablecitiescollective.com/namarchetti/42438/portugal-smart-city-ground (last accessed 27 May 2013).

Marz, N. and Warren, J. (2012) *Big Data: Principles and Best Practices of Scalable Realtime Data Systems*. MEAP edition. Manning, Shelter Island, New York.

Mattern, S. (2013) 'Methodolatry and the art of measure: the new wave of urban data science', *Design Observer: Places,* 5 November, http://designobserver.com/places/feature/0/38174/ (last accessed 15 November 2013).

Mayer-Schonberger, V. and Cukier, K. (2013) *Big Data: A Revolution That Will Change How We Live, Work and Think*. John Murray, London.

McCandless, D. (2010) 'Data, information, knowledge, wisdom', *Information is Beautiful,* 29 November, http://www.informationisbeautiful.net/2010/data-information-knowledge-wisdom/ (last accessed 24 July 2013).

McClean, T. (2011) *Not with a Bang but a Whimper: the Politics of Accountability and Open Data in the UK*. Paper prepared for the American Political Science Association Annual Meeting. Seattle, Washington, 1–4 September 2011. http://papers.ssrn.com/sol3/papers.cfm?abstract_id=1899790 (last accessed 19 August 2013).

McCreary, D. (2009) 'Entity extraction and the semantic web', *Semantic Web,* 12 January, http://semanticweb.com/entity-extraction-and-the-semantic-web_b10675 (last accessed 19 July 2013).

McKeon, S.G. (2013) 'Hacking the hackathon', *Shaunagm.net,* 10 October, http://www.shaunagm.net/blog/2013/10/hacking-the-hackathon/ (last accessed 21 October 2013).

McNay, L. (1994) *Foucault: A Critical Introduction*. Polity Press, Oxford.

Miller, H.J. (2010) 'The data avalanche is here. Shouldn't we be digging?', *Journal of Regional Science,* 50(1): 181–201.

Miller, H.J. and Han, J. (2009) 'Geographic data mining and knowledge discovery: an overview', in H.J. Miller and J. Han (eds), *Geographic Data Mining and Knowledge Discovery*. Taylor and Francis, London, pp. 3–32.

Miller, P. (2001) 'Governing by numbers: why calculative practices matter', *Social Research,* 68(2): 379–96.

Miller, P. (2010) *Linked Data and Government*. ePSIplatform Topic Report no. 7, http://epsi-platform.eu/content/topic-report-no-7-linked-data-and-government-0 (last accessed 14 August 2013).

Miller-Rushing, A., Primack, R. and Bonney, R. (2012) 'The history of public participation in ecological research', *Frontier in Ecology and the Environment,* 10(6): 285–90.

Mims, C. (2013) 'Coming soon: the cybercrime of things', *The Atlantic,* 6 August, http://www.theatlantic.com/technology/archive/2013/08/coming-soon-the-cybercrime-of-things/278409/ (last accessed 7 August 2013).

Minelli, M., Chambers, M. and Dhiraj, A. (2013) *Big Data, Big Analytics.* Wiley, Hoboken, NJ.

Mitchell, M. (1996) *An Introduction to Genetic Algorithms.* MIT Press, Cambridge, MA.

Mooney, P., Sun, H., Corcoran, P. and Yan, L. (2011) 'Citizen generated spatial data and information: risks and opportunities', *Proceedings of the 2nd International Conference on Network Engineering and Computer Science (ICNECS 2011),* Xi'an, Shaanxi, China, www.cs.nuim.ie/~pmooney/websitePapers/Mooney-et-all-Submitted-May2011.pdf (last accessed 28 January 2013).

Moore, G.E. (1965) 'Cramming more components onto integrated circuits', *Electronics,* 38(8), http://download.intel.com/museum/Moores_Law/Articles-Press_Releases/Gordon_Moore_1965_Article.pdf (last accessed 20 May 2013).

Moretti, F. (2005) *Graphs, Maps, Trees: Abstract Models for a Literary History.* Verso, London.

Morozov, E. (2013) *To Save Everything, Click Here: Technology, Solutionism, and the Urge to Fix Problems That Don't Exist.* Allen Lane, New York.

Morton, F. (2005) 'Performing ethnography: Irish traditional music sessions and new methodological spaces', *Social and Cultural Geography,* 6: 661–76.

Najmi (2004) 'Generations of computer', *Techi/Warehouse,* 13 August, http://www.techiwarehouse.com/engine/a046ee08/Generations-of-Computer (last accessed 20 May 2013).

Narayanan, A. and Shmatikov, V. (2010) 'Privacy and security: myths and fallacies of "personally identifiable information"', *Communications of the ACM,* 53(6): 24–6.

National Science Foundation (2012) *Core Techniques and Technologies for Advancing Big Data Science & Engineering (BIGDATA).* Programme solicitation NSF 12-499 http://www.nsf.gov/pubs/2012/nsf12499/nsf12499.pdf (last accessed 25 February 2013).

NISO (National Information Standards Organization) (2004) *Understanding Metadata.* Bethesda, MD, http://www.niso.org/publications/press/UnderstandingMetadata.pdf (last accessed 28 June 2013).

Nordhaus, W.D. (2002) *The Progress of Computing,* version 5.2.2, Yale University. http://www.econ.yale.edu/~nordhaus/homepage/prog_083001a.pdf (last accessed 17 January 2014).

Northcutt, C. (2012) 'Open data creates value', *NYI,* 28 August, http://www.nyi.net/blog/2012/08/open-data-creates-value/ (last accessed 28 January 2013).

OECD (2008) *OECD Recommendation of the Council for Enhanced Access and More Effective Use of Public Sector Information.* OECD, http://www.oecd.org/internet/ieconomy/40826024.pdf (last accessed 14 August 2013).

O'Carroll, A. and Webb, S. (2012) *Digital Archiving in Ireland: National Survey of the Humanities and Social Sciences.* NUI Maynooth and Digital Repository of Ireland, Dublin.

O'Carroll, A., Collins, S., Gallagher, D., Tang, J. and Webb, S. (2013) *Caring for Digital Content, Mapping International Approaches.* NUI Maynooth, Trinity College Dublin, Royal Irish Academy and Digital Repository of Ireland, Dublin.

O'Neill, J. E. (1995) 'The role of ARPA in the development of the ARPANET, 1961–1972', *IEEE Annals of the History of Computing,* 17(4): 76–81.

O'Reilly, T. (2005) *What is Web 2.0: Design Patterns and Business Models for the Next Generation of Software,* 30 September, http://www.oreillynet.com/pub/a/oreilly/tim/news/2005/09/30/what-is-web-20.html (last accessed 17 January 2014).

Ohlhorst, F.J. (2013) *Big Data Analytics: Turning Big Data into Big Money.* Wiley, New York.

Open Data Center Alliance (2012) *Big Data Consumer Guide.* Open Data Center Alliance, http://www.opendatacenteralliance.org/docs/Big_Data_Consumer_Guide_Rev1.0.pdf (last accessed 11 February 2013).

Open Knowledge Foundation (2012) *Open Data Handbook Documentation,* 1.0.0, http://opendatahandbook.org/ (last accessed 16 August 2013).

Open Scientist (2013) 'The levels of citizen science involvement – part 1', 23 January, http://www.openscientist.org/2013/01/the-levels-of-citizen-science.html (last accessed 28 January 2013).

Pentland, A. (2012) 'Reinventing society in the wake of big data', *Edge,* 30 August, http://www.edge.org/conversation/reinventing-society-in-the-wake-of-big-data (last accessed 28 January 2013).

Pérez-Montoro, M.G. and Díaz Nafría, J.M. (2010) 'Data', in J.M. Díaz Nafría, M.G. Pérez-Montoro and F.S. Alemany (eds), *Glossary of Concepts, Metaphors, Theories and Problems Concerning Information.* León: Universidad de León. http://glossarium.bitrum.unileon.es/Home/dato/data (last accessed 13 January 2014).

Piatetsky-Shapiro, G. (2012) 'From data mining to big data and beyond', *Inside Analysis,* 18 April, http://www.insideanalysis.com/2012/04/data-mining-and-beyond/ (last accessed 20 February 2013).

Picton, P.D. (2000) *Neural Networks,* 2nd edition. Palgrave Macmillan, Basingstoke.

Plumridge, B. (2012) 'Big data in a big brave world', *Wired,* 21 November, http://www.wired.co.uk/news/archive/2012-11/21/future-of-big-data? (last accessed 23 November 2012).

Pollock, R. (2006) 'The value of the public domain', *IPPR,* http://www.ippr.org/publication/55/1526/the-value-of-the-public-domain (last accessed 13 August 2013).

Pollock. R. (2009) The Economics of Public Information. *Cambridge Working Papers in Economics 0920.* http://www.econ.cam.ac.uk/research/repec/cam/pdf/cwpe0920.pdf (last accessed 13 August 2013).

Poovey, M. (1998) *A History of the Modern Fact: Problems of Knowledge in the Sciences of Wealth and Society.* University of Chicago Press, Chicago, IL.

Porter, T.M. (1995) *Trust in Numbers: The Pursuit of Objectivity in Science and Public Life.* Princeton University Press, Princeton, NJ.

Porway, J. (2013) 'You can't just hack your way to social change', *Harvard Business Review Blog,* 7 March, http://blogs.hbr.org/cs/2013/03/you_cant_just_hack_your_way_to.html (last accessed 9 March 2013).

Prensky, M. (2009) 'H. sapiens digital: from digital immigrants and digital natives to digital wisdom', *Innovate,* 5(3), http://www.innovateonline.info/index.php?view=article&id=705 (last accessed 12 October 2012).

Quintero, E. (2012) 'The data-driven education movement', *Shanker Blog,* 22 October, http://shankerblog.org/?p=7015 (last accessed 12 November 2012).

Rajaraman, A., Leskovec, J. and Ullman, J.D. (2012) *Mining of Massive Datasets*. Available at http://infolab.stanford.edu/~ullman/mmds.html, also available from Cambridge University Press.

Raley, R. (2013) 'Dataveillance and countervailance', in L. Gitelman (ed.), *'Raw Data' is an Oxymoron*. MIT Press, Cambridge, MA, pp. 121–46.

Rambam, S. (2008) *Privacy is Dead, Get Over It*. Presentation at the Last Hope Conference, New York. http://www.youtube.com/watch?v=Vsxxsrn2Tfs (last accessed 15 October 2013).

Ramirez, E. (2013) 'The privacy challenges of big data: a view from the lifeguard's chair', *Technology Policy Institute Aspen Forum*, 19 August, http//ftc.gov/speeches/ramirez/130819bigdataaspen.pdf (last accessed October 11 2013).

Ramsay, S. (2003) 'Toward an algorithmic criticism', *Literary and Linguistic Computing*, 18(2): 167–74.

Ramsay, S. (2010) *Reading Machines: Towards an Algorithmic Criticism*. University of Illinois Press, Champaign, IL.

Rezendes, C.J. and Stephenson, W.D (2013) 'Cyber security in the internet of things', *Harvard Business Review Blog*, 21 June, http://blogs.hbr.org/cs/2013/06/cyber_security_in_the_internet.html (last accessed 7 August 2013).

Rial, N. (2013) 'The power of big data in Europe', *New Europe*, 24 May, http://www.neurope.eu/article/power-big-data-europe (last accessed 27 May 2013).

Ribes, D. and Jackson, S.J. (2013) 'Data bite man: the work of sustaining long-term study', in L. Gitelman (ed.), *'Raw Data' is an Oxymoron*. MIT Press, Cambridge, MA, pp. 147–66.

Risen, J. and Lichtblau, E. (2013) 'How the US uses technology to mine more data more quickly', *New York Times*, 8 June, http://www.nytimes.com/2013/06/09/us/revelations-give-look-at-spy-agencys-wider-reach.html?hp&_r=3& (last accessed 8 July 2013).

Ritzer, G. and Jurgenson, N. (2010) 'Production, consumption, prosumption: the nature of capitalism in the age of the digital "prosumer"', *Journal of Consumer Culture*, 10(1): 13–36.

RLG and OCLC (2002) *Trusted Digital Repositories: Attributes and Responsibilities*. http://www.oclc.org/research/activities/trustedrep.html (last accessed 18 February 2013).

Robinson, S. (2003) *Simulation: The Practice of Model Development and Use*. John Wiley & Sons, Chichester.

Rogers, S. (2013) 'Twitter's languages of New York mapped', *Guardian*, 21 February, http://www.guardian.co.uk/news/datablog/interactive/2013/feb/21/twitter-languages-new-york-mapped (last accessed 3 April 2013).

Rooney, B. (2012) 'Big data's big problem: little talent', *Wall Street Journal: Tech Europe*, 26 April, http://blogs.wsj.com/tech-europe/2012/04/26/big-datas-big-problem-little-talent/ (last accessed 12 November 2012).

Rose, A. (2013) 'The internet of things has arrived – and so have massive security issues', *Wired*, 11 January, http://www.wired.com/opinion/2013/01/securing-the-internet-of-things/ (last accessed 7 August 2013).

Rose, N. (1996) *Inventing Our Selves: Psychology, Power and Personhood*. Cambridge University Press, Cambridge.

Rosenberg, D. (2013) 'Data before the fact', in L. Gitelman (ed.), *'Raw Data' is an Oxymoron*. MIT Press, Cambridge, MA, pp. 15–40.

Rubenking, N.J. (2013) 'Privacy is dead. The NSA killed it. Now what?', *PC Mag,* http://www.pcmag.com/article2/0,2817,2424193,00.asp (last accessed 15 October 2013).

Rubinstein, I.S. (2013) 'Big data: the end of privacy or a new beginning?', *International Data Privacy Law,* online first, http://idpl.oxfordjournals.org/content/early/2013/01/24/idpl.ips036.short (last accessed 15 July 2013).

Ruppert, E. (2012) 'The governmental topologies of database devices', *Theory, Culture Society,* 29: 116–36.

Ruppert, E. (2013) 'Rethinking empirical social sciences', *Dialogues in Human Geography,* 3(3): 268–73.

Salmon, F. (2014) 'Why the Nate Silvers of the world don't know everything', *Wired,* 7 January, http://www.wired.com/business/2014/01/quants-dont-know-everything/ (last accessed 8 January 2014).

Salus, P. (1995) *Casting the Net: From Arpanet to Internet and Beyond.* Addison Wesley, Reading, MA.

Sawyer, S. (2008) 'Data wealth, data poverty, science and cyberinfrastructure', *Prometheus: Critical Studies in Innovation,* 26(4): 355–71.

Schnapp, J. and Presner, P. (2009) *Digital Humanities Manifesto 2.0.* http://www.humanitiesblast.com/manifesto/Manifesto_V2.pdf (last accessed 13 March 2013).

Scherer, M. (2012) 'Inside the secret world of the data crunchers who helped Obama win', *Time: Swampland,* 7 November, http://swampland.time.com/2012/11/07/inside-the-secret-world-of-quants-and-data-crunchers-who-helped-obama-win/ (last accessed 19 November 2012).

Science Coalition (2013) *Sparking Economic Growth: Companies Created from Federally Funded University Research, Fueling American Innovation and Economic Growth,* October 2013, http://www.sciencecoalition.org/reports/Sparking%20Economic%20Growth%20FINAL%2010-21-13.pdf (last accessed 12 January 2014).

Schwartz, P.M. and Solove, D. (2011) 'The PII problem: privacy and a new concept of personally identifiable information', *New York University Law Review,* 86: 1814–94.

Selisker, S. (2012) 'The digital inhumanities?', *Los Angeles Review of Books,* 5 November, http://lareviewofbooks.org/article.php?type=&id=1146 (last accessed 4 April 2013).

Seni, G. and Elder, J. (2010) *Ensemble Methods in Data Mining: Improving Accuracy Through Combining Predictions.* Morgan & Claypool, San Rafael, CA.

Shah, N. (2013) 'Big data, people's lives, and the importance of openness', *DMLcentral,* 24 June, http://dmlcentral.net/blog/nishant-shah/big-data-peoples-lives-and-importance-openness (last accessed 25 July 2013).

Shah, S., Horne, A. and Capellá, J. (2012) 'Good data won't guarantee good decisions', *Harvard Business Review,* 90(4): 23–5.

Shneiderman, B. (1996) 'The eyes have it: a task by data type taxonomy for information visualizations', *Proceedings IEEE Visual Languages,* 96: 336–43.

Short, J.E., Bohn, R.E. and Chaitanya, C. (2011) *How Much Information? 2010: Report on Enterprise Server Information.* Global Information Industry Center, UC San Diego. http://hmi.ucsd.edu/pdf/HMI_2010_EnterpriseReport_Jan_2011.pdf (last accessed 1 October 2012).

Sicular, S. (2013) 'Big data is falling into the trough of disillusionment', *Gartner,* 22 January, http://blogs.gartner.com/svetlana-sicular/big-data-is-falling-into-the-trough-of-disillusionment/ (last accessed 26 February 2013).

Siegel, E. (2013) *Predictive Analytics.* Wiley, Hoboken, NJ.

Sigala, M. (2005) 'Integrating customer relationship management in hotel operations: managerial and operations implications', *International Journal of Hospitality Management,* 24(3): 391–413.

Silver, N. (2012) *The Signal and the Noise: The Art and Science of Prediction.* Penguin, London.

Singer, N. (2012a) 'You for sale: mapping, and sharing, the consumer genome', *New York Times,* 17 June, http://www.nytimes.com/2012/06/17/technology/acxiom-the-quiet-giant-of-consumer-database-marketing.html (last accessed 11 October 2013).

Singer, N. (2012b) 'F.T.C. opens an inquiry into data brokers', *New York Times,* 18 December, http://www.nytimes.com/2012/12/19/technology/ftc-opens-an-inquiry-into-data-brokers.html (last accessed 11 October 2013).

Singer, N. (2012c) 'Mission control, built for cities: I.B.M. takes 'Smarter Cities' concept to Rio de Janeiro', *New York Times,* 3 March, http://www.nytimes.com/2012/03/04/business/ibm-takes-smarter-cities-concept-to-rio-de-janeiro.html (last accessed 9 May 2013).

Singh, R. (2012) 'Crowdsourced geospatial data', *GIM International,* 26(9): 26–31.

Slee, T. (2012) 'Seeing like a geek', *Crooked Timber,* 25 June, http://crookedtimber.org/2012/06/25/seeing-like-a-geek/ (last accessed 18 September 2013).

Smolan, R. and Erwitt, J. (2012) *The Human Face of Big Data.* Sterling, New York.

Solove, D.J. (2006) 'A taxonomy of privacy', *University of Pennsylvania Law Review,* 154(3): 477–560.

Solove, D.J. (2007) '"I've got nothing to hide" and other misunderstandings of privacy', *Social Sciences Research Network,* http://ssrn.com/abstract=998565 (last accessed 16 July 2013).

Solove, D. (2013) 'Privacy management and the consent dilemma', *Harvard Law Review,* 126: 1880–903.

Stalder, F. (2002) 'Privacy is not the antidote to surveillance', *Surveillance and Society,* 1(1): 120–4.

Star, S.L. and Ruhleder, K. (1996) 'Steps Toward an Ecology of Infrastructure: design and access for large information spaces', *Information Systems Research,* 7(1): 111–34.

Star, S.L. and Lampland, M. (2009) 'Reckoning with standards', in M. Lampland and S.L. Star (eds) *Standards and Their Stories: How Quantifying, Classifying and Formalizing Practices Shape Everyday Life.* Cornell University Press, Ithaca, NY, pp. 3–24.

Starr, P. (1987) 'The sociology of official statistics', in W. Alonso and P. Starr (eds), *The Politics of Numbers.* Russell Sage, New York, pp. 7–58.

Steadman, I. (2013) 'Big data and the death of the theorist', *Wired,* 25 January, http://www.wired.co.uk/news/archive/2013-01/25/big-data-end-of-theory (last accessed 30 January 2013).

Strasser, B.J. (2012) 'Data-driven sciences: from wonder cabinets to electronic databases', *Studies in History and Philosophy of Biological and Biomedical Sciences,* 43: 85–7.

Strasser, C. (2013) 'Closed data ... excuses, excuses', *Data Pub: California Digital Library,* 24 April, http://datapub.cdlib.org/2013/04/24/closed-data-excuses-excuses (last accessed 18 September 2013).

Strohm, C. and Homan, T. (2013) 'NSA spying row in Congress ushers in debate over big data', *Bloomberg,* 25 July, http://www.bloomberg.com/news/2013-07-25/nsa-spying-row-in-congress-ushers-in-debate-over-big-data.html (last accessed 25 July 2013).

Strom, D. (2012) 'Big data makes things better', *Slashdot,* 3 August, http://slashdot.org/topic/bi/big-data-makes-things-better/ (last accessed 24 October 2013).

Sword, K. (2008) 'Contribution to: The Promise of Digital History' (roundtable discussion), *Journal of American History,* 95(2): 452–91.

Taleb. N. (2012) *Antifragile: Things That Gain From Disorder.* Random House, New York.

Taleb, N. (2013) 'Beware the big errors of "big data"', *Wired,* 2 February, http://www.wired.com/opinion/2013/02/big-data-means-big-errors-people/ (last accessed 9 February 2013).

TechAmerica Foundation (2012) *Demystifying Big Data: A Practical Guide to Transforming the Business of Government.* http://www.techamericafoundation.org/official-report-of-the-techamerica-foundations-big-data-commission (last accessed 25 February 2013).

Tene, O. and Polonetsky, J. (2012) 'Big data for all: privacy and user control in the age of analytics', *Social Sciences Research Network,* http://ssrn.com/abstract=2149364 (last accessed 15 July 2013).

Thomas, J.J. and Cook, K.A. (2006) 'A visual analytics agenda', *IEEE Computer Graphics & Applications,* 26: 10–13.

Thrift, N. (2004) 'Driving in the city', *Theory, Culture & Society,* 21(4/5): 41–59.

Townsend, A. (2013) *Smart Cities: Big Data, Civic Hackers, and the Quest for a New Utopia.* W.W. Norton & Co, New York.

Trumpener, K. (2009) 'Critical response I. Paratext and genre system: a response to Franco Moretti', *Critical Inquiry,* 36(1): 159–71.

Vanacek, J. (2012) 'How cloud and big data are impacting the human genome – touching 7 billion lives', *Forbes,* 16 April, http://www.forbes.com/sites/sap/2012/04/16/how-cloud-and-big-data-are-impacting-the-human-genome-touching-7-billion-lives (last accessed 27 February 2013).

Varian, H. (1996) 'Differential pricing and efficiency', *First Monday,* 1(2–5), http://firstmonday.org/ojs/index.php/fm/article/view/473/394 (last accessed 8 August 2013).

Verwayen, H., Arnoldus, M. and Kaufman, P.B. (2011) *The Problem of the Yellow Milkmaid: A Business Mode Perspective on Open Metadata.* Europeana, http://pro.europeana.eu/documents/858566/2cbf1f78-e036-4088-af25-94684ff90dc5 (last accessed 12 September 2013).

Vis, F. (2013) 'A critical reflection on big data: considering APIs, researchers and tools as data makers', *First Monday,* 18(10), http://firstmonday.org/ojs/index.php/fm/article/view/4878/3755 (last accessed 3 January 2013).

von Baeyer, H.C. (2003) *Information: The New Language of Science.* Harvard University Press, Cambridge, MA.

Wang, T. (2013) 'Big data needs thick data', *Ethnography Matters,* 13 May, http://ethnographymatters.net/2013/05/13/big-data-needs-thick-data/ (last accessed 3 January 2014).

Weber, R.H. (2010) 'Internet of things – new security and privacy challenges', *Computer Law & Security Review,* 26: 23–30.

Webster, T. (2011) 'Social media data dredging', *BrandSavant,* 22 March, http://brandsavant.com/social-media-data-dredging/ (last accessed 20 February 2013).

Weinberger, D. (2011) *Too Big to Know*. Basic Books, New York.

White House (2009) *Open Government Directive*. Executive Office of the President. http://www.whitehouse.gov/sites/default/files/microsites/ogi-directive.pdf (last accessed 19 September 2013).

Williford, C. and Henry, C. (2012) *One Culture: Computationally Intensive Research in the Humanities and Social Sciences*. Council on Library and Information Resources, Washington DC. http://www.clir.org/pubs/reports/pub151 (last accessed 6 January 2014).

Wilson, M. (2011) 'Data matter(s): legitimacy, coding, and qualifications-of-life', *Environment and Planning D: Society and Space*, 29: 857–72.

Wired (2008) 'The petabyte age: because more isn't just more – more is different', 23 June, http://www.wired.com/science/discoveries/magazine/16-07/pb_intro (last accessed 9 November 2012).

Wittgenstein, L. (1921[1974]) *Tractatus Logico-Philosophicus*, translated by D.F. Pears and B.F. McGuinness. Routledge, London.

Wu, M. (2012) 'The big data fallacy and why we need to collect even bigger data', *Tech Crunch*, 25 November, http://techcrunch.com/2012/11/25/the-big-data-fallacy-data-%E2%89%A0-information-%E2%89%A0-insights/ (last accessed 28 January 2013).

Wu, T. (2011) *The Master Switch: The Rise and Fall of Information Empires*. Vintage, New York.

Wyly, E. (in press) 'Automated (post)positivism', *Urban Geography*.

Yiu, C. (2012) *A Right to Data: Fulfilling the Promise of Open Public Data in the UK*. Policy Exchange Research Note, http://www.policyexchange.org.uk/publications/category/item/a-right-to-data-fulfilling-the-promise-of-open-public-data-in-the-uk (last accessed 14 August 2013).

Zelany, M. (1987) 'Management support systems: towards integrated knowledge management', *Human Systems Management*, 7: 59–70.

Zhang, J.., Hsu, M. and Li, L. (2001) 'Image mining: issues, frameworks and techniques', *CiteSeerx*, http://citeseerx.ist.psu.edu/viewdoc/summary?doi=10.1.1.4.8726 (last accessed 17 January 2014).

Zikopoulos, P.C., Eaton, C., deRoos, D., Deutsch, T. and Lapis, G. (2012) *Understanding Big Data*. McGraw Hill, New York.

INDEX

Renaissance xvi, 129, 141
repository 29, 33, 34, 41
representativeness 13, 14, 19, 21
Resource Description Framework (RDF) 53, 54
remote sensing 73–4, 105
RFID 74, 85, 90, 91, 169
rhetorical 3, 4, 185
right to
   be forgotten 45, 172, 187
   information (RTI) 48, 62
risk 16, 44, 58, 63, 118, 120, 123, 132, 158, 174,
   176–7, 178, 179, 180
Rosenberg, D. 1, 3
Ruppert, E. 22, 112, 157, 163, 187

sampling 13, 14, 27, 28, 46, 68, 72, 73, 77, 78, 88,
   100, 101, 102, 120, 126, 133, 138, 139, 146,
   149–50, 152, 153, 154, 156, 159
scale of economy 37
scanners 6, 25, 29, 32, 83, 85, 88, 89, 90, 91, 92, 175,
   177, 180
science xvi, 1, 2, 3, 19, 20, 29, 31, 34, 37, 46, 65, 67,
   71, 72, 73, 78, 79, 97, 98, 100, 101, 103, 111,
   112, 128–39, 140, 147, 148, 150, 158, 161, 165,
   166, 181, 184, 186
scientific method 129, 130, 133, 134, 136, 137–8,
   140, 147, 148, 186
security
   data 28, 33, 34, 40, 45, 46, 51, 57, 126, 157, 166,
      169, 171, 173, 174–5, 182, 187
   national 42, 71, 88, 116–7, 172, 176, 178, 179
   private 99, 115, 118, 151
   social 8, 32, 45, 87, 115, 171
segmentation 104, 105, 110, 119, 120, 121, 122, 176
semantic
   information 9, 10, 11, 105, 157
   Web 49, 52, 53, 66
sensors xv, 6, 7, 19, 20, 24, 25, 28, 34, 71, 76, 83, 84,
   91–2, 95, 124, 139, 150, 160
sentiment analysis 105, 106, 121,
Siegel, E. 103, 110, 111, 114, 120, 132, 158, 176, 179
signal 9, 151, 159
Silver, N. 136, 151, 158
simulation 4, 32, 37, 101, 104, 110–12, 119, 129,
   133, 137, 139, 140
skills 37, 48, 52, 53, 57, 63, 94, 97, 98, 112, 149,
   160–3, 164
small data 21, 27–47, 68, 72, 75, 76, 77, 79, 100, 103,
   110, 112, 146, 147, 148, 150, 156, 160, 166,
   184, 186, 188, 191
smart
   cards 90
   cities 91, 92, 99, 124–5, 181–2
   devices 83

smart *cont.*
   metering 89, 123, 174
   phones 81, 82, 83, 84, 90, 94, 107, 121, 155,
      170, 174
SmartSantander 91
social
   computing xvi
   determinism 144
   media xv, 13, 42, 43, 76, 78, 90, 93, 94–5, 96, 105,
      119, 121, 140, 150, 151, 152, 154, 155, 160,
      167, 176, 180
   physics 144
   security number 8, 32, 45, 87, 115, 171
   sorting 126, 166, 168, 175–8, 182
sociotechnical systems 21–4, 47, 66, 183, 185, 188
software 6, 20, 32, 34, 40, 48, 53, 54, 56, 63, 80, 83,
   84, 86, 88, 96, 132, 143, 160, 161, 163, 166,
   170, 172, 175, 177, 180, 189
Solove, D. 116, 120, 168, 169, 170, 172, 176, 178, 180
solutionism 181
sousveillance 95–6
spatial
   autocorrelation 146
   data infrastructure 34, 35, 38
   processes 136, 144
   resolution 149
   statistics 110
   video 88
spatiality 17, 157
Star, S.L. 19, 20, 23, 24
stationarity 100
statistical
   agencies 8, 30, 34, 35, 115
   geography 17, 74, 157
statistics 4, 8, 13, 14, 24, 48, 77, 100, 101, 102, 104,
   105, 109–10, 111, 129, 132, 134, 135, 136, 140,
   142, 143, 145, 147, 159
   descriptive 4, 106, 109, 147
   inferential 4, 110, 147
   non-parametric 105, 110
   parametric 105, 110
   probablistic 110
   radical 147
   spatial 110
storage 31–2, 68, 72, 73, 78, 80, 85–7, 88, 100, 118,
   161, 171
   analogue 85, 86
   digital 85–7
   media 20, 86
store loyalty cards 42, 45, 165
Sunlight Foundation 49
supervised learning 103
Supply Chain Management (SCM) 74, 99, 117–8,
   119, 120, 121